CONGRESS
AFTER INDIRA

'Zoya Hasan's important book on the life of the Congress post-Indira Gandhi draws its rationale from the unique position that the organisation occupies in terms of its longevity and "its role in the building of the Indian nation".'

—*Economic and Political Weekly*

'The book's distinctive feature is reflections on three inter-related themes of "policy, power and political change" from a political scientist's hindsight, but enriched with apt historical perspectives.'

—*The Hindu*

'Hasan has covered the period between 1984 and 2009 well in her book. Those interested in Indian politics would find it a useful and lucid read.'

—*Biblio*

'[T]he [Congress] party should do many of the things she recommends in order to become...as it was under Gandhiji and Nehru—the moral conscience of the nation—"modern, forward looking and compassionate", as Hasan puts it. Otherwise, India may prosper—but Indians won't.'

—*Outlook*

'In-depth studies on political parties are rare in India. *Congress after Indira* fills this void.'

—*Deccan Herald*

'Objective analyses of the [Congress] party and its role in India over the past few decades from a social science perspective are surprisingly rare...[this] book...contributes to filling this gap...Hasan's real point of departure is the recent past, particularly the period after the unexpected victory in the 2004 parliamentary elections that brought the Congress back to power on the national stage.'

—*Frontline*

'[E]xtracts from Zoya Hasan's lucid primer on the Congress after Indira Gandhi's assassination...explains why economic liberalisation, abandoned mid-way by Rajiv Gandhi, took off under P.V. Narasimha Rao.'

—*Mail Today*

'Political scientist, Zoya Hasan, chronicles the changes in policy, power and politics in the country with focus on the Congress party in the aftermath of Indira Gandhi's assassination, especially the "dualist structure" of its leadership.'

—*Business Line*

CONGRESS

AFTER INDIRA

Policy, Power, Political Change
(1984–2009)

ZOYA HASAN

OXFORD
UNIVERSITY PRESS

OXFORD
UNIVERSITY PRESS

Oxford University Press is a department of the University of Oxford.
It furthers the University's objective of excellence in research, scholarship,
and education by publishing worldwide. Oxford is a registered trademark of
Oxford University Press in the UK and in certain other countries

Published in India by
Oxford University Press
22 workspace, 2nd Floor, 1/22 Asaf Ali Road, New Delhi 110002

First Edition published in 2012
Oxford India Paperbacks 2015

ISBN-13: 978-0-19-945335-1
ISBN-10: 0-19-945335-7

Typeset in Adobe Garamond Pro 10.5/13.5,
at MAP Systems, Bengaluru 560 082, India
Printed in India by Repro India Limited

In remembrance of my father, Mohammed Khaliq Siddiqi,
and my uncles, Mohammed Atiq Siddiqi, Abdur Rashid,
and Azimuzzafar

Contents

Acknowledgements

This book began life as the Prem Bhatia Memorial Lecture given in New Delhi in 2004 and subsequently the Nirman Foundation Lecture at the British South Asian Studies Conference in London in 2006. The book developed from the arguments of these lectures which had taken shape amid the surprise return of the Indian National Congress to power in the 2004 elections. The dramatic election outcome, very few expected, was the starting point for examining transformation in the Congress, both in its policy and strategy, and in its organization and leadership. This book tracks political change in the period from 1984 to 2009; it does not discuss events and processes after the 2009 elections.

Given the absence of accessible written records of the contemporary Congress, this book depends heavily on interviews with those familiar with Congress politics. Over the last few years, I have had the privilege of talking to prominent leaders of the Congress Party and the United Progressive Alliance (UPA) government, civil servants, members of the Planning Commission, National Advisory Council, and various national commissions; editors and journalists; and political activists. These interviews provided a very useful archive of information and interpretation of the events and processes of our recent past. Although in many cases I have not mentioned names, I have drawn liberally from these interviews, and I thank the interviewees for their generosity and insights.

Beyond the specific issues addressed in the interviews, the book has benefited greatly from stimulating conversations with a large number of well-wishers, colleagues, and friends. For these conversations, I am grateful to Amrita Basu, France Bhattacharya, Praful Bidwai, Seema Chishti, Radhika Desai, Peter Ronald deSouza, Smita Gupta, Violette Graff, Ajay Gudavarthy, Gopal Guru, Masoodul Haq, Francine Frankel,

Arati Jerath, Pralay Kanungo, Harish Khare, A.K. Shiva Kumar, Harsh Mander, Pratap Bhanu Mehta, Ritu Menon, Saeed Naqvi, Dileep Padgoankar, Malini Parthasarathy, Prabhat Patnaik, Pamela Philipose, Rajan Prasad, Jean-Luc Racine, Radhika Ramaseshan, P. Sainath, Abhijit Sen, Jyotirmaya Sharma, E. Sridharan, Ravi Srivastava, Paranjoy Guha-Thakurta, Achin Vanaik, Siddharth Varadarajan, Vidhu Verma, and Max Zins.

For reading earlier drafts or some parts of the manuscript and offering valuable comments, I am indebted to V. Krishna Ananth, Christophe Jaffrelot, Gyanesh Kudesia, James Manor, and Srirupa Roy.

I am grateful to David Ludden, Amrita Basu, Kalyanakrishnan Sivaramkrishanan, Daud Ali, Janaki Bakhle, and Christophe Jaffrelot for inviting me to present some parts of the book at New York University, Amherst College, Yale University, University of Pennsylvania, Columbia University, and CERI-Sciences-Po Paris, respectively.

I want to especially thank Aftab Alam, Anita Tagore, and Poulomi Pal for providing excellent research assistance for this book.

Special thanks are also due to Adil Tyabji and Anjali Aggarwal for doing a superb job of editing the manuscript. I am much obliged to Nitasha Devasar of Oxford University Press for her wonderful support to this book as well as to other projects. As ever, my deepest gratitude is to Mushirul Hasan whose courage, integrity, generosity, and exemplary intellectual rigour continue to inspire me.

Abbreviations

ADB	Asian Development Bank
AEA	Atomic Energy Act
AIADMK	All India Anna Dravida Munnetra Kazhagam
AICC	All India Congress Committee
AIMIM	All India Majlis-e-Ittehadul Muslimeen
BHEL	Bharat Heavy Electricals Limited
BJP	Bharatiya Janata Party
BMAC	Babri Masjid Action Committee
BPL	Below Poverty Line
BRIC	Brazil, Russia, India, and China
BSP	Bahujan Samaj Party
CAG	Comptroller and Auditor General
CBGA	Centre for Budget and Governance Accountability
CES	Centre of Equity Studies
CII	Confederation of Indian Industry
CPIA	Consumer Prices Index for Agricultural Labourers
CPI	Communist Party of India
CPI (M)	Communist Party of India (Marxist)
CPP	Congress Parliamentary Party
Cr Pc	Criminal Procedure Code
CRPF	Central Reserve Police Force
CSDS	Centre for the Study of Developing Societies
CWC	Congress Working Committee
DAE	Department of Atomic Energy
DMK	Dravida Munnetra Kazhagam
DoPT	Department of Personnel Training
EGA	Employment Guarantee Act
EGS	Employment Guarantee Scheme
ENR	Enrichment and Reprocessing
EOC	Equal Opportunity Commission
FICCI	Federation of Indian Chambers of Commerce and Industry

GDP	Gross Domestic Product
GoM	Group of Ministers
IAEA	International Atomic Energy Agency
ICDS	Integrated Child Development Services
IMF	International Monetary Fund
ITI	Industrial Training Institute
IUML	Indian Union Muslim League
JMM	Jharkhand Mukti Morcha
JNNURM	Jawaharlal Nehru National Urban Renewal Mission
JPC	Joint Parliamentary Committee
JRY	Jawahar Rozgar Yojana
KC (J)	Kerala Congress (Joseph)
LJP	Lok Janshakti Party
LTTE	Liberation Tigers of Tamil Eelam
MDMK	Marumalarchi Dravida Munnetra Kazhagam
MEGS	Maharashtra Employment Guarantee Scheme
MGNREGA	Mahatma Gandhi National Rural Employment Guarantee Act
MKSS	Mazdoor Kisan Shakti Sangathan
MMA	Ministry of Minority Affairs
MNC	Multinational Corporation
MP	Member of Parliament
MSDP	Multi-Sectoral Development Programme
MSP	Minority Sub-Plan
MWA	Muslim Women's (Protection of Rights on Divorce) Act
NAC	National Advisory Council
NASSCOM	National Association of Software and Services Companies
NCERT	National Council for Educational Research and Training
NCEUS	National Commission for Enterprises in the Unorganized Sector
NCF	National Curriculum Framework
NCM	National Commission for Minorities
NCMP	National Common Minimum Programme
NCP	Nationalist Congress Party
NCPRI	National Campaign for People's Right to Information
NCRB	National Crime Records Bureau
NCRLM	National Commission for Religious and Linguistic Minorities
NDA	National Democratic Alliance
NDC	National Development Council
NES	National Election Study
NHRC	National Human Rights Commission
NIC	National Integration Council
NPT	Non-Proliferation Treaty
NREGA	National Rural Employment Guarantee Act

NREGS	National Rural Employment Guarantee Scheme
NRHM	National Rural Health Mission
NRI	Non-Resident Indian
NSG	Nuclear Suppliers Group
NSS	National Sample Survey
NSSP	Next Steps in Strategic Partnership
NSUI	National Students Union of India
OBC	Other Backward Class
PCC	Pradesh Congress Committee
PDP	Peoples Democratic Party
PDS	Public Distribution System
PMGSY	Pradhan Mantri Gram Sadak Yojana
PMK	Paattali Makkal Katchi
PMO	Prime Minister's Office
POTA	Prevention of Terrorism Act
PSU	Public Sector Undertaking
RAF	Rapid Action Force
RBI	Reserve Bank of India
RJD	Rashtriya Janata Dal
RLD	Rashtriya Lok Dal
RPI (A)	Republican Party of India (Athvale)
RPI (G)	Republican Party of India (Gavai)
RSS	Rashtriya Swayamsevak Sangh
RTI	Right to Information
SC	Scheduled Caste
SLP	Special Leave Petition
ST	Scheduled Tribe
TISS	Tata Institute of Social Sciences
TRS	Telangana Rashtra Samithi
UGC	University Grants Commission
UNRISD	United Nations Research Institute for Social Development
UNSC	United Nations Security Council
UPA	United Progressive Alliance
UPCC	Uttar Pradesh Congress Committee
VHP	Vishwa Hindu Parishad
WTO	World Trade Organization

Introduction

The political history of modern India is intimately intertwined with the history of the Indian National Congress, India's dominant party of government under Jawaharlal Nehru and his successors. It is unique not only for its longevity but also for its role in the building of the Indian nation. It played a crucial part in shaping modern India and establishing a democratic system. From the civil disobedience movement to Independence to the Emergency to economic reforms to the demolition of the Babri Masjid, the Congress has been at the very centre of historical events through its long innings. No other political formation is nearly as central as the Congress to India's present and future. The Congress is one of the most important, durable, and influential political parties in the world. No other political party, at least in the developing world outside Western democracies, can claim such a powerful and long innings in power.

Established in 1885, the 125-year-old party was born out of India's struggle for freedom from British rule. In the vanguard of the national movement, it was the natural party of governance after Independence in 1947. In the 65 years since then, it has run the central government in New Delhi for all but 12 years. In most general elections held prior to 1989, with the exception of those in 1977, it commanded an outright majority or emerged as the party with the highest number of seats in the Parliament. Since 1989, however, the Congress has steadily ceded ground to other political parties at the Centre and in the states. Thus, for long stretches of time, several states, notably West Bengal, Tamil Nadu, Uttar Pradesh, and Bihar, have been ruled by the Left or the regional parties. Other states have seen Congress governments alternate with those led by parties based on identities of caste, religion, and language.

The Congress inherited the legacy of the freedom struggle and laid the foundation for parliamentary democracy. As a movement that became a party, it encompassed virtually every shade of political opinion and social constituency of the nation. Mahatma Gandhi, in his speech to the All India Congress Committee (AICC) in November 1947, said: 'Congress is of Indians, of all those who inhabit this land, whether they are Hindus, Muslims, Christians or Sikhs.'[1] The Congress could therefore claim an authority, legitimacy, and representativeness which no other political party could. This resulted in a system of one-party dominance which Rajni Kothari famously termed the 'Congress system'.[2] It sought to establish unity through the pursuit of the common goals of secularism and economic development, assuring citizens of equal rights regardless of their caste and religion, and working to end poverty. Significantly, one-party dominance did not lapse into authoritarianism. Its domination was based on a concrete set of actions and achievements: an independent model of industrial growth; considerable reduction in large-scale feudal landholdings; growth in infrastructure; expansion in educational facilities and technical personnel; the initiation and construction of the public sector; and the provision of public services. This framework of development held out the promise of redistributive justice with an emphasis on the state's responsibility towards society.

This political system worked until the split in the Congress in 1969 when Indira Gandhi acted against the old guard, accusing them of being reactionaries and against progressive policies such as the nationalization of banks and abolition of privy purses. The consequence was a radicalization of the Congress in the short term and centralization of power in the long run, and also complete control over the cabinet and the party. The once robust Congress Party's roots withered and governance became less institutionalized, more personalized, and highly centralized. Indira Gandhi discarded the intraparty democracy of the old decentralized structure and placed individuals who were personally loyal to her at the head of Pradesh Congress Committees. It was clear that Indira Gandhi's lurch towards authoritarian rule had cost the party deeply in terms of its popular credibility in north India which had to suffer the worst excesses of the Emergency imposed in June 1975. It was a blow from which the Congress never really recovered. Its three-decade-long rule at the Centre was broken when the 1977 elections brought the Janata Party, a conglomerate of four parties [the Jana Sangh, Bhartiya Lok Dal, Congress (O), and the Socialist Party], to power. The Congress defeat was a defining moment in more ways than one: it was a bold assertion of sovereignty by the people; a validation of parliamentary democracy which Nehru had pushed; and a test run for the coalition politics that would subsequently emerge. After the formation of the Janata Party government, the backward castes emerged as a major force in national politics to the detriment of the Congress. Even though the Congress returned to power in 1980, the party's decline was unmistakable. In the 1984 elections, held after Indira Gandhi's assassination, it polled the highest vote and seat tally ever as a sympathy wave swept the country and brought her son Rajiv to power. The underlying trends, however, indicated an end of the Congress epoch in Indian politics.

Much of the responsibility for the decline of the Congress and the weakened governmental and administrative institutions can be attributed to Indira Gandhi's personal ambition and dynastic proclivities as she went about refashioning the party to suit her political interests. However, neither the need to reshape the Congress nor her capacity to do so was conceivable had the party not already been in serious and growing disarray. In short, the decline itself was not due to factors that were altogether internal to the Congress or because of Indira Gandhi's centralizing drive but essentially the result of paradigmatic changes in the polity, economy, and society. The Congress was both shaping and being shaped by societal changes. As the Congress was changing, so was India. The challenges facing the Congress were partly symptomatic of the growing democratization of traditional power relations throughout society, and partly the result of its own actions and inactions. Within the Congress itself, multiple sources of power had developed owing to the emergence of regional elites. Some of these regional leaders favoured rural interests, especially agriculture, and challenged the political marginalization of backward castes by the upper-caste-dominated Congress. Educated sections of the backward and lower castes had looked to the Congress to represent them but were now progressively more assertive and keen to use their numbers to gain leverage in the political system in opposition to the Congress.

All these trends were indicative of a great ferment in Indian society. Social and political change was aided by the reservation policy for the Scheduled Castes (SCs) and Scheduled Tribes (STs) in education and governmental employment which, despite slow and tardy implementation, had created a lower-caste elite of substantial size that had acquired education and joined non-traditional occupations and professions. This section formed the nucleus of a small but highly vocal political leadership which began to alter the public discourse. This process came to a head in the course of the Mandal Commission's proposal to extend reservations in jobs and education to the 'Other Backward Classes' (OBCs) in 1990, a course that was vehemently opposed by the upper-caste middle classes. The backward castes were questioning the way the country had been governed and, above all, their exclusion from bureaucratic and political power. These trends point to a social and political transformation which had given voice to previously marginalized groups and enabled them to gain access to the political system. In consequence, political power moved downwards from the old established elites to new groups who pushed for a politics of parity and equality. At the turn of the twenty-first century, the political landscape had changed so noticeably that lower-caste chief ministers were no longer rare; indeed, upper-caste chief ministers were rarer. The Congress did not initiate these changes but had to rapidly adjust to them. This notwithstanding, it gradually lost the support of the backward castes, SCs, and even Muslims who had constituted its most loyal supporters, as they began drifting away in several states. The latter two groups had constituted the very foundation of its power, and once they began shifting their loyalties to different regional parties, the Congress's political dominance was truly shaken.

Historically, the Congress had focused on Dalit issues and their aspirations as part of the freedom struggle. Reservations for SCs played a key role in cementing their loyalties to the Congress for almost three decades.[3] Dalit support enabled the party to rule India almost uninterrupted until 1989, when the emergence of the Bahujan Samaj Party (BSP), a party formed to support lower caste issues and aspirations, prompted many Dalits to desert the Congress in Uttar Pradesh. Its misfortunes in this state started with the growth and expansion of the BSP. The BSP's pro-Dalit agenda was not nearly as revolutionary as it once appeared but its impact was admittedly nothing short of radical. Indeed, the electoral landscape was changed drastically because of the elite bent of Congress politics and institutions, which lacked a Dalit agenda to neutralize the popular appeal of the BSP. The Madhya Pradesh Chief Minister Digvijay Singh's Bhopal Declaration was the only significant response to the Dalit assertiveness and consciousness.[4] By advancing the idea of diversity (the right of every Dalit to a fair share of resources, power, and wealth) the document began the process of assuring affirmative action in non-governmental fields. The Congress high command, however, remained ambivalent about this, which led many Dalits to conclude that it had nothing much to offer them beyond the constitutionally mandated reservation in the public sector.

Prior to the 1980s, the political impact of religion was limited and communal parties won few seats. Troubles in Punjab, Kashmir, and Assam had opened up the space to such tendencies. Most damaging was the fallout from Punjab where the Congress faced a secessionist challenge. Its greatest failure was in the way it approached the growing Hindu assertiveness spearheaded by the Bharatiya Janata Party (BJP) and Rashtriya Swayamsevak Sangh (RSS) combine. As the Congress resorted to ethnic appeals and flirted with religious politics to shore up its dwindling support, it was to eventually become the preeminent victim of these actions. It committed tactical errors in its approach to the politics of organized religion taking shape outside the party system. Above all, this created conditions conducive to the rise of the BJP, which was a crucial turning point in Indian politics as the BJP formed a government at the Centre in 1998, ending decades of erstwhile political isolation. Once in power with the BJP in control, the Sangh Parivar focused its attention on reorienting India's national identity in an exclusionary direction. Its growing influence posed a threat to secular democracy and the equality of all citizens under the law, the core of the Nehruvian consensus. With the emergence of a clear right-wing alternative at the Centre and regional parties in the states, the Congress found it difficult to occupy and define the middle ground as electoral competition was increasingly along communal and caste lines. These developments were undermining it in two ways: directly, by challenging the secular pluralist foundation of the political system, and indirectly, by shifting the political discourse away from development to identity issues. All in all, the Congress sought to remain broadly centrist, but the centre ground got squeezed.

Post 1989, the most important development which was to reshape India's destiny was the change in economic development strategy in 1991 under Prime Minister P.V. Narasimha Rao with Dr Manmohan Singh as his finance minister. The new economic policies declared a shift from a multi-class state to a narrow conception of the state more closely aligned with business, capital, and middle classes eager to embrace capitalism and abandon whatever was left of the idea of socialism. The shift posed a dilemma for the Congress: that of winning elections with policies which had little resonance with the poor. The party's problem was how to win majorities when the majority was poor and excluded from both the state and market, especially under the new policy dispensation.

The social and political changes sweeping through India hastened the fragmentation of the party system and the decline of the Congress and its replacement by coalition governments at the Centre since 1996. The economic consequences and political ramifications of economic liberalization surfaced at the same time as the assertiveness of the caste–class clusters, once part of the Congress coalition, clamouring for a voice and representation in state power. By 1989, some of these trends had begun to catch up with the Congress. Most importantly, it had lost its character as an umbrella party able to mobilize majorities at the national level. In an extremely diverse society, where parties have pursued a politics of social cleavages, this erosion was inevitable. All the same, from a catch-all party, the Congress was now a party with a distinct and more limited base. It is well known that although its support base varies from state to state, there were discernible broad patterns. The Congress seems to be least popular among upper castes and OBCs. In class terms, the Congress voter was likely to be an economically marginalized citizen. It performed well in states where it was the party of the underprivileged; whenever it lost its grip on the marginalized, it was pushed to the margins.

THE AIM

This book seeks to analyse important aspects of political change at a moment when India is at once a rising power with an expanding middle class and a poor, unequal, and misgoverned country through the story of the shifts in the politics and strategy of the Congress Party. It assesses the impact of the transformation in economy, society, and polity on the Congress, and its response to these changes. It takes as its point of departure the Congress comeback in the 2004 parliamentary elections to investigate the structure and direction of change within the party and its governance agenda, essentially in its policy and strategy and in its organization and leadership after Indira Gandhi. It provides an interpretation of contemporary Congress politics in the context of the challenges thrown up by the process of political and economic change.

Disproving predictions that it would be down to double-digit figures in the 2004 elections, the Congress was back in power as the single largest party and heading the UPA. For the first time it headed a coalition government at the Centre in 2004, which was a significant development from the standpoint of Congress politics. The BJP's defeat was a mandate for the Congress to negotiate its way in a period of rapid change as the party had done when it began its career after Independence in 1947 and reinvented itself from a movement to government under the leadership of Nehru.

Since 1989, immense changes have occurred in the political system and policies and strategies of parties. Once the Congress ceased to be the fulcrum of the political system, it could not always shape politics and policy, it was reacting to them. The decline of the Congress was met by two important developments: the rise of the BJP and the growing importance of regional parties and the Left parties. In addition to the dwindling organizational base, the lack of ideological clarity and political purpose left the Congress with an image of ambiguity and confusion, but more disturbingly, an impression that it lacked political direction. The Congress under Sonia Gandhi's leadership reversed several of these tendencies and was thereby able to recover some of the lost ground.

The political recovery was however dependent on the Congress's ability to sharpen the focus on economic and political inclusion which helped to renew its relevance in rapidly changing circumstances. Between 2004 and 2009, the Congress walked the 'middle path' and has pursued a wide range of social welfare and distributive policies and social legislation to project itself as an all-encompassing and accomodating party. This 'middle path' was premised upon the proposition that it is possible to pursue policies that stress both growth and equity, and that economic reforms and distributive justice can go hand in hand. Part of this revamp was evident in the introduction of the right to employment, while the other part was the declared interest in an altered foreign policy including, most significantly, engaging the United States and strengthening the strategic content of the relationship, which included the nuclear deal as a prominent element. The passage of the National Rural Employment Guarantee Act (NREGA) and the signing of the India–US nuclear deal signify the Congress leadership's dual approach of seeking to appeal to the elite and the middle-class constituency while at the same time trying to assuage the economic majority. Another aspect of this approach was the dualist structure of leadership with Prime Minister Manmohan Singh leading the government and Sonia Gandhi being the president of the Congress Party. While Manmohan Singh would ensure that growth and economic reforms were at the top of the government's agenda, Sonia Gandhi would continually highlight issues of distributive justice and poverty alleviation.

The narrative unfolds at the national level as the Congress has the status of being the principal party with a national presence. As a party, it favours a centralist approach and the top-most leadership takes all significant decisions. It makes methodological sense therefore to focus on the national–central level. State-level issues and local-level concerns do come periodically into prominence, but the Congress focus is self-consciously central/national despite the decentring of and regionalization of politics since 1989, and the party makes it a point to emphasize that it is the only truly national party. This book is not a historical account of the Congress, and it does not provide an account of the party before Rajiv Gandhi's prime-ministership or claim to offer an exhaustive or even detailed interpretation of all aspects of its politics after Indira Gandhi. It is not a history of the party organization, which would be difficult to construct as records of the decision-making bodies are not available. It is a thematic account of political processes and the discursive and policy practices that shaped the thinking and approach of the Congress, and through it this book provides an interpretation of the politics of change in India and how this shaped the development of Congress, especially under the UPA.

THE DESIGN

This book is organized in eight chapters. The first two chapters set out the changes in the Congress strategy since the party was swept to power in 1984 in the aftermath of Indira Gandhi's assassination. The first chapter begins with the Congress's handling of the religious politics in the context of the Shah Bano and Ayodhya controversies (1984–96) which set the stage for its decline in the 1990s; the second chapter deals with economic liberalization (1986–96) which too produced its share of discontents and contributed to party decline in the 1990s. It then moves on to political changes, processes, and policies that reversed this process and began the revival of the Congress. The 2004–9 period marks a distinct phase as it was heading a coalition government at the Centre with the direct participation of regional parties and the outside support of the Left parties. The next six chapters concentrate on this period of transition.

Chapters 3 and 4 examine how this came about and how the Congress adjusted to the realities of coalition politics and the government–party relationship under the UPA arising out of Sonia Gandhi's decision to decline the post of prime minister in 2004, and what impact, if any, this had on organizational change. Chapter 5 tracks the overall policy change and the attempt to reconcile equity with growth. Chapters 6, 7, and 8 examine the Congress's political–policy response to three critical issues: rural inequalities, minority development, and the India–US nuclear deal. The approach to these issues signals major departures, and all three impacted its core social constituencies: the poor, the minorities, and the middle classes that the Congress was keen to court in the process of forging a new social coalition. Finally, the book concludes by looking at the challenges of sustaining a policy-driven reinvention of the party.

As noted earlier, the records of the Congress Party are either unavailable or are not maintained in the way they were during the first two decades after Independence. This book has therefore had to rely on reportage in newspapers and news magazines which provide a rich day-to-day account of political developments and debates, and the pros and cons of political and policy options and analysis. However, important insights on changing Congress politics and strategy have come from a series of interviews of leading politicians and policymakers over the past few years.

NOTES

1. Cited in the Political Resolution of the 83rd Plenary Session of the Congress Party, New Delhi, 19 December 2010. Available at http://www.congress.org.in/new/political_resolution_83rd_plenary_delhi.pdf (accessed on 24 December 2010).
2. See Rajni Kothari, 'The Congress System in India', *Asian Survey*, August 1964.
3. The Indian Constitution, in the chapter on Fundamental Rights, enshrines the principle of non-discrimination by enabling the state to make special provision for the advancement of any socially and educationally backward classes of citizens or for the SCs and STs [Article 15(4)]. Such a transformative provision was added by the Constitution (First Amendment) Act, 1951.
4. Bhopal Declaration adopted unanimously by the Bhopal Conference: Charting a New Course for Dalits for the 21st Century, held at Bhopal, Madhya Pradesh, India, 12–13 January 2002.

1 Ayodhya and the Politics of Religion

The story of the Indian National Congress after Indira Gandhi's prime-ministership cannot but begin with the crisis leading to the demolition of the Babri Masjid in Ayodhya on 6 December 1992. One can scarcely overemphasize the significance of this date in India's history in the post-Indira period and the challenge it posed to a secular polity which was up against the forces of religious obscurantism and communalism. The Congress's periodical willingness to play the communal hand whenever this suited its tactical interests clearly weakened the party, and, along with it, secularism. Stanley Tambiah points to the Ayodhya dispute as 'an extremely condensed symbol' of a range of problems facing the Congress from the late 1980s into the 1990s which resulted in its terminal decline.[1] It is imperative to take stock of these terrible events because

one thing is clear: if India is to resolve its ethnic conflicts and work for a harmonious balance in its ethnic and cultural fibre, political opportunism and expediency cannot be allowed to go uncurbed. To permit this would distort the logic of development and the thrust of federal and democratic institutions. The problem is not with the institutions and the common people in India, but with a leadership that surrenders values and larger gains for short-term, selfish advantages.[2]

This chapter is not concerned with religious politics per se or political mobilization by Hindutva organizations (which is well known and well documented) but with the position and response of the Congress and its governments at the Centre to the aggravation of this dispute from 1986 to 1996, which had the result of seriously weakening the party. An appreciation of its role in giving a fillip to majority and minority sentiment from 1986 onwards and then accommodation of this sentiment, which paved the way for the Sangh Parivar and its allies to accomplish their objective of demolishing the Babri Masjid in Ayodhya, is essential for an understanding of the decline of the Congress. The destruction and violence the Masjid's demolition wreaked led to a structural shift in the centre of gravity in Indian politics from the left of centre to the right of centre. It helped the BJP to become the number-one opposition to the Congress and eventually resulted in its rise to power at the Centre in 1998. Importantly, the Ayodhya dispute and the way it spiralled out of control destroyed the Congress in north India and also redefined politics and underlined the vital need to keep religious identities outside the political arena. The edifice of secular democracy had never been under graver threat than in this period.

UNRAVELLING THE SECULAR FABRIC

From the early 1980s, a series of events, some unintended, others calculated, helped anti-secular forces to gain a foothold in the political system and destabilize and challenge Congress dominance. The unravelling of the secular fabric began with the demands for regional autonomy in Punjab and the form in which the Congress responded to these. To counter the popularity of the Akali Dal, its regional rival, the Congress leaders decided to play 'the Hindu card' in this state. Indira Gandhi refused to take stern action against Sant Jarnail Singh Bhindranwale (Sikh preacher-turned-extremist), thereby allowing him to run amuck and turn his rage against Hindus.[3] The Congress expected the Hindu reaction in north India to consolidate behind the party and also help it regain political support in the rest of the country. However, the attacks orchestrated from the Golden Temple in Amritsar against Hindus spun out of hand, and could only be contained after she ordered the army to eject the militants who had taken control of the shrine. The Sikh separatists, led by Bhindranwale, were accused of amassing weapons in the Golden Temple. As a consequence, the first week of June 1984 'witnessed Operation Bluestar, an unprecedented attack by the state on a place of worship'.[4]

The news of Indira Gandhi's assassination plunged New Delhi and other parts of the country into a rage of Hindu violence against Sikhs. While she lay in state at Teen Murti House, mobs went on the rampage through the streets of the capital and elsewhere over the following three days, killing some 3,000 Sikhs. The violence was entirely one-sided, in that Hindus attacked Sikhs. The Delhi police did little to stop or apprehend the rioters 'who roamed the streets, killing and burning at will'.[5] In some instances, the police actively joined in the mayhem, in others it turned a blind eye.[6] The home minister, Rao, did not call in the army on 31 October. Following the deployment of the army, almost three days after the onset of the riots, was order fully restored. This was only after Rajiv Gandhi swung into action in the face of gross dereliction of duty at the highest echelons of the government.

The violence, arson, and looting that took place for three days that followed the assassination of Indira Gandhi was organized and well planned. Investigative reports by civil society groups found evidence that in several areas, local residents, Congress activists, and leaders of the lower echelons of the party were involved in commandeering buses to transport enraged Hindus from the slums to the areas they attacked and provided them with paraffin and weaponry. The uniform pattern of attacks suggests that the objective was to teach the Sikhs a lesson. Most of the reports spoke of the failure of the police and the inertia and indifference of the official machinery to take action against mobs led by local Congress politicians and hoodlums.[7] The Nanavati Commission which submitted its report in 2007 documented evidence against some members of the ruling Congress for instigating mobs to kill Sikhs in their constituencies.[8] Many reports and analysis of the 1984 pogrom have noted that far from being spontaneous expressions of anger at the assassination of Indira Gandhi, the killing of Sikhs was a well-organized action by some Congress leaders.[9] Those who covered the riots generally believe that what Delhi witnessed for 72 hours was not an instance of Hindu–Sikh riots but 'Congress–Sikh riots', or rather 'Delhi Congress–Sikh riots', as *The Indian Express* editor Shekhar Gupta described it much later in the context of the Gujarat violence.[10]

However, even as the riots were dying out on 3 November, Delhi's Lieutenant-Governor P.G. Gavai was fired and the serving Union Home Secretary M.M.K. Wali was removed. The political careers of Congress leaders, H.K.L Bhagat, Jagdish Tytler, and Sajjan Kumar who were accused of involvment in the violence never recovered from the taint of 1984. The party gradually distanced itself from these leaders, and this explains why it ended up developing an attitude of contrition, which was expressed when Jagdish Tytler had to quit the cabinet on charges that he helped the anti-Sikh mobs, and the party did not let him contest the 2009 parliamentary elections because he had not been exonerated of these charges.[11] In 2009, the Congress also denied an election ticket to Sajjan Kumar, the other major politician accused of instigating rioters in 1984.

Rajiv Gandhi remarked that 'when a mighty tree falls, it is only natural that the earth around it does shake a little'.[12] It took a long time for the Congress to live down the impact of this remark and its government to apologize for the massacre of Sikhs. It was a Sikh, Prime Minister Manmohan Singh, who tendered an apology to the community over the 1984 violence in August 2005.[13] He said: 'My head hangs in shame.'[14] The carnage in Bombay in 1992 and in Gujarat in 2002, each accounting for thousands of brutal murders, cannot be properly understood without reckoning with the far-reaching legacy of what happened in Delhi in the wake of Indira Gandhi's assassination and the failure to punish the guilty, especially as it happened in the heart of the capital.

RISE OF RAJIV GANDHI

Rajiv Gandhi was sworn in as prime minister within hours of Indira Gandhi's assassination. Elections were held in November 1984. When the results were out in December, the Congress had swept the polls, capturing 48 per cent of the popular vote and 77 per cent of the seats in the Lok Sabha.[15] The party won 401 seats, far more than they had ever done under Jawaharlal Nehru or Indira Gandhi. In 1984, the Congress occupied a dominant position in the Lok Sabha and in many Vidhan Sabhas. The BJP was reduced to two seats in the Parliament and was totally wiped out in the Hindi-speaking states. This victory happened even though the Congress did not possess a strong organization and remained structurally weak in the states.

India Today declared Rajiv Gandhi's unprecedented electoral mandate 'a historic win; one that India is not likely to ever see again'.[16] However, as one of the prime minister's advisors admitted: 'The victory was as much his late mother's as his own.'[17] The polls were dominated by the sympathy generated by Indira Gandhi's assassination. The election campaign presented Rajiv Gandhi as the only bulwark against the forces of disunity. The campaign, wrote one commentator, 'capitalized on the growing mass insecurities' and 'Mrs Gandhi's assassination was equated in the public mind with an assault on the Indian state and that perception was constantly reinforced'.[18] It played upon anti-Sikh sentiments: 'India could be your vote away from unity or separation'[19] ran the punch line of one advertisement featuring Rajiv Gandhi. Promises to safeguard the nation against external threats to unity aroused an emotional response from voters of diverse backgrounds. But a year after the famous victory, the Congress lost the assembly elections in Punjab, Assam, Karnataka, Andhra Pradesh, West Bengal, and Tamil Nadu. By the end of 1985, it ruled only in Bihar, Gujarat, Haryana, Himachal Pradesh, Madhya Pradesh, Maharashtra, Orissa, Rajasthan, and Uttar Pradesh. The Congress had become the party of the Hindi heartland and the neighbouring states, while opposition parties were in control of the southern and eastern states. This, however, changed dramatically in the 1990s when Congress power shifted to the south after its terminal decline in the north.

The prime minister was eager to break new ground in various aspects of economic and foreign policy as well as domestic politics. He promised to 'propel the country into the twenty-first century' through principled politics, efficient government, and modern technologies. Towards this end, his government passed the 52nd Amendment to the Constitution, an anti-defection law that banned defectors from political parties joining another party and retaining their seats unless at least a third of the legislative party split from the parent party. He also initiated the exercise to amend the Constitution to provide a constitutional status and mandate for holding of elections to local bodies but the 73rd and 74th Amendments did not pass muster in Parliament. Eventually, the Narasimha Rao government reworked the Amendments which became law as the Constitution 73rd and 74th Amendments in 1993.[20]

Rajiv Gandhi was keen to break away from his mother's more confrontationist approach towards opposition parties to one of accommodation and reconciliation.[21] He searched for political solutions in Punjab and Assam, and displayed a willingness to give up power in these states in order to restore peace and normalcy.[22] In July 1985, Rajiv Gandhi and Sant Harcharan Singh Longowal signed an accord, agreeing to the transfer of Chandigarh to Punjab within a specified time frame, assuring a fair share of river waters to Punjab, and committing the government to a review of Centre–state relations. This did not, however, bring the turbulence in Punjab to an end and Longowal was assassinated a month later. In the face of strong opposition in Punjab and Haryana, the accord was never implemented.[23] Besides, this strategy of entering into accords with moderate elements to contain ethnic secessionisms did not bring extremism to an end, and in fact resulted in losses at the polls. The accord reached with Assamese agitators on the issue of illegal Bangladeshi immigrants was followed by losses in the Assam elections of 1985.

Expectations about reviving the Congress were high when Rajiv Gandhi became the prime minister. He, however, frittered away the advantage within two years. Far from invigorating the party, he functioned as though he could minimize the role of the organization or dispense with it altogether. He persisted with the centralized decision-making structure and, what is more, power was concentrated in the hands of a small group of inexperienced personal advisors. The dominant advisors came from outside politics, infused with a corporate culture. Two of them, Arun Nehru and Arun Singh, played a key role in decision-making on several important and controversial issues even though they had 'not the foggiest idea of politics'.[24] The cabinet was frequently reshuffled, and there were repeated changes in state leadership, with two individuals alternating in brief spells as chief minister during Rajiv Gandhi's five-year tenure in the crucial states of Uttar Pradesh and Madhya Pradesh. Bihar, similarly, had three different chief ministers; Maharashtra had four; and Gujarat, Haryana, and Rajasthan had two each. In fact, no Congress chief minister, with the exception of J.B. Patnaik in Orissa, was allowed to complete a full five-year term. The massive mandate for the Congress in the 1984 elections had led 'Rajiv Gandhi to believe that he had the latitude to act independently without realizing that any action against powerful interests and entrenched attitudes would provoke opposition'.[25]

Rajiv Gandhi, in a remarkable speech commemorating the centenary of the Congress in Bombay in December 1985, mounted a sweeping critique of the party organization and pointed out the weakness in its functioning. He denounced the power-brokers, as he called them, 'who dispense patronage to convert a mass movement into a feudal oligarchy'.[26] He spoke of Congress party bosses 'who thrive on the slogans of caste and religion', and of 'cliques ... enmeshing the living body of the Congress in their net of avarice'.[27] He complained of Congress operatives and their 'self-aggrandizement, their corrupt ways, their linkages with vested interests ... and their sanctimonious posturing' and said that 'corruption is not only tolerated ... but even regarded as a hallmark of leadership'.[28] He appointed his close associate Arjun Singh as the party vice-president, who, along with new general secretaries was given the responsibility of reorganizing the party. Having thus launched a frontal attack on power-brokers, he was, however, unable to get rid of them. In the end, all he was able to achieve was to replace Indira Gandhi's coterie with his own.

Two years later, very little had been accomplished. Whilst Rajiv Gandhi's speech was 'revolutionary', it did not go down well as the power-brokers, who had vested interests, would not allow him to implement it.[29] For all practical purposes, the effort ended there and virtually no evidence exists to show that he took steps to begin the process of implementing the radical thoughts he had enunciated in his Bombay speech. His avowed goal of restructuring the party to make it more democratic had stalled. Party elections were announced and postponed on at least five occasions during his term in office, and it proved impossible to hold them during his lifetime. The Congress remained leader-driven and completely dependent on him. As Congress president, he launched a membership drive in March 1986 but was unable to end the fraudulent practice of enrolment of bogus members given the enormous disarray of party records, including hundreds of thousands of names of bogus members.[30] This forced him to cancel party elections. Following this, he was advised not to hold party elections because bogus membership would lead to the election of the very power-brokers who Rajiv Gandhi wanted to check.[31]

By mid-term, Rajiv Gandhi's grip over his own party had weakened considerably. Like his mother, he depended upon the formal institutions of the state and not the party to mobilize people. The Congress had ceased to exist as a political organization in many states and was riddled with corruption and factionalism. Senior leaders were disgruntled and unhappy with the direction the party was taking. Pranab Mukherjee, finance minister in Indira Gandhi's cabinet and a dissident leader at the time, was expelled, while the party's working president, Kamlapati Tripathi, was forced to step down after he expressed sympathy for dissidents. Tripathi blamed the ad hoc and inept handling of party matters by Rajiv Gandhi and his advisors for the decline of the Congress in assembly elections.[32] He criticized the frequent changes in the party and administration for 'injecting uncertainties in the whole system'.[33]

In the end, the party's electoral appeal came to depend upon 'the discrete charms of the Nehru–Gandhi dynasty'.[34] It was, however, to Rajiv Gandhi's credit that he did recognize that only a strong organization anchored in people's support, and not the charisma of an individual or his family, could help the party to grow. However, the failure to translate the electoral victory in 1984 to further success in state assembly elections reduced his capacity to cope with organizational restructuring, dissidence within the party, and the storm brewing without.

PLACATING RELIGIOUS SENTIMENT:
SHAH BANO AND AYODHYA

Halfway through his five-year term as prime minister, Rajiv Gandhi had faltered in most of his major initiatives. What had, however, created the greatest problems for him and the Congress was the compromising overtures and tactics that he was advised to adopt towards the demands of the various religious communities and their sundry anxieties. This did not mitigate political disagreement, but rather provoked and aggravated tension. One of the cardinal mistakes was to get directly involved in the controversy over the role of the state in regulating the personal law of religious minorities, and that at a time when Hindutva politics were on the rise. The timing of this initiative was obviously wrong. The prime minister, concerned about losing Muslim support, decided to enact the Muslim Women's (Protection of Rights on Divorce) Act (MWA) of 1986.[35] This was done to revoke the landmark Supreme Court judgement which granted a maintenance allowance to Shah Bano, a 73-year-old Muslim divorcee, to be paid by her husband under the Criminal Procedure Code (Cr Pc). The Court ruled that Section 125, as part of criminal rather than civil law, overrode all personal law and was uniformly applicable to all women, including Muslim women. At stake in this case was the right of a divorced Muslim woman to claim maintenance from her former husband under the Cr Pc. The judgement saw significant political mobilization, but the trigger was not the substance of the ruling itself. Earlier court rulings too had granted maintenance to divorced Muslim women, so it was the Supreme Court's going out of its way to regret that a uniform civil code had remained a 'dead letter' and also invoking the authority of the Quran to justify maintenance that incensed the Muslim leaders, and the case became such a hot potato.

This controversy sparked off a huge political uproar, demanding exclusion of Muslim women from the purview of the Cr Pc, to which otherwise all citizens have recourse. Acting on the advice of the clergy, the Congress government took the decision to nullify the court's verdict and enact the MWA, declaring that Muslim women would not have recourse to the provisions of the Cr Pc in regard to maintenance in the event of divorce. Rajiv Gandhi succumbed to pressure from Muslims leaders in his own party to pass this statute. This one piece of legislation which allowed Muslim personal law to prevail in reversal of the court decision ruined his reputation for modernity and progressiveness, and the move inflamed Hindu sentiments. It became a bone of contention between Muslim conservatives and critics of the government. The new law created problems not only for sex equality but also for non-discrimination on grounds of religion: Muslim women alone were denied this remedy under the criminal code.

The compromise in surrendering Muslim women's rights was part of the larger ideological shake-up in this period, resulting in a closer entanglement of politics and religion. The conciliatory response to Muslim misgivings against the court verdict tipped the balance in favour of opposition parties who campaigned against it.[36] For his part, Rajiv Gandhi felt that a purely liberal position was not compatible with the position of traditional communities as all communities in India have discriminatory practices. 'Proponents of ungrounded liberalism maligned Rajiv Gandhi but he felt uneasy that the Supreme Court judgement was part of a campaign of derision of Muslim personal law which they hold as divine,' explains Mani Shankar Aiyar, a close aide of the prime minister.[37] The immediate imperative appeared to him to be to reassure substantial segments of the Muslim minority that constitutional safeguards for their personal law were not being eroded; that they were not being called upon to subject the Shariat to civil jurisdiction as the price to be paid for continuing as equal citizens of the country. Significantly, the Congress accepted that Muslims must decide the 'true' interests of their community and any reform of such practices has to be undertaken by the community itself.

This excessive regard for Muslim sensibilities on personal law provoked an indignant reaction that India would be overrun by a rapidly rising Muslim population propagated by multiple wives. There was strong opposition from the middle classes, from Hindus more generally, and from the women's movement, which regarded the MWA as a concession to Muslim fundamentalism and a break from secularism. This was a blessing for the BJP which for the first time experienced a conjunction of interests between the party and the middle classes which agreed that India's Muslims were being pampered by the Congress. For long the BJP had sought to demonstrate that the Congress was 'pseudo-secular' because it had been interventionist with regard to the reform of Hindu personal laws while it refrained from interfering with those of Muslims. To the BJP and many other people outside the BJP circles, the Shah Bano episode was a touchstone of this. The passage of the MWA gave them a significant opportunity to revitalize this critique and further condemn the double standards of the state's constitutional law and jurisprudence. The political fallout was severe. Having done this, the Congress felt compelled to mollify Hindu militants demanding concessions on the Ayodhya dispute.

During this period, the BJP and its affiliates launched a nationwide campaign to construct a Rama temple at the site of the Babri mosque in Ayodhya. Hindu activists had been claiming that the mosque stood at the exact spot believed to be the birthplace of Lord Rama, and its use by Muslims was sacrilegious. A campaign to unlock the gates of the mosque and for the construction of a Rama temple at Ayodhya was launched by the Vishwa Hindu Parishad (VHP) in 1984. The stir took a popular militant turn when it made the liberation of Rama's birthplace the cornerstone of its programme, which was supported by the BJP and the RSS. The unresolved dispute in Ayodhya seemed to offer an opportunity for Hindu nationalism to garner support for the BJP. The historic moment was primarily the outcome of a series of events in the late 1980s that created a conducive climate for the growth of sectarian politics.

The District and Sessions Judge of Faizabad, K.M. Pandey, ordered the locks of the Babri mosque, which had remained padlocked for decades, to be opened for Hindu worshippers on 1 February 1986. Arun Nehru, one of the chief advisors of the prime minister, was thinking in terms of a quid pro quo to appease the Hindu militants in exchange for the concession to Muslim clerics on the MWA. The unlocking of the gates was 'manipulated through a judicial order' with the aid of the Uttar Pradesh government.[38] The opperatives seized on the Ayodhya controversy to pre-empt the VHP plan for a large-scale agitation with little grasp of the explosive situation this would create. Significantly, this came as a surprise to the VHP because they feared that they were about to lose their most important issue for mobilization.[39] The Congress did not take into account that the VHP would view this concession as the first step towards the demolition of the Babri Masjid, which is in fact how it perceived it. Together, these two decisions—the revocation of the Shah Bano verdict and the reopening of the gates to the mosque in Ayodhya—were part of a 'grand' strategy to arrest its declining hold over Hindu and Muslim votes.

By the autumn of 1989, the atmosphere had become surcharged with tension when the VHP announced plans to perform *shilanyas* (consecration) in different parts of the country and carry bricks, manufactured for the purpose, to Ayodhya to lay the foundation stone of the Rama temple. In the face of this, the Congress government allowed the VHP to perform shilanyas at the disputed site. Rajiv Gandhi had taken a legalistic rather than a political position, which meant that there could be no objection to a Rama temple but the mosque must be protected. The shilanyas ceremony took place in November 1989, just days before the commencement of the parliamentary election. Unlike the opening of the gates to the Babri Masjid, which was supposed to have been undertaken under a court order, there was no such justification this time, except the hope that there would be a turnaround in the Hindu vote. Even the assassination of Indira Gandhi had not driven home the dangers of this approach. It was as if the Congress had forgotten all this within a span of just a few years.

The party leadership reckoned that it could not afford to lose the initiative to the BJP and the Hindu support it was aiming for.[40] Allowing the shilanyas to take place at the disputed site, although Rajiv Gandhi later admitted this was done under the erroneous impression that the area fell outside the disputed land,[41] proved to be a breaking point. This tactical surrender had set the party on a perilous course but the political strategists continued to believe that the Congress would stand to benefit from this in the impending elections.[42] That did not happen because the BJP, VHP, and RSS launched a campaign to convince Hindus that the shilanyas had been the result of their efforts to compel the Uttar Pradesh government to concede to their demand. On the other hand, these actions inflicted serious damage on the Congress's political base in Uttar Pradesh and inflamed Muslim sentiment. Violence had broken out in the prime minister's Sultanpur constituency just hours before his visit in November 1989. Rajiv Gandhi reiterated his party's commitment to secularism in his speech attended by just 100 persons, an indication of which way the wind was blowing. He tried to assure the Muslim community that the Babri Masjid was safe. The leadership was in damage control as the situation had spiralled out of hand.

Rajiv Gandhi wanted to be present in Ayodhya at the time of the shilanyas but his handlers disabused him of the idea.[43] In the end, he did not go to Ayodhya but instead went on a *sadbhavna yatra* which aimed at undoing the damage caused by opening the gates of the mosque and the shilanyas. Had he followed through with his decision to go to

Ayodhya, he may well have been able to thwart the political coalescence of the opposition that removed him from power a few months later. Post shilanyas, Congress leaders were keen to harness the political advantages opened by the Ayodhya controversy even if that meant brushing aside secular principles and the prime minister's assurances. In the event, Rajiv Gandhi launched his party's election campaign with a meeting at Ayodhya–Faizabad on 3 November 1989. He was under pressure to start the campaign from Faizabad and not Nagaur as was earlier decided.[44] It was widely expected that he would assert on this occasion his own and his party's commitment to secularism but he instead promised to establish Rama Rajya. This was apparently not part of the draft of the speech and was added later in Faizabad.[45]

Senior Congress leader from Uttar Pradesh, Kamlapati Tripathi warned that this craven approach would destroy the unity and integrity of the country and the only course open to the party was mass mobilization to counter the VHP moves. Needless to say, the party leaders did not heed this advice as it was keen to undercut the BJP's temple campaign with its own gestures to appease Hindu sentiment but it backfired as the Sangh Parivar rapidly seized the initiative. The leadership was playing the Ayodhya card in the fond hope that RSS votes would go to the Congress.[46] It was hoping to outmanoeuvre the BJP by roping in the VHP on its side. It was only much later that it realized that it was alienating Muslims and by no means winning over Hindus. It tried to contain the damage by shifting the issue to the legal terrain. The principal consequence of this process was the acceleration of communal polarization, contributing to a groundswell of support for the BJP and a point of no recovery for the Congress which had completely lost the plot. The leadership admitted that permitting the shilanyas was a mistake, but it was too late to retrieve the ground it had lost.

THE END OF CONGRESS MAJORITY

Rajiv Gandhi had come to power with an unprecedented mandate, but as the general elections of 1989 approached, the Congress was hard-pressed to maintain its supremacy. It faced three serious challenges; the first from regional parties which were well-entrenched in Assam, Andhra Pradesh, Tamil Nadu, and Punjab, and the Communist Party of India (Marxist) [CPI (M)] in West Bengal. The second came from the Hindu right and the rising influence of the BJP which had hitched its fortunes to the Ayodhya campaign. The third challenge to Rajiv Gandhi came from his former cabinet colleague, V.P. Singh. Before the 1989 election, Rajiv Gandhi and his government were overwhelmed by a corruption scandal on major defence contracts. The most devastating was the Bofors contract for 155 mm howitzers. The charges of payoff were pressed by the defence minister, V.P. Singh, who later resigned from the cabinet. The prime minister compounded the problem by expelling Singh from the Congress in June 1987, and the latter subsequently became the focal point of the anti-Congress campaign. This situation resembled that which had existed before Indira Gandhi imposed the Emergency, with non-Congress parties coming together to oppose it. V.P. Singh emerged as the symbol of opposition unity and thus opened up the prospect of an alignment of opposition parties with the single objective of removing the Congress from power.

Of the three challenges confronting the Congress, the Ayodhya movement was the most serious in the long run for the party and its political bases which were destroyed by courting the Hindu vote through concessions to this movement. It set the stage for the communalization and polarization of politics in north India. Relations between Hindus and Muslims were tense, not least because of the incidence of communal riots and the resulting loss of lives and property. In 1989 alone, 500 people were killed in a series of riots that erupted in several parts of the country, notably Uttar Pradesh, Karnataka, Bihar, Madhya Pradesh, Gujarat, Maharashtra, and Rajasthan.[47] The home ministry officially classified 100 districts as 'hypersensitive' areas of communal tension.[48] The period also marked 'the beginning of a dangerous phase in which religion had come to be accepted as part of electoral politics and religious issues played a decisive role in political events'.[49] The Congress's ill-conceived attempts to manipulate the religious sentiments of both communities did not go down well with the voters. The BJP was the chief gainer as it had throughout supported Hindutva politics with greater conviction. In the 1989 parliamentary elections, it wrested 86 seats and won 12 per cent of the vote across the country in comparison with 7.5 per cent in 1984 on the basis of an avowedly Hindu plank.[50] The Congress lost both Hindu and Muslim votes, its seats declining from 415 in 1984 to 197 in 1989. The results were a rebuff to the Congress which remained the largest party in Parliament but was unable to form a government. Meanwhile, the BJP was all set to replace the Congress in Uttar Pradesh.

BJP'S AYODHYA FORMULA TO REPLACE THE CONGRESS

The political response to the Ayodhya movement combined with the Hindutva appeal convinced the BJP that they had at last found a formula to replace the Congress as the dominant political party in Uttar Pradesh, then the pathway to power at the Centre.[51] The party saw a great opportunity for expansion in the post-1989 phase of political instability and electoral stalemates. In the short run, it opened up the prospect of changing both the ideological discourse and institutional politics in favour of the majoritarian idea of India as a Hindu nation, quite contrary to the Congress's pluralist, non-parochial idea of India. The objective of the Sangh Parivar's orchestrated movement and violence against Muslims was to impose majoritarian domination over the polity and to convert the demographic majority of Hindus into an electoral majority.[52]

L.K. Advani, the president of the BJP, started a *rath yatra* that commenced from Somnath in Gujarat and had a final destination of Ayodhya. The yatra, which was to awaken the Hindu masses in favour of a Rama temple, began on 25 September 1990. Advani made it a point to emphasize that '[t]his [rath yatra] is a crusade against pseudo-secularism and minorityism which I regard as a political issue. Don't be under the misconception that I have become religious,' later reiterating, 'I am a politician.'[53] The rath yatra traversed eight states, stoking religious emotions and polarization in equal measure, to demand the construction of a Rama temple. In 1991, for the first time, it emerged as the single largest opposition party in the Parliament and won elections in four state assemblies, forming the governments in Uttar Pradesh, Madhya Pradesh, Rajasthan, and Himachal Pradesh. Electoral support for the BJP had grown unprecedentedly.

By the time the Congress government was formed in 1991 after it returned to power in the wake of the assassination of Rajiv Gandhi by Sri Lankan Liberation Tigers of Tamil Eelam (LTTE) while camping in Sriperambudur, the battle lines were clearly drawn around the secular–communal divide with the Ayodhya issue at the centre of it. It is important to note the political context which framed these changes. The early 1990s were a time of 'painful transition' for the Congress. It was the most traumatic period in its post-Independence history when a party with close to three-fourths majority could no longer muster a majority of seats, and it had to govern as a minority in need of allies. The popular vote had declined to 36.5 per cent, but a divided opposition allowed it to win 232 seats. It gained another 18 seats from an alliance with the All India Anna Dravida Munnetra Kazhagam (AIADMK) and support of small parties and splinter groups. It was only in late 1993 that it achieved a majority and even then by winning over defectors. The communal expediency of the Congress, particularly on the Ayodhya issue in the face of the threat and competition it faced from the BJP and its affiliates, had cost the party dearly in the 1991 parliamentary elections; it began to lose the support of its traditional constituencies, especially Muslims. Meanwhile, the OBCs shifted almost completely to the Janata Dal and regional parties which had actively pushed for the adoption of the Mandal Commission recommendations in 1990 by V.P. Singh. A few months later, Congress governments in almost all the states which went to the polls were replaced by non-Congress coalitions.

The BJP continued with its campaign for the construction of a grand Rama temple that it had promised its supporters. This resulted in the greatest crisis the Congress government faced, which was an upshot of its decision to remove the padlocks from the gates of the Babri Masjid. These concessions intensified political mobilization rather than, as the Congress might have hoped, containing it. At the same time, it was confronted with the loss of Muslim support as a consequence of these very concessions. Even so, it continued with the ill-advised strategy. The context was, however, more polarized than earlier. The party had to countenance a formidable challenger in the BJP which was more adept than it in playing religious politics but even then the leadership refused to recognize the pitfalls of its placatory approach towards the VHP.

From the standpoint of the Congress, the critical question is whether the Narasimha Rao government could have saved the Babri Masjid? The central government could indeed have prevented the demolition had it shown the requisite political will and interest in doing so and taken timely action in the light of intelligence reports and available information of the build-up to the destruction.

After reaping the benefits of the VHP-led mobilization on Ayodhya, the BJP government in Uttar Pradesh formed in 1991 was under pressure from the VHP and its restive supporters to implement the promise of building a Rama temple. The intentions of the state government were evident from the steady takeover of the surrounding land, demolition of all other structures on it, and withdrawal of various security arrangements to protect the mosque from December 1991 onwards.[54] The state government's objective was to transfer the land to the VHP to start construction by way of *kar sewa* on a portion of it outside the disputed area on the assumption that once construction began it could not be stopped even if the court verdict went in favour of Muslims.[55] However, the Waqf Board challenged the land acquisition in the Allahabad High Court which ruled that it could not allow the construction of a temple on this land until all sides of the case had been heard.[56] The VHP was unwilling to be constrained by legal stipulations but camouflaged this by its categorical assurance to the National Integration Council (NIC) on 2 November 1991 to protect the mosque till a final solution to the dispute was found. The BJP did not therefore oppose the NIC resolution but the kar sewa continued unabated.[57]

The BJP government's intentions of building a Rama temple were explicit and unequivocal from the very outset even if there is no agreement on the extent to which the demolition was planned. Uttar Pradesh Chief Minister Kalyan Singh had no intention of stopping the kar sewa even if that led to the demolition of the mosque.[58] Moreover, Rao could not have been unaware of the BJP's two-fold strategy of assuring the central government and the courts that it would not violate the judicial order, while the Sangh Parivar organizations continued to mobilize *kar sewak*s to press ahead with the plans to demolish the Babri Masjid.[59]

The Congress government at the Centre could have stepped in the day the state government began demolishing the buildings on the acquired land but did not act.[60] Arjun Singh felt that the government lost its opportunity by not acting at the critical moment when the demolitions commenced.[61] It was an obvious misjudgement which was justified to 'avoid a confrontationist approach' and on grounds of the binding commitments obtained by the Supreme Court from the Uttar Pradesh government to safeguard and protect the disputed structure in Ayodhya. The prime minister chose to ignore the court's observation that 'the Centre was free to take such action as it may deem appropriate'.[62]

Rao did not heed warnings regarding the threat to the mosque. He reiterated the commitment of the Congress given in its election manifesto to finding a solution to the dispute, and if an agreed solution was not possible, then a legal solution had to be found.[63] He focused on negotiations with an assortment of sadhus and sants and the Sangh

Parivar, and receiving assurances from them that the mosque would not be harmed. From the beginning of September to almost the end of November 1992, over 90 meetings were held between Hindu and Muslim delegations, achieving nothing other than bringing the leaders of the Babri Masjid Action Committee (BMAC) and VHP to the negotiating table.[64] As a legal way out of the imbroglio, he proposed referring all pending cases to the Supreme Court.[65] The chief minister summarily rejected the idea in the meeting with the prime minister on 30 November 1992 and declared that he was prepared only to accept a non-binding advisory reference under Article 143. In the event, the Congress government was left with no alternative other than central intervention. This line of action was not, however, seriously considered as a strategic decision had been taken to allow the BJP government in Uttar Pradesh to continue in spite of mounting evidence of a threat to the mosque. The NIC meeting on 23 November 1992, which the BJP decided to boycott, extended its whole-hearted support and cooperation in whatever steps the prime minister considers essential in upholding the Constitution and the rule of law and in implementing Court orders.[66]

The build-up to the demolition was obvious from late November 1992. Reports prepared by senior Intelligence Bureau officials sent to the offices of the Prime Minister, Home Minister S.B. Chavan, and Home Secretary Madhav Godbole highlighted the catastrophic situation unfolding in Ayodhya during the week preceding the demolition as the kar sewaks were highly charged.[67] The Attorney General pointed out in the Supreme Court that the situation in Ayodhya had reached a 'boiling point'.[68] The number of people congregating in Ayodhya was rising rapidly: from 500 on 25 November to 175,000 on 30 November to over 2 lakh by 5 December.[69] As senior and retired police officer N.S. Saxena explains:

The initial error, deliberate or unforeseen, was to allow 200,000 people to congregate. Once this was done, the security forces became helpless as they had specific orders not to fire. The huge unruly mob could not be stopped from vandalism without killing not tens but several hundreds. Obviously no government in India would agree to kill several hundreds of its citizens.[70]

Rao was later asked: 'Were you told by your advisors that once a mob of two lakhs had gathered, there was no way you could control it.' He replied: 'I don't agree at all. Five lakhs people come here and collect at the Boat Club. They come and go and nobody notices. You see, that is what I said, this is a country of crowds. Just because two lakh people have come doesn't mean anything new.'[71]

This response was hardly surprising as Rao was opposed to the dismissal of the Uttar Pradesh government even though there was actionable intelligence that it would not and could not control crowds of 5 lakh after having allowed them to gather there in contravention of court orders. Not many were convinced by the state government's assurance that only a symbolic kar sewa will take place. The home ministry was convinced that the only way the mosque could be saved was to take it over and impose president's rule, and had made all preparations for such an eventuality. The law ministry was consulted and it had concurred.[72] On 30 November, Rao asked the home secretary to bring up a cabinet note which, according to Madhav Godbole, 'was kept ready every day'.[73] The question was of getting clearance from the top, which never came.[74]

In its 13 December 1992 issue, one week after the demolition, the RSS mouthpiece, the *Organiser*, wrote:

The Sangh Parivar played its cards well in this battle of wits with the PM.... It was decided to devise a strategy to confront the Centre while avoiding a clash with the judiciary. It was as part of this strategy that the UP government filed [an] affidavit in the Supreme Court ... that the government would not allow violation of the court's orders.[75]

Rao narrates in detail his reasoning and response to the Ayodhya crisis in his posthumously published book *Ayodhya: 6 December 1992*.[76] He trusted the Uttar Pradesh government's assurances about the protection of the Babri Masjid despite his admission that 'the situation had step-by-step been allowed to escalate to a point where construction activity was proceeding despite Court orders restraining it, and the state government said that it was helpless to stop the activity.[77] Rao allowed all this to continue unchecked even though in his own words 'the situation had become very critical and the state government had expressed its inability to do anything', culminating in the demolition of the mosque in Ayodhya.[78] His account provides sufficient evidence of the gradual escalation of construction activity despite court orders restraining it and his full knowledge of it, and the state government refusing to do anything to stop it. Rao relied on the strategy of legal constraints to prevent the demolition, and he had accepted the assurances given by Kalyan

Singh that the mosque would be protected. Yet, he did not agree to the imposition of president's rule because according to him promulgation of Article 356 would be justified only when the government of the state failed in its constitutional duty to protect the structure, 'and it is not possible to invoke the provision to serve a preventive purpose in time'.[79] A chapter in Rao's book on why Article 356 was not invoked pleads that the Centre can intervene in a state only after imposing president's rule and, in this case, the Centre could not do so because the state government had given an assurance that it would protect the mosque.[80]

The Supreme Court accepted the state government's assurances,[81] the governor gave Rao similar assurance in his appraisal, so according to him there was nothing to show that the state government did not intend to what it had assured. 'If it turned out otherwise how can I be blamed?' he asks.[82] He justified his inaction by putting the entire blame on Kalyan Singh and his betrayal stating that '[t]he UP government and the BJP, the party of the state government, would have to be held completely responsible for the wanton vandalism perpetrated on the secular credentials of the nation on that unfortunate day'.[83] Excessive fear of public disapproval was perhaps weighing on Rao's mind in not taking action under Articles 355 or 356.[84]

Rao government chose not to act even though 'it had the Constitution on its side, it had the requisite security forces at its command, and it had been forewarned sufficiently in advance by the intending evil-doers themselves'.[85] The pious concern for propriety when the entire constitutional order was under threat was bizarre. Even the Left parties, the most strident critics of the imposition of Article 356 by the Centre on the ground that it has been misused to blunt opposition to the central government, ridiculed the prime minister's stand on its use in this instance. Jyoti Basu, chief minister of West Bengal, telephoned the prime minister on 4 December 1992 'to inform him that there was apprehension that Babri Masjid may be attacked and hence something has to be done to protect it'.[86] A year later Basu and Harkishan Singh Surjeet asked him why nothing was done and he repeated his line that he had no reason to disbelieve the assurances of the chief minister that no harm would be done to the mosque.[87] The Left leaders felt that the government was using this as an alibi to avoid taking stringent action against the BJP government in a timely and effective manner. Rajeev Dhavan, senior advocate and counsel for the BMAC, charged that:

It was not the text of the Constitution which shortchanged the prime minister. It is the prime minister and his colleagues who have shortchanged the nation.... Time and again the policy of the Congress (and indeed of Mr Rao) was to impose politically motivated preemptive rather than redemptive President's rule for low, debased and often, absurd, narrow, unworthy political gains. The prime minister's newly discovered excuse for not acting decisively to save the Masjid is, with respect, perverse.... The decision to impose President's Rule is a political decision to be taken for sound political reasons to save the Constitution from lapsing.[88]

The Congress government was thus rightly accused of failing to discharge its constitutional obligations.

POLITICAL ENTENTE WITH THE BJP

It was clear that it was political considerations and not constitutional propriety that constrained Rao from imposing president's rule which was the only way of halting the demolition. The 1991 election had not delivered a clear majority for the Congress. Even though Rao was later able to 'manufacture a majority', he was unsure about the stability of his government. He feared that it 'could be voted out any time if the non-Congress parties chose to close ranks'.[89] He opened lines of communication with Hindu sadhus involved in the temple agitation and subsequently developed an informal understanding with the BJP, which effectively lasted for the entire period of his term. The BJP's support was a useful cushion to ensure the continuation of the government. Thus, in a number of instances, Rao would take the support of the BJP and tailor his decisions to ensure this. In the Places of Worship Special Provisions Bill of 1991, which imposed a status quo on all places of worship as they existed in August 1947, the government excluded the Babri Masjid/ Rama temple, presumably to assuage the BJP and its supporters.[90] It is significant that the BJP and its associates did not launch an agitation against it. They protested by abstaining on the day of the voting, which in fact ensured the smooth passage of the legislation. In other words, 'Ayodhya became a good tool to perpetuate his power by cultivating and appealing to the Hindu vote', especially because the Muslim vote had been lost to the Congress.[91] Rao's great mistake was, however, the attempt to mobilize the Hindu vote on terms set by the BJP rather than on the basis of the Congress as a party of national unity which could adjust and accommodate the majority and minority under its capacious umbrella. Rao's opportunism betrayed both the pluralism and the secular ethos of his own party.

In the political sphere, Rao thought he could frustrate the BJP by denying it the privilege of a frontal conflict against 'pseudo-secularism'. He calculated that his approach would frustrate the BJP's designs to emerge as the sole custodian of Hindu interests, and that this would reduce religious polarization. It was a high-risk strategy that came undone because the VHP understood his game and jumped the gun. Rao clearly fell into the Sangh Parivar's trap. He acknowledges that:

To the BJP also goes the dubious credit of not only hijacking the political process right into the religious ambit, but to some extent dragging other parties along with itself on the same path, if only to counter the BJP attack. The net result, however, has been that the admissibility as well as the respectability of the communal card have both been accepted, at least by necessary implication, on both sides, obviously for opposite reasons. And once the admissibility of the issue was accepted, everyone was stopped to some extent from disowning it.[92]

According to his own reasoning, calls for a crackdown underestimate the extent to which Hindutva would have benefited from a backlash.[93] He observed that the spectre of Ayodhya had haunted the Congress since the time of the shilanyas:

The BJP's pseudo-religious movement could not have sustained itself on a purely religious plane; to flourish politically it needed a political reaction: I cannot escape the uneasy feeling that we Congressmen [while in government] supplied it with just that. We also let our own religious susceptibilities go by default, with the same subconscious inhibition that any expression of religious sentiment on our part, even if we felt strongly would be seen to be non-secular. As a result the BJP became the sole repository and protector of the Hindu religion in the public mind.[94]

Under these circumstances, the Rao government came to perceive the demolition of the mosque to have been a lesser evil than having to take the responsibility for casualties that would have resulted from police action against the kar sewaks who had assembled at Ayodhya.[95]

Rao believed it was legitimate to use most of the land at the disputed site for various activities so long as the mosque itself was not threatened. It was, however, precisely those activities that generated the momentum for the eventual demolition. Basically, he favoured the construction of the temple without dismantling the mosque while the Sangh Parivar was not averse to the demolition of the Babri Masjid to make way for temple construction; indeed, to them it was clear that elimination of the mosque

was necessary for the construction of the temple. Both, however, agreed
that the religious sentiments of Hindus were paramount in the dispute and
these could not be ignored; both agreed that some kind of temple would
have to be built at Ayodhya, though Rao himself would have preferred
it to be adjoining the mosque. In the case of the Congress, the dilemma
was much greater because it did not want to displease Muslims either and
also wanted to defend its secular record against the BJP's denunciation
of it as pseudo-secularism. On the one hand, the Congress wanted to
position itself as the facilitator of a compromise, and to that extent could
never take a clear ideological position; on the other, it wanted to position
itself as a defender of secularism. At no stage did the party clarify what
this meant in practice. This dual strategy could not work after the rise of
the BJP which was using religious politics, especially Ayodhya, to gain
political power. The party wanted to capitalize on the Ayodhya issue, and
in doing so it created a tiger that it could not dismount.

On 6 December 1992, the Babri Masjid was demolished by Sangh
Parivar activists in brazen disregard of the stay order of the Supreme
Court. Even after the demolition, it took 40 hours before the Central
Reserve Police Force (CRPF) and Rapid Action Force (RAF) moved
in and took control of the site. The kar sewaks continued to run riot
following the dismissal of the Kalyan Singh government. Although the
central government took over the state administration after dismissing
the Uttar Pradesh government on 6 December, it left the disputed
area under the control of vandals for 36 hours, which enabled them to
complete the mission of erecting a makeshift temple on the site of the
demolished mosque.

The demolition ignited communal passions across the country,
leading to violence and rioting. Over 2,000 persons were killed in riots
and many more were injured. Violence spread to cities and towns, and
Muslims were the principal victims, not only in Ayodhya but also in other
cities. The central government failed to provide them protection from
the rampaging mobs and, above all, failed to provide a healing touch
to the injured Muslim psyche. The government banned the RSS, VHP,
and Bajrang Dal under the Unlawful Activities Prevention Act of 1967
on the day after the demolition.

The Uttar Pradesh government resigned on 6 December 1992,
followed by a proclamation by the president dissolving the legislative
assembly of the state. This was followed by the dismissal of the other three

BJP governments of Rajasthan, Madhya Pradesh, and Himachal Pradesh on the charge that they had lent support to the communal organizations. This led critics to argue that Rao had acted too little before the event and too much after it.[96] The ban on communal organizations was ineffective in curbing the activities of Hindu organizations, especially the RSS.[97]

The other three state governments that had been dismissed challenged the validity of the proclamations in the high court, and the cases were subsequently transferred to the Supreme Court. Apart from examining the use and abuse of Article 356 of the Constitution in imposing president's rule in the states and the scope of judicial review, the judges were asked to examine the concept of secularism in the context of imposition of president's rule in the three BJP-ruled states. The nine judges of the Supreme Court in the Bommai case accepted the central government's proclamations against these state governments because '[t]hey could not be trusted to adhere to secularism when they had admittedly come to power on the political plank of constructing Shri Ram Mandir on the site of the mosque by relocating the mosque elsewhere which meant destroying it and then reconstructing it at another place.'[98]

The judges used the Representation of People Act 1951, Section 29A, under which a political party is registered by the Election Commission if it undertakes to adhere to the Constitution, to pin down these state governments. The manifestos of the BJP and its sustained campaign for the Ramajanmabhoomi temple on the site of the mosque were accepted by the judges as proof of contravention of the Representation of the People Act, 1951.[99] The unanimous opinion of the judges was that the dismissal of these governments was constitutional. The judgement affirmed that if state governments violate the principles of secularism as enshrined in the Constitution, they can be dismissed.[100] Justice Sawant underlined that: 'Secularism is a part of the basic structure of the Constitution. The acts of a state government which are calculated to subvert or sabotage secularism as enshrined in our Constitution, can lawfully be deemed to give rise to a situation in which the Government of the State cannot be carried on in accordance with the provisions of the Constitution.'[101]

The framework of secularism was interpreted to stress the integral relationship between secularism, democracy, and the state in the Constitution. Constitutionally, it dealt a major blow to the mixing of religion and politics.

'SOUTHERN STRATEGY' AND NORTHERN DECIMATION

The Ayodhya movement changed the dynamics of electoral politics as the Congress lost the support of both Hindus and Muslims which undermined its monopoly over political power. In the 1991 election, Advani's rath yatra and the anti-reservation sentiments among the upper castes opposed to V.P. Singh's decision to extend reservation in central government employment to the backward castes (see Chapter 3) were the key factors in almost doubling the BJP's vote share and increasing its seats to 120. At no point before 1989 had the BJP gained even a tenth of the national vote. In 1996, its vote share increased to 20.3 per cent, in 1998 to 25.8 per cent, and in 1999 to 23.8 per cent. It crushed the Congress in Uttar Pradesh which was critical to political power in Delhi. Rao's inaction in the Babri Masjid–Ramajanmabhoomi catastrophe has to share the blame for the party's complete erosion in Uttar Pradesh.

Rao's and Congress's responsibility for the Ayodhya crisis and the violence that surrounded it cannot be minimized. Many politicians and parties expressed disapproval, even disgust, at the failure to take stronger action against political violence. There was dismay at the reluctance to challenge Hindutva groups and in defending pluralism and national unity against communal politics. Two former prime ministers, V.P. Singh and Chandrasekhar, attacked Rao after the demolition of the Babri Masjid. V.P. Singh demanded that Rao, jointly with Kalyan Singh, be put on trial for 'criminal negligence'.[102] Chandrasekhar said that Rao's culpability is no less and charged him with 'deliberate dereliction of duty'.[103] Opposition parties charged the Congress government with failure to discharge its constitutional obligations; the Left parties stated in Parliament on 3 December 1992 that the central government would not be allowed to continue if it was incapable of stopping the kar sewa. They were, however, unable to corner the Congress after the demolition. Instead of insisting on Rao's resignation as a minimum, the non-BJP opposition decided to combine with the Congress to launch a campaign against communal forces, without insisting that it change its leadership for its failure to avert the demolition.

Rao was the target of trenchant criticism from a section of the Congress, led by Arjun Singh, for not doing enough to prevent the demolition. The prime minister was attacked for implicitly supporting the Hindutva forces in their demolition project. There were serious disagreements within the party over the decision to engage in negotiations with the VHP rather than take any strong measures to prevent the kar sewa. The subsequent decisions to dismiss the BJP governments and ban extremist organizations such as the RSS were taken largely at the insistence of cabinet ministers who were opposed to Rao's irresolution. Arjun Singh resigned from the cabinet in December 1994 but it was two years too late to underscore the point that in spite of his repeated warnings the central government had failed to protect the Babri Masjid. He was later expelled from the party after which he released his confidential correspondence with the prime minister on the matter. The truth, however, remains that in the crucial days leading to the demolition, the Union cabinet remained a passive spectator to the prime minister's dithering and eventual acquiescence in the demolition. While several senior ministers later put the entire blame on Rao, none of them were able to compel him to adopt a viable course of action to prevent the demolition.

The conflict with Arjun Singh related to events leading to the demolition, and whether there was wilful neglect and deliberate inaction as a result of an understanding between Rao and the BJP–RSS to build the Rama temple at the disputed site and rebuild the mosque. His equivocal strategy on Ayodhya played right into the hands of the BJP.[104] In a letter to Rao, Arjun Singh stated that 'the whole gravaman of the charge of betrayal and perfidy against the BJP/VHP combine springs from the negotiations that were held from July 1992 till the last day before the demolition of the mosque.... It is obvious that something transpired which gave us reason to further trust the bonafides of the BJP, VHP and RSS combine.'[105]

Arjun Singh had raised some inconvenient questions about the White Paper published by Rao's government in March 1993 and whether it was meant to set out all the facts before the people to judge the issues in totality for themselves. The government's White Paper laid the blame squarely on the state government and Kalyan Singh who had instructed the police not to open fire. It did not discuss the contingency plans prepared for dealing with the dire situation.[106]

However, a powerful section of Congressmen from the southern states as well as a few leaders from the north strongly backed Rao. Political support for the Congress had grown in south India because Rao was the first Congress prime minister from a southern state and also because of his painstaking effort to strengthen the southern base. He believed that the BJP was principally a Hindi-belt party, and therefore it would be easy to confine it to that region. The rest of the country would provide a fair measure of support and strength in numbers that the Congress needed to remain in power. Rao's short-range tactics, which some contemporary commentators described as a 'southern strategy', were also responsible for further debilitating the Congress in north India.[107]

From 1992 to 1996, subtle efforts were underway to play down the northern base of the Congress, and this accelerated the long-term decline of the Congress in north India.[108] The assumption regarding the party's southern base was completely misplaced because the Congress rapidly conceded space to regional parties in Tamil Nadu and Andhra Pradesh, and later in Karnataka.[109] Meanwhile, in the north, especially in Uttar Pradesh, little was done to appeal to the public or organize mass opposition against the BJP's unbridled exploitation of religion. The danger of communal politics could only have been dealt with through determined opposition by the public as well as the central government led by the Congress. The party, rather than leading public opinion, was waiting for it to shift, or even worse, was involved in its appeasement. There were, however, some influential leaders who recognized the perils of opportunism and not taking a clear stand against the BJP's communal politics which had been the greatest gainer from the wavering and tentativeness plaguing the Congress.[110]

THE DEMOLITION AND ITS AFTERMATH

In December 1992, Prime Minister Narasimha Rao stated that Babri Masjid would be restored at the same spot. Rebuilding the mosque was impossible as the government had failed to prevent the installation of a makeshift temple at the disputed site. Subsequently, without any reference to his promise of building a mosque, he gave an assurance that a temple would be constructed. He did not specifically say that the mosque would not be rebuilt but moved the focus to the temple.[111] He was aware that the courts will not allow this and yet he could take the credit for having respected Hindu sentiments.

Shifting from the hasty promise to rebuild the mosque to an assurance that the temple could be constructed without any reference to the mosque, the central government introduced a special statute for the acquisition of the disputed Ramajanmabhoomi–Babri Masjid site and adjacent areas and a reference on the historical status of the

area. The Acquisition of Certain Area at Ayodhya Act 1993 shifted the
focus to the temple even as the government imposed a statutory freeze
of the 'position' on the site, which included continuance of worship at
the makeshift temple that had been illegally constructed on the site of
the mosque.[112] This Act was challenged in the Supreme Court as anti-
federal, discriminatory, and violating the due process of law.[113] Rejecting
the presidential reference as to whether a Hindu temple had originally
existed at the site where the Babri mosque had been built in 1528, the
majority judgement permitted prayer which was limited to the makeshift
temple.[114] The judgement took recourse to the doctrine of comparative
significance of practices across religions to argue that the acquisition of
the property of a mosque did not constitute an abridgement of Muslims'
right to freedom of religious belief and practice.[115] On the crucial issue
of immunity from acquisition of a mosque, the majority judgement drew
a distinction between places of worship of particular significance and
ordinary places of worship, and to the latter the constitutional protection
of religious freedom would not automatically apply.[116] The judgement
observed that the right to practice, profess, and propagate under Article
25 does not necessarily include the right to acquire, own, or possess
property. This means that while mosques can exist as a matter of law,
no mosque in India enjoys constitutional protection under Articles 25
and 26 of the Constitution.[117]

The Congress leadership's approach at every step was guided by a
desire to upstage the Sangh Parivar in the hope of garnering Hindu
support. Rao's policies were the most opportunistic in this regard. He
was hobnobbing with sants and sadhus who constituted the vast middle-
level leadership that expanded the reach of the BJP. This he explained
in terms of 'the undeniable fact that while Hindu masses were swayed
by their devotion to Rama and their intense desire for the temple, the
political forces behind the issue could not care less for the temple'.[118] He
was trying to display a holier-than-thou attitude in comparison with the
BJP and hijack its agenda. His calculations, however, failed, trumped by
the BJP. He made no attempt to protect the Babri Masjid and could not
prevent the expansion of the BJP. At the same time, he alienated Muslims,
most of whom have not forgiven him and the Congress. 'Worse still, he
turned his back on decades of Congress secularism and acted as though
he was the first BJP Prime Minister of India.'[119]

Even as we blame the Congress government at the Centre for serious errors of judgement at every stage of this controversial movement, from the opening of the locks to the demolition of the mosque and allowing the construction of a makeshift temple in its place, we cannot equate these mistakes with the premeditated role played by the Sangh Parivar in plotting and executing the demolition. The Liberhan Commission fixed political responsibility on the top BJP leaders, concluding that the demolition was no act of spontaneous vandalism but a pre-planned conspiracy.[120] The question was whether the UPA government could translate responsibility and culpability into a legal framework. At the best of times, the Congress and its governments have never demonstrated a strong interest in ensuring the punishment of those involved in communal crimes.[121] The findings of the Srikrishna Commission of Enquiry into the 1992–3 communal killings in Mumbai, which took place after the demolition when Congress was in power, have remained largely unimplemented. Going by the law of probability, there are good reasons to believe the Liberhan findings will also meet the same fate. The UPA government's action taken report did not fix culpability.[122]

The demolition of the Babri Masjid was a defining moment in modern Indian history, emphasizing as it did a new place for the sentiment of the majority in the life and politics of the nation. The Congress seemed inhibited not only by Rao's approach of not confronting the BJP but also by the more widespread fear of losing Hindu votes in north India. Even though it pulled back from riding the tiger of Hindu fundamentalism, the party was keen to take advantage of religious sentiment but ended up creating a space for religious politics to play a more central role in public life. Its indecisiveness stemmed from a persisting doubt about the principle of depoliticization of religion as an essential ingredient of secular politics in a plural society. The Congress's real failure lay in its unwillingness to confront the seriousness of the challenge posed by communal politics to the structure of the national polity. It undermined its secular credentials by giving one concession to a particular community and then offsetting it by granting concessions to other communities in a process that left both the Hindu and Muslim communities feeling they had lost something. The party was reduced to a pale shadow of its former dominance, plummeting to a position of having to seek alliances to come to power even at the Centre. These events ruined its political base, particularly in the Hindi heartland, and had the result of creating space for new contenders. The BJP's influence rose exponentially while the Congress failed to devise a counter-strategy to regain lost ground. This political failure lies at the heart of the problem: from the beginning of the 1980s under Indira Gandhi, the party effected a tilt away from the left of centre, then to a confused dalliance with both Hindu and Muslim communalism under Rajiv Gandhi, and finally a marked swing to the right of centre under Rao, culminating in the destruction of the Babri Masjid.

The fallout from events in Ayodhya was bitter recrimination of the Congress from Muslims who felt betrayed by the prime minister's decision not to impose president's rule and prevent the demolition. The demolition was regarded by most people to be a seminal tragedy; a frontal attack on the secular state and the Constitution. Twenty years have passed since the demolition of the Babri Masjid. The Supreme Court in its judgement of 1994 called it

an act of national shame. What was demolished was not just a structure, but the faith of the minorities in the sense of justice and fairplay of the majority. It shook their faith in the rule of law. A 500-year old structure that was defenceless and whose safety was a sacred trust in the hands of the state government was demolished.[123]

Those responsible for the defiance of law, however, refuse to accept their responsibility. In the Lok Sabha debate on the Liberhan Report, the BJP leaders were 'defiant in their insistence that the "disputed structure" met its brutal end because kar sewaks were at the end of their patience'.[124] The UPA home minister, P. Chidambaram, rejected the BJP's argument that spontaneous action by kar sewaks led to the demolition. 'The RSS controlled every aspect of [the] Ayodhya movement, and it has no shame or remorse over what happened. It was a pre-planned, cold-blooded destruction of the mosque,' he said.[125] Significantly, the home minister acknowledged that Rao had made a 'wrong political judgment' in 1992 in believing the then Uttar Pradesh government that led to the demolition of the mosque in Ayodhya, and that was partly to blame for the demolition.[126]

The demolition was a watershed for Indian nationhood; a deviation from the consensus that the fundamental goals of the state were economic development and social transformation, and that religion would not be permitted to define identity and should therefore not determine public policy. The central challenge posed by the demolition was not just about the place of minorities in the nation's body politic, not even about the relationship between secular politics and religion, but fundamentally about the violation of the Constitution and the rule of law. It was the most blatant act of defiance of law in modern Indian politics. That is why it was extremely important to fix criminal responsibility for the demolition of the mosque.

NOTES

1.   Stanley Tambiah (1997), *Levelling Crowds: Ethnonationalist Conflicts and Collective Violence in South Asia*, Vistaar Publications, New Delhi, p. 247.

2.   Ibid.

3.   Sumit Ganguly (2003), 'The Crisis of Indian Secularism', *Journal of Democracy*, vol. 14, no. 4, October, pp. 11–25.

4.   Ramachandra Guha (2007), *India after Gandhi: The History of the World's Largest Democracy*, Picador, London, p. 575. The army launched this operation to remove Sikh separatists from the Golden Temple complex. This attack inflamed the Sikhs and eventually led to the assassination of Indira Gandhi on 31 October 1984 by two of her Sikh bodyguards who avenged the storming of the Golden Temple by the security forces.

5.   Mark Tully and Satish Jacob (1985), *Amritsar: Mrs. Gandhi's Last Battle*, Rupa & Co., Delhi, p. 5.

6.   Ibid., p. 4.

7.   People's Union for Democratic Rights and People's Union for Civil Liberties (1984), *Who Are the Guilty? Report of a Joint Inquiry into the Causes and Impact of the Riots in Delhi from 31 October to 10 November, 1984*, PUDR & PUCL, New Delhi.

8.   'Justice Nanavati Commission of Inquiry' (1984 Anti-Sikh Riots), Report, Volume 1, Ministry of Home Affairs, New Delhi, 2007. Available at mha.nic.in/pdfs/Nanavati-II_eng.pdf (accessed on 16 January 2012).

9.   See, for example, Manoj Mitta and H.S. Phoolka (2007), *When a Tree Shook Delhi: The 1984 Carnage and Its Aftermath*, Roli Books, New Delhi.

10.   Shekhar Gupta, '72 Hours, 21 Years Later', *The Indian Express*, 13 August 2005.

11.   Jagdish Tytler, Minister for Overseas Indian Affairs, resigned on 11 August 2005 following his indictment by the Nanavati Commission appointed by the NDA government in May 2000 to probe the anti-Sikh violence, which submitted its report on 10 February 2005. The Nanavati Commission report mentioned that there was 'credible evidence' that Tytler 'very probably had a hand in organizing anti-Sikh attacks'. Prime Minister Manmohan Singh

promised in the Lok Sabha that the UPA government would reopen and re-examine specific cases mentioned in the probe report.

12.   Rajiv Gandhi's speech cited in Mani Shankar Aiyar (ed.) (1997), *Rajiv Gandhi's India*, 4 vols, UBSPD, New Delhi.

13.   Sikhs were able to get an apology from Prime Minister Manmohan Singh, the resignation of Jagdish Tytler, and enhanced compensation to all the victims 21 years after the incident because of public pressure and follow-up by civil society groups in the Sikh community. On this, see Editorial, 'The Politics of Apology and 1984', *The Hindu*, 16 August 2005.

14.   Text of Prime Minister Manmohan Singh's statement in the Rajya Sabha during the debate on the adjournment motion regarding action taken. Report of the government on Nanavati Commission. Available at pmindia.nic.in/RS%20 speech.pdf (accessed on 4 June 2009).

15.   Election results are available in David Butler, Ashok Lahiri, Prannoy Roy (1991), *India Decides: Elections 1953–1991*, Living Media India, New Delhi.

16.   Dilip Bobb (1985), 'Spring in the Air', *India Today*, 15 August.

17.   Quoted in 'A Historic Mandate', *India Today*, 15 January 1985.

18.   James Manor (1988), 'Parties and Party System', in Atul Kohli (ed.), *India's Democracy: An Analysis of Changing State–Society Relations*, Princeton University Press, Princeton, p. 83.

19.   Ibid.

20.   The Constitutional (73rd Amendment) Act, 1992, came into force on 24 April 1993 to provide constitutional status to the panchayati raj institutions. This Act was extended to panchayats in the tribal areas of seven states, namely, Andhra Pradesh, Gujarat, Himachal Pradesh, Maharashtra, Madhya Pradesh, Orissa, and Rajasthan in 1996. The panchayati raj system exists in all the states except Nagaland, Meghalaya, and Mizoram. The Act aims to provide a three-tier system of panchayati raj for all states having a population of over 2 million, to hold panchayat elections regularly every five years, and to provide reservation of seats for SCs, STs, and women.

21.   Francine Frankel (2005), *India's Political Economy: 1947–2004, The Gradual Revolution*, 2nd edition, Oxford University Press, New Delhi, pp. 678–9.

22.   Aiyar, *Rajiv Gandhi's India*.

23.   After Longowal's death, combined with powerful opposition both in Punjab and Haryana, the Accord was never implemented. It ran into rough weather over the question of Chandigarh and the sharing of river waters.

24.   Interview with Natwar Singh, MP, Rajya Sabha, Minister of External Affairs, May 2004–December 2005, New Delhi, 20 December 2009.

25.   Myron Weiner (1987) 'Rajiv Gandhi: A Mid-Term Assessment', in Marshall Bouton (ed.), *India Briefing*, Westview Press, Boulder, CA, pp. 22–3.

26.   Inaugural speech by Rajiv Gandhi at the Congress Centenary Session, Bombay, 28 December 1985. Available at www.congresssandesh.com/ rajivgandhi/rajivgandhi.html (accessed on 6 July 2009).

27.   Ibid.

28.   Ibid.
29.   According to Arjun Singh, the speech was written by Rajiv Gandhi himself. Before going to Bombay, Arun Singh, a close aid of the prime minister, showed the draft to Arjun Singh and asked for his opinion. He said the speech was historic but that none of it would go down well with the Congress apparatus. He, therefore, advised caution. Interview with Arjun Singh, MP, Rajya Sabha, 2000–2006, 2006–2011; Minister of Human Resources and Development, 2004–2009, New Delhi, 10 October 2009.
30.   Frankel, *India's Political Economy*, p. 678.
31.   Paul Kreisberg (1987), 'Gandhi at Mid-Term', *Foreign Affairs*, Summer, p. 1061.
32.   For details of Working President Tripathi's letter indicting Prime Minister Rajiv Gandhi's handling of the government and ruling party, see report by K.K. Katyal, 'Stemming a Trend', *Frontline*, 14–27 June 1986.
33.   From November 1984 to January 1986, nine party general secretaries were appointed and removed. Information from Tripathi's letter cited in Ibid.
34.   Sukumar Muralidharan, 'A Difficult Legacy', *Frontline*, vol. 15, no. 2, 24 January–6 February 1998.
35.   For a discussion of the Shah Bano case and the Supreme Court ruling, see Zoya Hasan (ed.) (1998b), 'Minority Identity, State Policy and the Political Process', in *Forging Identities: Gender, Communities and the State in India*, Kali for Women, New Delhi.
36.   Ibid., p. 67.
37.   Interview with Mani Shankar Aiyar, MP, Fourteenth Lok Sabha, 2004–2009; Minister of Petroleum and Natural Gas, 2004–2006; Minister of Panchayati Raj, 2004–2009; Minister of Youth Affairs and Sports, 2006–2008; Minister of the Development of North-Eastern Region, 2008–2009, New Delhi, 17 December 2009.
38.   Ibid.
39.   Narasimha Rao (2006), *Ayodhya: 6 December 1992*, Penguin Viking, New Delhi, p. 37.
40.   Ibid., p. 49.
41.   Interview with Aiyar.
42.   Interview with Arjun Singh.
43.   Ibid.
44.   Prime Minister Jawaharlal Nehru launched panchayati raj from Nagaur in Rajasthan on 2 October 1959. In view of Rajiv Gandhi's commitment to panchayati raj, it had symbolic value.
45.   Interview with Aiyar.
46.   Interview with Digvijay Singh, Chief Minister of Madhya Pradesh, 1993–2003; General Secretary, AICC, New Delhi, 6 December 2009.
47.   Information given in Krishna Ananth (2010), *India since Independence*, Pearson, New Delhi.
48.   Frankel, *India's Political Economy*, p. 686.

49.   Shekhar Gupta (1990), 'The Gathering Storm', in Marshall Bouton and Philip Oldenberg (eds), *India Briefing*, Oxford University Press, New Delhi, p. 25.

50.   Butler *et al.*, *India Decides: Elections 1953–1991*.

51.   Frankel, *India's Political Economy*, p. 712.

52.   Rajeev Bhargava (2002), 'Liberal, Secular Democracy and Explanations of Hindu Nationalism', *Journal of Commonwealth and Comparative Politics*, vol. 40, no. 3.

53.   Cited in Martha Nussbaum (2007), *The Clash within: Democracy, Religious Violence and India's Future*, Harvard University Press, Cambridge, MA, p. 175.

54.   Rao, *Ayodhya*, pp. 90–1.

55.   Ibid., p. 92.

56.   Later, the Supreme Court reiterated the orders of the High Court restraining parties from any construction on this land. Ibid., pp. 92–3.

57.   Ibid.

58.   For details, see A.G. Noorani, 'Silent Spectator', *Frontline*, vol. 23, no. 10, 20 May–2 June 2006.

59.   Cited in Smita Gupta, 'Asleep at the Wheel?' *Outlook*, 7 December 2009.

60.   Nilanjan Mukhopadhyay (1994), *The Demolition: India at the Crossroads*, HarperCollins, New Delhi, p. 337.

61.   Interview with Arjun Singh.

62.   Rao, *Ayodhya*, p. 94.

63.   Ibid., p. 95

64.   Ashis Nandy, Shikha Trivedi, Shail Mayaram, and Achut Yagnik (1995), *Creating a Nationality: Ramjanmabhoomi Movement and the Fear of the Self*, Oxford University Press, New Delhi, p. 185.

65.   Rao, *Ayodhya*, p. 100.

66.   NIC Resolution reported in *The Times of India*, 24 November 1992.

67.   Madhav Godbole (1996), *Unfinished Innings: Recollections and Reflections of a Civil Servant*, Orient Longman, New Delhi, p. 357.

68.   Rao, *Ayodhya*, p. 113.

69.   N.S. Saxena's statement in *The Telegraph*, 6 January 1993 cited in Noorani, 'Silent Spectator'.

70.   Ibid.

71.   Rao, interview to *India Today*, 15 January 1993.

72.   Godbole, *Unfinished Innings*, p. 358.

73.   Ibid., p. 372.

74.   Gupta, 'Asleep at the Wheel?'

75.   See *Organiser*, 13 December 1992, quoted in Noorani, 'Silent Spectator'.

76.   Rao, *Ayodhya*, p. 93.

77.   Ibid., p. 94.

78.   Ibid., Chapter 6, 'Ayodhya 1992: The Building Blocks of Dispute' which provides ample evidence that the structure was not safe despite assurances, pp. 92–141.

79.   Ibid., p. 179.

80. Ibid., Chapter 7, 'Why Article 56 Not Invoked', pp. 167–81.

81. Ibid., 170.

82. Ibid., p. 166.

83. Ibid.

84. The kar sewa in 1990 led to police firing ordered by chief minister Mulayam Singh Yadav, which resulted in the death of some kar sewaks. The VHP published a list of 59 names. There were rumours, and even newspaper reports, that over 100 people had died. On 27 December 1990, the Chandrashekhar government stated in Parliament that only 15 'kar sewaks' had died in the police firing in Ayodhya and even challenged those who were projecting a larger figure to come out with a single additional name. Reported in S.P. Singh and Venkitesh Ramakrishnan, 'When the "Dead" Came Back', *Frontline*, vol. 27, no. 1, 2–15 January 2010.

85. Editorial, 'Ayodhya and After', *Economic and Political Weekly*, vol. 27, no. 49/50, 5–12 December 1992, p. 2619.

86. Jyoti Basu's telephone conversation cited in Noorani, 'Silent Spectator'.

87. Ibid.

88. Rajeev Dhavan, 'Why Blame Article 356', *Hindustan Times*, 26 December 1992.

89. Katyal, 'Clearer Lines, Unclear Future', *The Hindu*, 21 December 1992.

90. Manju Parikh (1993), 'The Debacle at Ayodhya: Why Militant Hinduism Met with a Weak Response', *Asian Survey*, vol. 33, no. 19, July, pp. 173–84. Also see *Economic and Political Weekly*, Editorial, 'Ayodhya and After'.

91. Interview with Arjun Singh.

92. Rao, *Ayodhya*, p. 188.

93. Ibid.

94. Ibid., p. 48.

95. Ibid.

96. Yubraj Ghimre and R. Pathak, 'Too Much Too Late', *India Today*, 11 December 1992.

97. Parikh, 'The Debacle at Ayodhya'.

98. *S.R. Bommai vs Union of India* [(1994) 2 SCR 644: AIR 1994 SC 1918: (1994) 3 SCC1].

99. Cited in Tambiah, *Levelling Crowds*, p. 447.

100. Ibid., p. 446.

101. Justice Sawant cited in ibid., p. 448.

102. Noorani, 'Silent Spectator'.

103. Ibid.

104. There is a view that had Arjun Singh resigned from Rao's cabinet on the day of the Ayodhya demolition, it would have lent greater credibility to his rebellion. Singh did resign as minister for human resource development from the cabinet but two years later. His critics argued that it was surprising that Rao's most strident critic on the Ayodhya question wavered at the decisive moment. Singh disagreed with this view and suggested that he gave priority to national

interests and the party than his personal interest. Interview with Arjun Singh, New Delhi, 10 October 2009.

105.   Arjun Singh's letter to the cabinet secretary, 10 January 1991; reproduced in *Frontline*, 26 February 1993.

106.   Noorani, 'Silent Spectator'.

107.   Muralidharan, 'A Difficult Legacy'.

108.   Interview with Arjun Singh, 20 November 2009.

109.   In 2006, the BJP for the first time formed a government in Karnataka, a process which can be traced to the developments that began in the 1990s.

110.   Some leaders like Arjun Singh who were prepared to take on the BJP in these regions were left out in the cold during the reorganization of the party in early 1993, even though he had won the Congress Working Committee (CWC) elections with the highest number of votes, followed by Sharad Pawar.

111.   Rajni Kothari, 'Supreme Court Verdict: A Political Analysis', *Mainstream*, 29 October 1994.

112.   Dhavan (1994), 'The Ayodhya Judgment: Encoding Secularism in the Law', *Economic and Political Weekly*, vol. 29, no. 48, 26 November.

113.   Ibid., p. 3035.

114.   Supreme Court Cases (1994) 6SCC. *Ismail Faruqui vs Union of India* with writ Petition No. 86 of 1994 *Jamaiat-Ulama-E-Hind and Another vs Union of India and Others*, 405. Available at www.excellsoft.com/se1.pdf (accessed on 13 January 2012).

115.   Dhavan, 'Ayodhya, Act III: Hard Talk, Real Solutions', *The Times of India*, 17 March 2002.

116.   Two dissenting judges, P.N. Bharucha and A.N. Ahmadi, differed sharply from their colleagues and thought that this status quo favoured the Hindu groups.

117.   Dhavan, 'Ayodhya, Act III'.

118.   Rao, *Ayodhya*, p. 185–6.

119.   Vir Sanghvi, 'Manmohan–Sonia Core Unit', *Hindustan Times*, 10 September 2006.

120.   The Liberhan Commission of Inquiry, led by retired High Court judge, M.S. Liberhan, to investigate the destruction of the Babri Masjid was constituted on 16 December 1992 by the home ministry. The report was submitted to Parliament on 24 November 2009. The commission was originally mandated to submit its report within three months. It proved to be one of India's longest-running inquiry commissions (took 17 years and 48 extensions) and submitted its report to the UPA government on 30 June 2009 about the events and circumstances leading up to the demolition of the Babri Masjid in 1992. It took the government another five months to table the report in the Parliament on 24 November 2009, and that too after a newspaper published portions of the report. It accepted Rao's explanation that Article 356, enabling the imposition of President's Rule could not be used for preventive purposes and that its object was to enable the Union of India to take remedial action consequent upon a breakdown of constitutional machinery.

The Liberhan report dismisses the theory of a spontaneous upsurge. Liberhan Commission of Enquiry Report is available at www.sacw.net/article1247.html (accessed on 23 August 2011). In Chapter 10, the report makes a definitive statement about culpability:

It stood established before me beyond reasonable doubt that the Joint Common Enterprise was a preplanned act for demolition under the immediate leadership of Vinay Katiyar, Paramhans Ramchander Dass, Ashok Singhal, Champat Rai, Swami Chinmayanand, S.C. Dixit, B.P. Singhal, and Acharya Giriraj. They were the local leaders on the spot and the executors of the plan conceived by the RSS. The other leaders [L.K. Advani, Murli Manohar Joshi, and others] cannot be absolved of their vicarious liability and were willing collaborators, playing the roles assigned to them by the RSS. Their informed support for the Ayodhya campaign, fortified by their physical presence during the grand finale of the prolonged campaign, is irrefutably established. ('India: Liberhan Commission of Enquiry Report'. Available at www.sacw.net/article 1247.html)

121. Siddharth Varadarajan, 'Little Men Reenact Ayodhya Chaos inside Parliament', *The Hindu*, 9 December 2009.

122. Action taken report submitted to the Parliament in March 2010. Liberhan Commission Report tabled in parliament on 24 November 2009. Reported in Venkitesh Ramakrishnan, 'Demolition by Design', *Frontline*, vol. 26, no. 25, 5–18 December 2009.

123. Supreme Court judgement, *Ismail Faruqui* v. *the Union of India*, 24 October 1994.

124. *The Hindu*, Editorial, 10 December 2009.

125. Ibid.

126. 'Rao Govt Had Made Wrong Political Judgement: PC', Home Minister quoted in *The Indian Express*, 8 December 2009.

2 Economic Liberalization and Its Discontents

The development model promoted by the Congress governments for three decades after Independence was a template of state-led, import-substituting industrialization in which both private and public sectors played key roles. The centrepiece of the framework was the primacy given to the interventionist state with a sizeable public sector, especially in areas of infrastructure and basic industries. However, the key role of the state and planned economy did not imply an opposition to capitalism. The large numbers of public sector undertakings (PSUs) were expected to complement and support private enterprise, rather than displace it. This mixed economy paradigm operating in a multi-party democracy attracted worldwide attention.

In 1991, 'India fundamentally altered its development strategy', and from that year the government initiatives to restructure the basis of the economy 'ended four decades of planning and have initiated a quiet economic revolution'.[1] Widely seen as a definitive shift in India's economic paradigm, the framework of economic liberalization introduced systemic changes, from self-sufficient, state-driven development to much greater dependence on the private sector and export promotion to increase growth.[2] This shift, which found influential support from international financial institutions, was ranked by a leading World Bank economist of the time as being among the most important events of the twentieth century alongside the collapse of the Soviet Union and China's institution of market reforms.[3]

This chapter recounts the economic crises and political processes spurring the dramatic change of economic policy, which constitutes a watershed in India's economic history. It is specifically concerned with how this played itself out and the degree to which it was induced by policy choices of political leaders acting in response to a changing domestic and international environment, and the degree to which it was induced by structural determinants. It is essentially an attempt to look at the broader question of the politics of economic liberalization than to assess the merits and demerits of liberalization per se, which is best left to economists. The purpose is to understand the changing role of the political elite and the continuities and discontinuities in economic policy from Rajiv Gandhi to Rao and its impact on the fortunes of the Congress and, in the years that followed, the impact on the support the party enjoyed among the marginalized and disadvantaged groups. The policy regime ushered by liberalization enhanced the global outreach of the economy and economic growth. India's slow growth of 3 per cent to 4 per cent had increased to an average rate of 6 per cent per annum in this period. Rapid economic growth was, however, accompanied by rising inequalities, and the share of the poor in it was inadequate.[4] The obvious consequences have been regional and class disparities which led to serious political ramifications for the Congress.

PRE-HISTORY OF ECONOMIC LIBERALIZATION

A major ideological shift took place in the early 1990s from a state-regulated economy to a market-centred one. Economic liberalization in 1991 placed emphasis on decontrol and deregulation. The basics of this policy change commenced in the early 1980s during the period when Indira Gandhi (1980–4) was prime minister and later during Rajiv Gandhi's prime-ministership (1984–9). This economic transition was made possible by a turn around in the Congress strategy that had actually begun during her last term in office (1980–4), when she moved away from *garibi hatao* to creating an environment in which the industrial sector would take the lead in economic development. Indira Gandhi's government began to change the traditional anti-capitalist approach to embrace a pro-business orientation. Increasing growth and production were to become the hallmark of policy from 1980 onwards. As economic growth became the principal state goal, for the first time she downplayed redistributive concerns, the significance of planning and the Planning Commission, and public sector industries, and focused on policies favouring the industrial sector, encouraging private investment, and supporting business groups to achieve this goal.[5] The new policy gave a series of concessions to the industrial sector in order to maximize production, and as part of this reorientation 1982 was labelled as the year of productivity. The push for an industry-friendly environment had come from technocrats who began to dominate policymaking from this period. Three powerful committees headed by respected bureaucrats who were 'well regarded by the Indian business community' were entrusted with the task of making suggestions with regard to implementation of the blueprint of this growth-first policy, which had the imprimatur of the Federation of Indian Chambers of Commerce and Industry (FICCI).[6] As a follow up, the central government did away with restrictions on the expansion of big business and encouraged them to enter areas hitherto reserved for the public sector.[7] Liberalization at this stage did not involve opening up the economy internationally in terms of free movement of capital, goods, or finance.[8] Also, there was no attempt at privatization of the public sector or cutbacks in public expenditures. The policy was still quite statist but more explicitly growth-oriented. Rather, liberalization aimed at loosening government controls in the functioning of the private sector and gradually building greater reliance on the latter. *The Times of India* noted editorially: 'A change of considerable significance is taking place in India ... the emphasis has shifted from distributive justice to growth.'[9]

The adoption of economic liberalization marked a departure from policies of self-sufficient development independent of world capitalism and using the state to improve the lot of its people. These changes occurred in a context in which the significance of capitalism in agriculture and industry had progressively grown. When Rajiv Gandhi became the prime minister, he altered economic policy even further as 'his advisors decided from the outset to emphasize a break with the past'.[10] During his term in office, the technocratic leadership once again was in the forefront of pushing economic reforms and was committed to liberalization and deeply believed in its desirability. His political advisors and confidants like Arun Nehru and Arun Singh had worked as executives in multinational corporations (MNCs), and influential economic advisors like Manmohan Singh, Montek Singh Ahluwalia, and Raja Chelliah were known protagonists of economic liberalization.

Within months of assuming office, Rajiv Gandhi created the impression that 'he was prepared to go well beyond the limited liberalization initiated by his mother'.[11] He declared his government's approach to be one that would involve a judicious combination of deregulation, import liberalization, and easier access to technology. Taken together, he had in effect proposed a partnership between the government and business to accelerate plans for the modernization of industry.[12]

The Prime Minister announced a slew of policies to accelerate industrial growth: liberalizing imports, providing initiatives for exports, permitting import of technologies, encouraging foreign investment through joint ventures, deregulating the economy in order to make it more competitive.[13] Even though he was unwilling to dispense with state intervention, there was a great deal of bit-by-bit economic reform through a political process of diffusing resistance to liberalization. Some of the measures sought to alter the relationship between the state and market in economic development and thus commenced a steady transition to delicencing, deregulation, and privatization. The monopoly of PSUs was diluted by small-scale backdoor privatization or by allowing industrial firms to have captive power plants and so on. Labour laws and job security were not changed on paper; in practice, employers got away with many changes: workers pushed out by voluntary retirement schemes, widespread use of contract labour, unviable units closed down through various manoeuvres, work being sub-contracted to small-scale units.

The reformist trend was strengthened by the budget of 1985–6, hailed as the most important one in 30 years. The budget reduced corporate and wealth taxes, provided tax breaks to exporters, and eliminated licencing restrictions on investments. The number of industries exempted from licencing was substantially increased, large business houses were encouraged to participate in high-technology industries, and tax concessions for the corporate sector and urban upper middle classes were introduced. Major support for these policies came from industrial and commercial groups and the upper middle classes. It especially aroused the hopes of the middle classes as it gave them greater purchasing power. The managerial style of the government and the focus on modern technology manifest in Rajiv Gandhi's eagerness to expand India's computer industry and telecommunications resonated with these groups even as they invited opprobrium from old-style politicians.

There was considerable opposition to the budget from the Left parties and other opposition parties. There were objections even from sections of the business community and bureaucracy, and certainly the public sector companies, especially those engaged in capital goods; the trade unions too were unhappy.[14] However, the strongest criticism came from within the Congress. Atul Kohli has analysed in detail the policy changes and the strong opposition they evoked within the Congress and pointed out that the party's rank and file were not prepared to accept the paradigm shift.[15] The Left elements within the Congress, as well as those attached to the concept of a socialist pattern of society, refused to accept departures from Nehru's policy of self-reliance and Indira Gandhi's pro-poor programmes. They echoed the broadside of the Left parties that Rajiv Gandhi was 'pro-rich'.[16] Organized labour and their unions opposed any attempt at the corporatization or privatization of public assets.

The plenary session prior to the Congress Party's centenary celebrations in 1985 witnessed open expressions of dissatisfaction over abandoning socialism as an explicit goal.[17] Very briefly, in May 1985 the prime minister and his advisors took an economic resolution for presentation first to the CWC, prior to its presentation to the AICC session in Bombay for ratification, and this faced rough weather in the party. The resolution was presented by Finance Minister V.P. Singh in an effort to obtain the party's backing for these policy initiatives. It did not mention socialism and used language that seemed to signify a shift in economic strategy, indicating that this was 'both necessary and justified'.[18] Many members saw this as a move away from socialism and opposed the economic resolution for fear of political and electoral consequences of abandoning it. These leaders conveyed their apprehension that liberalization of the economy and opening it up to foreign investment and multinationals would not go down well with people who were largely concerned about livelihood issues which will be adversely affected by these changes. In the end, the revised resolution passed by the AICC deleted a critical sentence which had stated: 'In the process of continued development, the policy instruments relevant to one stage cannot be treated as permanently sacrosanct.' It was replaced by another passage that restated the Congress's commitment to the goal of achieving socialism.[19]

These doubts gained momentum after the setbacks the Congress suffered in the 1985 elections in 11 states. Rajiv Gandhi was placed on the defensive following defeats in the assembly elections in Madhya Pradesh, Gujarat, Uttar Pradesh, and Bihar in particular. When faced with criticism that the party had abandoned Nehruvian policies that made it electable, he quickly reverted to the more cautious policy of the mixed economy. Rajiv Gandhi while making piecemeal policy changes insisted that his government was continuing the traditional Congress programme of the mixed economy in which the public sector would control the 'commanding heights' of the economy.[20] He actually went on to increase public investment in anti-poverty programmes, and this was more substantive than it had been in the 1970s during the heyday of garibi hatao.[21] A combination of pro-poor commitment and a mild dosage of economic reform was the distinctive feature of the last phase of his government. Advocacy of economic liberalization, therefore, remained minimal during Rajiv Gandhi's term of office because of the critical reaction to his endeavour to introduce it. Indira Gandhi, on the other hand, had initiated important liberalizing initiatives with nominal political opposition because her socialist credentials were well established as was her pro-poor commitment, whereas Rajiv Gandhi was a novice in politics, as were many of his advisors who evidently lacked political judgment on important issues.[22] However, throughout the 1980s, economic reform was a major area of contention and despite attempts at liberalization of the economy, India remained a state-dominated and state-controlled economy, both internally and externally.

THE ELITE'S CHANGE OF HEART

The Congress government which came to power in the aftermath of Rajiv Gandhi's assassination was successful in introducing much greater economic reforms than the previous one even though the latter had enjoyed a three-fourths majority in Parliament.[23] The new government did not enjoy majority support when it came to power in July 1991. It added some more seats in March 1992 but was still short of a majority until Rao created one in 1994. This government was able to push reforms from which Rajiv Gandhi had to back away. Despite differences in interpretation and the politics surrounding the origins of economic liberalization, there is little doubt that there was a far-reaching transition underway that went far beyond what had been attempted prior to 1991.[24] Significantly, this change occurred under Rao, only the second non-Nehru–Gandhi family prime minister in a Congress government (the first was Lal Bahadur Shastri). These reforms transformed the policy environment, the nature of the state, and most notably, government–business relations.

When the Congress government took charge, India faced a balance of payments crisis. Bimal Jalan, former finance secretary, described this period as 'among the cruelest in India's post-Independence economic history', and the subsequent economic reforms measures as 'one of the most momentous periods in India's economy since Independence'.[25] The severe fiscal crisis left the government on the brink of a meltdown.[26] The government could not finance essential imports, and as foreign exchange reserves fell to the equivalent of two weeks' imports, it transferred gold to British banks as collateral to stem speculation about an imminent default. To show how low India's creditworthiness had sunk, the International Monetary Fund (IMF) insisted on physical transfer of gold and Montek Singh Ahluwalia, then secretary in the government, had to accompany the consignment.[27] 'This came as a shock to average Indians who for centuries had placed their trust in gold as the ultimate security,' notes Arjun Singh.[28] The notion that the country was in effect pawning its gold abroad sent shock waves through society and polity. It was a defining experience, it would seem, for both policymakers and the people. This event 'supposedly drove home the indispensability of economic reforms and eventually influenced its acceptability'.[29] Under such circumstances, it was much easier to argue that the only recourse was to go the IMF, and that this would entail policies of macroeconomic adjustment.

The fiscal crisis was attributed to large government expenditures in the 1980s, especially the economic mismanagement of the National Front governments in power from 1989 to 1991. The government had shied away from domestic resource mobilization as direct tax rates were progressively reduced while indirect taxes, which already contributed three-fourths of total revenues, could not be raised any further. Inadequate resource mobilization was compounded by a profligate increase in public expenditure on defence, loan waivers, and subsidies, and this was not matched by higher levels of productivity or taxation. Expensive imports of weapons systems for the defence sector, much of it financed by borrowings from abroad, played a key part in the accumulation of external debt. In 1990–1, total public debt was 76 per cent of the gross domestic product (GDP), and interest payments reached 20 per cent of the total expenditure of the central government; and debt service amounted to 21 per cent of current account receipts.[30] In the same year, the current account deficit in the balance of payments, financed by borrowings from abroad, was higher than 2.5 per cent of GDP. The increased public spending in the

1980s had brought the economy to the brink of disaster which, the Congress leadership argued, necessitated a complete change of policy to meet the crisis.[31]

The timing of the 1991 economic reforms was also significant in pushing towards a relatively smaller role for the state in the development process, and a much larger one for the private sector. From the mid-1980s, global factors favoured the introduction of economic reforms and their continuance. The global scene witnessed the collapse of the Soviet Union and East European socialist regimes, which raised questions with regard to both the desirability and feasibility of socialist models. In this context, leading policymakers and technocrats began to argue that the end of the Cold War required India to restructure both its internal and external economic and foreign policies. China was also opening up its economy to foreign capital and moving towards a market economy, and cumulatively these developments built up a case for changing the basic parameters of Indian policy too. A sense of inevitability grew and this made a major contribution to the acceptance and continuance of the 1991 reforms. By contrast, earlier there had been internal constraints, essentially political, that had prevented Rajiv Gandhi's attempt at liberalization from taking wing.

While the fiscal crisis confronting the economy in terms of liquidity and declining foreign exchange reserves has not been questioned, Prabhat Patnaik and C.P. Chandrasekhar have argued that 'the foreign exchange crisis could have been managed'.[32] The Congress government maintained that there was no alternative to the IMF loan and nothing short of strong corrective measures would help the economic recovery and prevent insolvency. CPI (M) leader E.M.S. Namboodripad characterized the official argument as 'like a thirsty man taking a cup of poison on the plea that there is no alternative with which he can quench his thirst'.[33] The fact is that the elaborate package of economic restructuring was 'really not necessary to meet what was merely a crisis of liquidity'.[34] The foreign exchange crunch was not by itself responsible for the paradigm shift; it was the excuse, not the grounds, for the structural adjustment. The policy change which went well beyond a compelling response to the financial crisis came about more because of internal pressures and because of the role played by some business leaders in arguing for economic reforms to serve their private and corporate interests, than as a response to external influences.[35]

The change in direction was propelled by the liberalization lobby: technocratic leaders, the bureaucracy, and business groups who saw in the crisis an opportunity to dump state intervention and bring in market reforms.[36] This lobby considered fire-fighting measures insufficient and favoured a wholesale transformation of the policy process based on the alternative intellectual assumption about the benefits of capitalism and the benign nature of the global capitalist order. The influence of this significant minority had grown since the early 1980s, and by early 1990 they were strongly represented in the policy team that presided over India's economic transition. Several of these members had been socialized into neo-liberal ideas or had worked in international financial institutions, and the impact of this experience on their thinking and decisions cannot be minimized.[37] To these groups, the interventionist state and the policy of import-substituting industrialization had run their course.[38] To them, the domestic constraints pointed to the need to move from an inward to an outward orientation, from public investment to private sector–driven growth, from emphasis on heavy industry and agriculture to services and technology.

The most remarkable aspect of the Congress government's response to the liquidity crisis was that the policy redesign it favoured went beyond economic stabilization.[39] Resource mobilization as an alternative to going to the IMF was ruled out on the grounds that the imperative was a credible stabilization programme with the prior backing of international financial institutions.[40] Dr Manmohan Singh was a strong advocate of this position, and had argued for 'bold measures' to 'convert this crisis into an opportunity to build a new India, to do things which many people before us have thought and said should be done, but somehow were never done'.[41] Arguing for an across-the-board revision in policy, he insisted that

it was time to think big, not to shrink.… Stabilization plus a credible structural adjustment programme would shorten the period of misery. It would release the innovative spirit, [the] entrepreneurial spirits which were always there in India in [such] a manner that our economy would grow at a much faster pace, sooner than most people believed.[42]

In any event, the World Bank and the IMF had moved beyond economic stabilization to push for structural adjustment to minimize regulation and alter the relationship between the market and the state in favour of the former. As it turned out, the Congress government negotiated a structural adjustment loan with the World Bank–IMF to restore confidence in India's repayment capacity. A further IMF loan of $1.4 billion under the Compensatory and Contingency Finance Facility followed soon after, along with loans from the World Bank and the Asian Development Bank (ADB). This was not a historically necessary phenomenon but it might have been difficult to carry out under different political circumstances.[43] An important effect of the crisis was to strengthen the position of the policy elite backing the proposal for wholesale change.

THE NEW ECONOMIC REGIME

Deregulation, liberalization, and decontrol were effected at a rapid pace after 1991. Ironically, successive Congress governments, which had been running what the IMF described as 'one of the most regulated economies in the world',[44] decided to quite effortlessly embrace globalization and integration into the world economy. To achieve this objective, Rao had gone outside politics to appoint as finance minister the distinguished economist and technocrat, Manmohan Singh, who is widely regarded as the architect of India's economic reform programme.[45]

Although Manmohan Singh had been a part of the economic policy establishment since 1971 and was an active participant in policymaking in the earlier dirigiste dispensation, he played the most critical role in repudiating this model. Described as the economist's economist in the government, he was the only person to have held every important position in the Government of India, including the posts of secretary, economic affairs, in the Ministry of Finance; governor, Reserve Bank of India (RBI); chairman, University Grants Commission (UGC); deputy chairman, Planning Commission; and finance minister;[46] and has had two terms as prime minister. He was able to bring about not just a policy shift but also a change from the entire complex of ideas of inward orientation, state regulation, and public ownership—which had enjoyed ideological hegemony in the country for several decades—to a much more outward-oriented economy.[47] Of all the policymakers, Singh's influence has been the most significant since 1991, especially because he succeeded too in changing the political mindset of his party.[48] As finance minister, he opened a new era in India's political economy, 'significantly freeing the economy from state intervention'.[49]

Manmohan Singh ended his very first budget speech with the now famous quote from Victor Hugo: 'No power on earth can stop an idea whose time has come'. And then went on to say:

I suggest to this august House that the emergence of India as a major economic power in the world happens to be one such idea. The emergence of India as a major global power, [an] economic power, is an idea whose time has come. I sincerely believe that if we did the things that I was saying to parliament that they should do, no power on earth could stop the realization of this idea.

That served as the launch of an unprecedented and ambitious liberalization programme. Manmohan Singh stood the country's traditional economic thinking, which for a long time was governed by the powerful idea of planned economic development and the necessity of state intervention on its head. This marked a departure from import-substituting industrialization, especially in areas of infrastructure and basic industries. The view informing this policy in the 1950s and 1960s believed that excessive integration with the world economy significantly disadvantaged late industrializers, necessitating a role for the state in developing countries. By the end of the 1970s it was evident that Nehru's vision of rapid economic growth based on the development of heavy industry, import substitution, and social justice had failed largely because the existing power structures did not allow the development of a large internal market. On the other hand, the Congress's class character made it very difficult to push through policies such as land reform that would have resulted in structural change facilitating the emergence of a more egalitarian social structure and an expansion of the domestic market. An attempt was therefore made to find an alternative growth strategy based on economic liberalization.

Globalization and liberalization of the economy in the period 1991–6 covered both the internal and external dimensions and especially changed the state's relationship with the private sector and the international economy. The package covered a combination of short-term stabilization measures and medium-range and long-term economic reforms aimed at structural adjustment. Economic reforms included substantial changes in industrial economy, investment, trade, and opening up to the outside world. The government de-licenced most industries, the private sector was allowed into sectors hitherto reserved for the state, foreign investment was permitted in 34 areas from which non-Indian capital had been excluded in the past, foreign investors were granted the right to acquire majority shareholdings in Indian companies, and in key sectors, such as power, 100 per cent foreign ownership was allowed.[50] Among the changes, internal deregulation proceeded unhindered, while the opening up to the global market was modest to begin with and gathered momentum later, whilst curbs on public spending were held back in response to public pressure.[51] Two other reforms—privatization of public sector companies as a way of generating funds and labour reforms—which were repeatedly discussed, were not pursued for fear of political repercussions, especially opposition from labour and trade unions. The government claimed that trade, investment, and infrastructure reforms of 1991 had brought about an unprecedented strong economic performance driven by the private sector boom. 'These economic reforms taken together constitute a comprehensive and thoroughgoing overhaul of the economic regime,' asserts Raja Chelliah.[52] On the whole, it was facilitated by careful political calibration of the liberalization process to suit the needs of Indian capital. By the mid-1990s reforms had turned India into an emerging market even as the pace of change was dictated by political considerations and hence modest by global standards.

FEEBLE POLITICAL OPPOSITION

Economic liberalization raised objections throughout the country, even though the Congress was careful that it did not go too far or too fast.[53] Liberalization came in for extensive disapproval on the ground that they were ushered in without a thorough debate and vote in the Parliament. There was, therefore, criticism that liberalization policies had violated democratic norms; that there were no discussions even in the cabinet; that they were pushed through by bureaucratic decisions; that the follow-up measures were not transparent.[54] True, economic policies of liberalization were authorized by an executive decree but there was sufficient opportunity to debate them in the Parliament and outside as most of the reform measures were introduced via the national budget. The budgets for 1992 and 1993 reflected most clearly the policy of economic liberalization. They reduced and simplified direct taxes, removed wealth tax from financial investments, and indexed the capital gains tax.[55] The substantive criticism of the budgets of 1991, 1992, and 1993 was scathing; several arguments were made in the Lok Sabha debates against the loss of sovereignty to the World Bank and IMF. A second set of criticisms pertained to the pro-rich orientation of these policies.

Even as the opposition parties and leaders were incensed over several aspects of liberalization policies and denounced the Congress for taking an IMF loan that imposed conditions on India, they were not prepared to rock the boat and vote against the budget. The Left and Janata Dal, which amongst them had 108 seats, were on the horns of a dilemma. As hostilities escalated between the BJP and Congress leading to the worst Hindu–Muslim violence since Independence (1991–3), significant sections of the opposition, especially the Left, had to at the very time respond to the rise of Hindu nationalism.[56] Against the backdrop of the Ayodhya movement and the demolition of the Babri Masjid in December 1992, these parties were increasingly anxious to distance themselves from the BJP and unwilling to coordinate with it to defeat the Congress in the Parliament. The Ayodhya issue had sparked off polarization of the electorate on communal lines and posed serious threats to political secularism (Chapter 1). Consequently, the conflict between secularism and communalism developed into the primary contradiction in the politics of this period; indeed, it was to dominate politics until the defeat of the BJP-led NDA in 2004. Hence, the paramount concern of the non-Congress parties was to contain the BJP, and this was given precedence over their long-standing hostility to the Congress and its economic reform agenda. In the emerging contest between the Congress and BJP, a secular coalition was formed to defeat the Hindu nationalists.

Although the Left parties were resolutely opposed to liberalization, they were even more opposed to the BJP and its communal agenda during this period and were concerned not to allow the BJP to further it by exploiting differences in the secular camp.[57] The BJP, on the other hand, was tactically opposed to liberalization, but this was secondary to its principal objective of trying to build a united Hindu community and was eager to displace caste which was fast emerging as a major axis of mobilization as it feared that during this time this would undercut its efforts to forge such unity. In effect, economic reforms were crowded out of mass politics by issues of national identity and Hindutva that during this time aroused greater passion and anxiety.[58] The primacy of secular politics and the need to contain the BJP's further expansion was one important reason why economic liberalization did not face significant hurdles even though the Congress lacked a majority in the Parliament.

Just the same, most political parties expressed disapproval with the economic policies but they did not organize major or sustained protests against them. The Congress government was able to make the most of the fear of the BJP in the early 1990s to neutralize the opposition to economic reforms. Despite ideological objections, there was no real political pressure to overturn economic reforms. This was also because powerful groups, such as the business community, who stood to benefit backed the liberalization policy, and others in the middle classes who did not benefit immediately saw themselves as potential beneficiaries. Both these constituencies pressed for change of the earlier model which had served their interests very well but they revolted against it because of the sense that it had run its course and needed to be reformed.[59]

THE CHANGED GOALPOST

As it happened, the Congress government went ahead with liberalization which triggered multiple changes, most notably in the sectoral structure of industry, with a major expansion of the technologically advanced segment of industry and the rapid growth of medium- and small-scale enterprises in comparison to traditional small-scale industry.[60] All this was a prelude to the huge growth of the corporate sector. The market shares of the public and private sectors began to change in key sectors of the economy as the private sector surpassed the public sector in investment. By 1996, private paid-up capital exceeded that of the public sector for the first time since 1972.[61] Proliferation of the capitalist class had taken place in the years of import-substituting growth and subsequently with the entry of new entrepreneurs. It led to a change in the structural character of business with the balance shifting away from big business in favour of small- and medium-sized groups. The emergence of a more modern segment of business, as against the family-based industrial enterprises of the earlier era, came about through the establishment of new companies and also changes in the process of accumulation.[62] For example, a number of these business groups accumulated capital in the agriculturally successful areas of southern and western India.[63] These groups had a strong interest in the abolition of state regulation which had facilitated and offered protection to monopolies and oligopolies. Many of them wanted to use foreign and technological collaboration to enter the industrial sector. They were among the most vocal supporters of liberalization and globalization. On the other hand, big business, whose monopoly had been threatened by the proliferation of capital, was keen to reverse their decline by expansion abroad. The change in the overall structure of industry created the conditions for this outcome, without which it would not have been possible.[64]

India's average growth rate after the implementation of economic reforms had grown at a rate of 6.3 per cent per annum in the period from 1992–2001, which was much higher than in the early decades of the 1960s and 1970s.[65] This was largely due to the 11.7 per cent growth of industry and the construction sector and the 7 per cent growth of the services sector.[66] More remarkably, 'this is the first time that a growth rate of this magnitude was not due to exceptional agricultural growth'.[67] In 1995–6, the *Annual Economic Survey* was able to claim that 'India recorded one of the fastest recoveries from a macroeconomic and balance of payments crisis'.[68] It also stated that 'the growth achieved in the post-crisis period was a noteworthy achievement by international standards and was more sustainable than the growth in the immediate pre-crisis period'. Although the survey claimed rapid expansion of public employment, job creation was not very good.

The main push underlying sustained growth was the active pro-business orientation of the state and its commitment to the promotion of entrepreneurship-led growth that developed into a central feature of the political economy with emphasis on business and private investment as its engine of growth.[69] Economic liberalization led to a change in the balance of forces among public, private, and foreign capital, resulting in a much greater role for business groups and the corporate sector than ever before. The success in establishing the dominant role of the public sector in industrial development was the most powerful symbol of Nehru's legacy. It was indelibly associated with the political goals of a self-reliant economy whose roots lay in the freedom struggle. All this had changed appreciably by the mid-1990s under the Congress government.

BUSINESS, MIDDLE CLASS, AND BUREAUCRATIC SUPPORT

Once economic liberalization took off, the strongest support for it came from the corporate sector and middle classes, the very groups that grew around the state and had been the greatest beneficiary of the earlier regime of state intervention.[70] Within a few years, limited government and economic liberalization came to be viewed as a panacea for India's economic problems. Prior to 1991, business had little influence in shaping public policy as such. After economic liberalization, these groups were able to exert direct influence on the broad macro-level economic policies of the government. Their access to the policy process and the political system became more direct.[71] As business and politicians drew closer, they evolved a mutually beneficial relationship at both formal and informal levels. Apex industrial bodies of industry, especially the Confederation of Indian Industry (CII) as the representative body of the up-and-coming business and industry groups developed a close rapport with the government and became the most powerful and effective lobbying organization in the country, with deep roots in all major economic ministries, the Ministry of External Affairs, and the Prime Minister's Office (PMO).[72] Since 1991, the CII played the most influential role in shaping economic policy and successfully lobbied for further liberalization of economic policies. Big business had open access to the highest level of policymaking, the PMO. The Prime Minister's Economic Advisory Council included all the big industry actors, and became more active and met regularly. Major strategic support for economic liberalization came from the bureaucratic and technocratic elite manning the ministry of finance, the cabinet secretariat, and the PMO.[73] This was especially the case with the finance ministry, which acquired the status of a super-ministry after the process of economic reforms and bureaucrats owing allegiance to the World Bank and IMF ideology were the most influential. Many of them began arguing that the state had over-extended itself in the economy far beyond the limits of its administrative capacity. Some of the rising entrepreneurs, in collusion with growing breed of on-the-rise politicians, bureaucrats, technocrats, and advisors, were the key promoters of economic reforms throughout this period.[74]

A related development of enormous significance was the emergence of the non-resident Indians (NRIs), especially American NRIs, as a powerful influence in policymaking. They were the richest ethnic minority in the US and some of this wealth and clout was being recycled in the Indian economy. As one of the largest diaspora in the world, it had roots in every country but was especially important and influential in the US. By and large, the number and magnitude of NRI deposits and investments grew rapidly and had a huge impact on the policy orientation of both the government and the business community. The NRIs were an important source of capital inflow, but they were important too because of their close links to the dominant groups within political parties and the establishment.[75]

The growing middle classes whose real incomes increased with the consumption-led boom of the 1980s and through the first decade of this century, were the principal driving force behind liberalization. The entrepreneurial middle classes, who increasingly questioned the state's control over the economy, as well as the professional middle classes turned away from the Congress in the 1980s because they thought that the statist model of development was incapable of providing economic opportunities for which they yearned with increasing intensity over time. The surge in economic growth led to an increase in the size and influence of the middle classes.[76] After economic liberalization, this group had a political voice that was far greater than its share of the population and hence it was able to influence economic policy to its own advantage.

POLITICAL DISCONTENT

India moved from 'Hindu rate of growth' to a respectable growth of 5 per cent to 6 per cent per annum beginning with the 1980s.[77] On the other hand, the increased employment opportunities and incomes mostly benefited the social elites and middle classes who had turned against the earlier model of state-led economic development.[78] Hence, only those economic liberalization measures that buttressed their interests were pursued while those that affected the masses, such as reform of agriculture, human development, or inflation control, were not attempted or did not go very far.[79] The vast majority of people in the rural areas were not in favour of these economic changes which brought them no direct or indirect benefit.

The Congress, with a concentration of its support among the rural poor, was particularly sensitive to the impact of liberalization on rural voters. The setback suffered by the party in the assembly elections from 1993 to 1995 in Uttar Pradesh, Rajasthan, Delhi, Andhra Pradesh, Karnataka (1993–4) and in Gujarat, Maharashtra, and Bihar (1995) was a cause of worry because many viewed it as a vote against these policies as the benefits did not reach the poor. The fear of losing their vote put the leadership on the defensive. At stake was the question of the pace of liberalization and whether it was causing hardship to the poor and disadvantaged, leading to an increase in disparities and injustices. It was felt that governments which introduced social welfare policies to offset the hardships being faced by people had a good prospect of winning elections.

In the earlier decades, welfare and development were the foremost issues in Congress discourse. Until liberalization, the poor saw it as their party, 'however much economists might have seen the party's policies as doing little to actually remove poverty'.[80] The party's success was also due in no small measure to its strategy of consensus and accommodation, with the policy of self-reliance and social welfare acting as the political glue of this entente. Moreover, it had mobilized support and maintained its dominance largely as a party committed to the promotion of state intervention. Hence, its political support depended upon its capacity to work a statist model of development which disbursed public goods and services. This changed with the dismantling of a state-led model of development. In so far as liberalization reduced the remit of the state, it lost the support of the underprivileged who depended on state support, which could be one of the reasons for its declining performance in the elections in the 1990s. As early as 1992 Rao and Manmohan Singh had come under attack within the Congress for the decision to liberalize the economy and thus deviating from established policies. Rao had conceded in his intervention at the AICC meeting in Tirupati (1992) that that the process of globalization could badly hurt those at the lower rungs of the economy. Not surprisingly, he made very little attempt to persuade the public of the purposes and benefits of liberalization. Indeed, he himself did not make a case for economic liberalization in the election campaign in 1996.[81] Though these changes produced considerable prosperity for the middle classes, the Congress did not offer an unapologetic defence of these policies because it was worried that the benefits had bypassed the poor, its main support base. According to Vayalar Ravi, the idea of market economy was originally not a Congress idea; rather, it was initiated and adopted under pressure from international agencies. Political opposition came to the forefront on the larger ideological questions of state intervention, economic sovereignty, and the policy of self-reliance as sections of the party began expressing unease over departures from these policies.[82]

Seeking to reassure groups that felt threatened by economic liberalization, prominent leaders, including Rao, Manmohan Singh, and the deputy chairman of the Planning Commission, Mukherjee, all sought to fend off the unease by emphasizing continuity with the past. These policies were adopted, they argued, because the earlier ones were not yielding results but they were in line with the economic policies of Rajiv Gandhi. Sonia Gandhi, subsequently in 2009, was to reiterate this argument when she affirmed that her husband had scripted the course of economic policies that were followed by the Rao government: 'Rajiv did not stay with us to see his dreams being realized but we can see his stamp in the party manifesto for 1991 elections. That became the basis for economic policies for the next five years. These policies gave a new direction and strength to our economy and our society.'[83]

As Finance Minister, Manmohan Singh was under pressure to explain the increased reliance on international institutions and why the Congress had given up on state intervention. Whilst he did not see the economic reforms as entirely new, at the same time he admitted that in some ways reforms were a departure from past policies but in other ways a continuation of the policies of Indira Gandhi and Rajiv Gandhi.[84] He conceded that the party was not prepared for this drastic change and therefore one reason for the disquiet was that major changes were brought about quite suddenly. However, on the whole he defended economic liberalization was a continuation of what Rajiv Gandhi had left off in the hope that this would put a stop to the complaints the critics in the party made:

But fortunately Rajiv Gandhi did a great service to our country, because he wrote the 1991 election manifesto of our party. In that election manifesto he had clearly recognized the need for economic reforms of the type which we undertook. It was an easy task for me to convince the sceptics in the party that I was not doing anything that was against the party. It is a legacy left to us by Rajiv Gandhi.

This argument did not fully convince the critics but it silenced them for quite some time.[85]

One key issue at the centre of the debate was whether the Congress government was being true to its Nehruvian inheritance. The market-oriented policy regime was a reversal of Nehru's policy of state-led development, but interestingly it was projected by the dominant group as a case of 'continuity with change'. However, leaders like Priya Ranjan Das Munshi, Vayalar Ravi, and Bhagwat Jha Azad disagreed and insisted that Nehru's policies had been thrown overboard in the push for globalization.[86] Mukherjee denied the charge that the Congress was compromising India's economic sovereignty. Like Manmohan Singh, he maintained that economic reforms were an extension of earlier policies and the departures only concerned details. To bolster his argument, he reminded his colleagues that the party had not given up on the importance of the public sector which was evident from its increased share of investment in the Eighth Five Year Plan (1992–7). He pointed out that the Congress vision, even in the heyday of Nehruvanism, was of a mixed economy and not total social control of production.[87] In this way, these leaders reiterated their commitment to welfare and for compatibility between nationalism and entrepreneurship. Rao later stated that liberalization, 'when it was conceived, it was meant as a means to transform the society—purely as a socio-political process than as a business ploy. We tried other means for over four decades. If we discovered inadequacies in the means, we thought we should change, by all means. And the change we did, but most certainly, for the same purpose.'[88] In brief, for the votaries of policy change, liberalization was simply an alternative means to the goal of self-reliance rather than the abandonment of it. Not many leaders were won over by this explanation.

The period of economic reform was a testing time for the Congress. The discontent triggered by liberalization cast doubts on the fairness of these policies as the poor sections began to move away from the party. Its vote share declined from 48.1 per cent in 1984 to 31 per cent in 1996; its seats declined from 415 to 136.[89] In more than a quarter of parliamentary constituencies, Congress candidates did not even finish as runners up. Evidently, liberalization was seen by the masses at large as an attempt to dilute the party's social commitment to the deprived sections of society. The Antony Committee later appointed by the Congress president to investigate the reasons for the party's debacle in the 1999 parliamentary elections acknowledged the disjuncture between politics and economics in India.[90] It observed: 'The stark political fact was that the programme of economic reforms had its highest appeal among the urban bourgeoisie. It has not proved a vote catcher in the ranks of the poor.'[91] The discontinuity between the 'socialistic pattern of society', which for half a century had been the official position of the Congress, and the post-reform priorities with an emphasis on the promotion of the private sector had confused most Congressmen and women.[92] The party needed to contain the political pressures generated by those who were left out by the market-based model of development as this would put at risk the support of the poor for the Congress. While a large section of party leaders and rank and file was concerned about the popular disapproval of liberalization, the real problem was that there was no serious discussion of an alternative development strategy that would aim to bring improvement in the living conditions of the masses. The main concern was not to be seen to be breaking from past policy regardless of whether it would lead to an improvement in standards of living.

Economic liberalization went on to rewrite the rules of engagement between domestic and foreign private capital and the state in favour of greater freedom for the private sector and private accumulation. It, however, did so without totally compromising the notion of economic sovereignty. India was seen as an example of a prudent yet extensive programme of global economic integration and domestic deregulation, and sound macroeconomic management.[93] This last point has been noted by many observers of India's liberalization trajectory who argued that India was able to avoid the pitfalls of reforms that broke many other countries. Taken as a whole, 'their [Rao–Singh] reforms,' James Manor argues, 'were cautious and limited by international standards, but by Indian standards quite startling. Their cumulative impact eventually produced a substantial revision of relations between the state and market forces.'[94] By Indian standards, the change was dramatic but in a comparative context it was still quite modest.[95]

Despite its cautious character, liberalization provoked popular discontent, yet it continued to get the full backing of the Congress because the political alliance of powerful groups prevailed over opponents of liberalization as they continued to be the dominant force in policy circles. This underlines the changed policy priorities of the Congress leadership. Both the central and state governments under Congress rule were unwilling to roll back policies of economic liberalization, and this further set back egalitarian ambitions such as redistributive policies.

NOTES

1. World Bank, Country Operations, Industry and Finance Division, Country Department II, South Asia Region, *India Country Economic Memorandum—Five Years of Stabilisation and Reform: The Challenges Ahead*, 8 August 1996, cited in Rob Jenkins (1999), *Democratic Politics and Economic Reform in India*, Cambridge University Press, Cambridge, p. 1.

2. See T.J. Byres (ed.) (1997), 'Introduction: Development Planning and the Interventionist State versus Liberalization and the Neo-liberal State: India, 1989–1996' in *The State, Development Planning and Liberalization in India*, New Delhi: Oxford University Press.

3. Cited in Prabhat Patnaik, 'India: A Setback for Neoliberalism', International Development Associates, 9 June 2004. Available at www.macroscan.org/archive/archive_macro.htm (accessed on 24 June 2009).

4. See, for example, Angus Deaton and Jean Drèze (2002), 'Poverty and Inequality in India: A Reexamination', *Economic and Political Weekly*, vol. 37, no. 36, 7–13 September, pp. 3729–48; Abhijit Sen and Himanshu (2004), 'Poverty and Inequality in India', *Economic and Political Weekly*, vol. 39, 18 and 25 September, p. 4247 and pp. 4361–75.

5. Atul Kohli (2009a), 'Politics of Economic Growth in India, 1980–2005, Part I: The 1980s', in *Democracy and Development: From Socialism to Pro-Business*, Oxford University Press, New Delhi, pp. 140–64.

6. Ibid., p. 154.

7. Ibid., p. 152.

8. Ibid.

9. Editorial in *The Times of India*, 22 February 1981, cited in ibid., pp. 152–3.

10. Ibid., p. 159.

11. Francine Frankel (2005), *India's Political Economy: 1947–2004, The Gradual Revolution*, 2nd edition, Oxford University Press, New Delhi, p. 586.

12. Kohli (2009b), 'Politics of Economic Liberalization in India', in *Democracy and Development in India: From Socialism to Pro-Business*, pp. 200–1.

13. The shift was manifest in the major policy documents of the period: Seventh Plan, Government of India (1987), *Economic Survey 1986–7*, Ministry of Finance, New Delhi.

14. Kohli, 'Politics of Economic Liberalization in India', pp. 200–6.

15. Ibid.

16. Frankel, *India's Political Economy*, p. 586.

17. Kohli, 'Politics of Economic Liberalisation in India', p. 202.

18. Frankel, *India's Political Economy*, p. 586.

19. Ibid., p. 586.

20. Ibid., p. 587.

21. Even though this extensive intervention did not create durable social opportunities for people at large, officially the proportion of people living in poverty declined from 59 per cent in the early 1970s to 39 per cent in the second half of 1980s. 'Government of India Poverty Estimate for 1999–2000', Press Information Bureau, 22 February 2001.

22. Kohli, 'Politics of Economic Liberalization in India', p. 222.

23. For an explanation of why this was so, see Ashutosh Varshney (2007a), 'Mass Politics or Elite Politics? India's Economic Reforms in Comparative Perspective', in Rahul Mukherji (ed.), *India's Economic Transition: The Politics of Reforms*, Oxford University Press, New Delhi.

24. See Stuart Corbridge and John Harriss (2000), *Reinventing India: Liberalization, Hindu Nationalism and Popular Democracy*, Oxford University Press, New Delhi; and Jos Mooij (2005), *The Politics of the Economic Reforms in India*, Sage Publications, New Delhi.

25. Bimal Jalan (1992), *The Indian Economy*, Oxford University Press, New Delhi, p. vii.

26. According to Finance Minister Manmohan Singh, 'foreign exchange reserves were no more than a billion dollars, that is, roughly equal to two weeks' imports'. Manmohan Singh, interview, PBS, 2 June 2001. Available at http://www.pbs.org/wgbh/commanding heights/hi/resources/pdf_index.html.

27. In the first week of November 2009, the RBI bought 200 tonnes of gold. Meghnad Desai, a strong advocate of economic reforms, described it as '… the redeeming moment. I recognize that this was a technical operation and 200 tonnes is not much by the standards of a Central Bank. But it was still symbolic that after 18 years India had now come back and had to be seen as a solvent and indeed a well-endowed country.' Meghnad Desai, 'The Golden Hindustan', *The Indian Express*, 8 November 2008.

28. Interview, Arjun Singh.

29. Interview, ibid.

30. Frankel, *India's Political Economy*.

31. Governments in the 1980s under both Rajiv Gandhi and V.P. Singh had resorted to deficit financing by borrowing heavily from financial institutions within the country and abroad.

32. Prabhat Patnaik and C.P. Chandrasekhar (1995) 'Indian Economy under "Structural Adjustment"', *Economic and Political Weekly*, vol. 30, no. 47, 25 November, pp. 3001–13, esp. p. 3001.

33. E.M.S. Namboodripad's statement cited in Frankel, *India's Political Economy*, pp. 593–4.

34. Arjun Sengupta (1995), 'Financial Sector and Economic Reforms in India', *Economic and Political Weekly*, vol. 30, no. 1, 7 January, pp. 39–44, esp. p. 40.

35. Corbridge and Harriss, *Reinventing India*, pp. 155–7.

36. Mitu Sengupta (2008), 'How the State Changed Its Mind: Power, Politics and the Origins of India's Market Reforms', *Economic and Political Weekly*, vol. 43, no. 21, 24–30 May, pp. 35–42.

37. Baldev Raj Nayar (1998), 'Political Structure and India's Economic Reforms of the 1990s', *Pacific Affairs*, vol. 71, no. 3, Autumn, pp. 335–58.

38. Sunita Kale (2009), 'Inside Out: India's Global Reorientation', *India Review*, vol. 8, no. 1, January–March, pp. 43–64, esp. p. 50.

39. Nayar, 'Political Structure and India's Economic Reforms of the 1990s'.

40. Manmohan Singh (1993), 'India's Economic Policies: The Past Experiences and the New Initiatives', in Debandra K. Das (ed.), *Structural Adjustment in the Indian Economy*, Deep & Deep, New Delhi.

41.   Manmohan Singh, interview given to PBS on 2 June 2011. Available at http://www.pbs.org/wgbh/commandingheights/hi/resources/pdf_index.html (accessed on 9 January 2012).

42.   Ibid.

43.   Sengupta, 'How the State Changed Its Mind', pp. 40–1.

44.   IMF statement cited in Nayar, 'Political Structure and India's Economic Reforms of the 1990s', p. 335.

45.   On Manmohan Singh's position, see C.T. Kurien (1996), *Economic Reforms and the People*, Madhyam Books, New Delhi.

46.   For an account of Manmohan Singh's contribution to policymaking, see Isher Judge Ahluwalia and I.M.D Little (eds) (1998), 'Introduction', in *India's Economic Reforms and Development: Essays for Manmohan Singh*, Oxford University Press, New Delhi.

47.   Until 1991, Manmohan Singh was seen as an establishment economist who had endorsed the 'socialist' policy framework of the Indian government. Even as the South Commission's Secretary General in the late 1980s, he had articulated the economic aspirations of the developing countries and been critical of the IMF and World Bank.

48.   Ahluwalia and Little, *India's Economic Reforms and Development*, p. 5.

49.   Byres, *The State, Development Planning and Liberalization in India*, p. 5.

50.   Kohli, 'Politics of Economic Growth in India', p. 171.

51.   Ibid.

52.   Raja Chelliah (1996), *Towards Sustainable Growth: Essays in Fiscal and Financial Sector Reforms in India*, Oxford University Press, New Delhi, p. 3.

53.   See public opinion survey, 'Tails You Lose: Where Is the Much-vaunted "Trickle-down Effect"?' *Outlook*, 28 February 1996.

54.   For a discussion of the political processes and skills involved in ensuring the sustainability of economic reform in a democracy such as India, see Chapters 5 and 6 in Jenkins, *Democratic Politics and Economic Reform in India*.

55.   Varshney, 'Mass Politics or Elite Politics? India's Economic Reforms in Comparative Perspective', p. 155.

56.   Ibid., p. 157.

57.   Ibid., p. 156.

58.   Ibid., p. 158.

59.   Corbridge and Harriss, *Reinventing India*, p. 160.

60.   Harish Damodran (2008), *India's New Capitalists: Caste, Business and Industry in a Modern Nation*, Permanent Black, Delhi.

61.   Ibid.

62.   Jorgen Pedersen (2000), 'Explaining Economic Liberalization in India: State and Society Perspectives', *World Development*, vol. 28, no. 2, February, pp. 265–82.

63.   Ibid.

64.   Ibid., p. 276.

65.   Frankel, *India's Political Economy*, p. 595.

66.   Government of India (1996), *Economic Survey of India, 1995–96*, Ministry of Finance, Economic Division. Available at ieo.org/surv001.html.

67.   Kohli, 'Politics of Economic Growth'.

68.   Ibid.

69.   Ibid.

70.   For the reasons why Indian capital backed liberalization, see C.P. Chandrasekhar and Jayati Ghosh (2002), *The Market That Failed: A Decade of Neoliberal Economic Reforms in India*, Leftword Books, New Delhi, pp. 31–7.

71.   Stanley Kochanek (1996), 'Liberalization and Business Lobbying in India', *Journal of Commonwealth and Comparative Politics*, vol. 34, no. 3, pp. 155–73.

72.   Ibid.

73.   Kurien (1994), *Global Capitalism and the Indian Economy*, vol. 6, *Tracts for the Times*, Orient Longman, New Delhi.

74.   Pedersen, 'Explaining Economic Liberalization in India', p. 274.

75.   Chandrasekhar and Ghosh, *The Market That Failed*.

76.   For an analysis of the middle classes, see E. Sridharan (2004a), 'The Growth and Sectoral Composition of India's Middle Class: Its Impact on the Politics of Economic Liberalization', *India Review*, vol. 3, no. 4, October, pp. 405–28.

77.   Arvind Panagariya (2002), 'India in the 1980s and 1990s: A Triumph of Reform', 6 November. Available at http.www.imf.org.

78.   Corbridge and Harriss, *Reinventing India*, p. 145.

79.   Ibid.

80.   Mani Shankar Aiyar (2003), 'Can the Congress Find a Future', *Seminar*, no. 526, June, pp. 14–22.

81.   Frankel, *India's Political Economy*, p. 594.

82.   Ibid., p. 586.

83.   'Sonia Ignores P.V. Narsimha Rao, Says Rajiv Scripted Economic Reforms', *The Times of India*, 28 December 2009.

84.   Manmohan Singh discussed the history of India's industrial policy and economic reform, the impact of globalization, and the role of government in the economy in an interview to PBS on 2 June 2001. See interview, Manmohan Singh.

85.   Ibid.

86.   For details of the debate in the Congress, see V. Bijukumar (2006), *Reinventing the Congress: Economic Policies and Strategies since 1991*, Rawat Publications, New Delhi, pp. 112–16.

87.   Cited in ibid. p. 78.

88.   Narasimha Rao (2000), 'Essence of Liberalization: Means to Transform Society, Not a Business Ploy', The Second J.R.D. Tata Memorial Lecture delivered in New Delhi on 1 November 1999, *Mainstream*, 10 June 2010.

89. In more than a quarter of parliamentary constituencies Congress candidates did not even finish as runners up.

90. After the 1999 elections, when the Congress won just 114 seats in the Lok Sabha, putting up its worst performance in a general election up to that date, Sonia Gandhi appointed a committee under A.K. Antony to look into the party's drubbing. The report was submitted to the Congress president in November 1999.

91. *Congress Sandesh* (2000), 'Antony Committee Report', January. Available at www.congresssandesh.com/dec_jan_issue/cwc.html.

92. Ibid.

93. Chandrasekhar and Ghosh (2007), 'Recent Trends in Employment in India and China: An Unfortunate Convergence?' *MacroScan*, 5 April. Available at www.macroscan.org/anl/apr07/pdf/india_china.pdf.

94. James Manor (2011a), 'The Congress Party and the "Great Transformation"', in Sanjay Ruparelia, Sanjay Reddy, John Harriss, and Stuart Corbridge (eds), *Understanding India's New Political Economy: A Great Transformation?* Routledge, London, p. 205.

95. On this, see Nayar (2001b) 'Opening Up and Openness of Indian Economy', *Economic and Political Weekly*, vol. 36, no. 37, 15–21 September, pp. 792–815.

3   Regime Change and Working a Coalition

The 1996 election marked the end of the Congress epoch in Indian politics. From 1989 onwards, it had ceased to be the central pole around which political competition was structured. The 1990s was a period of transition from one-party dominance to a multi-party system. Two important developments defined this period: the rise of the BJP and the growing significance of lower-caste-dominated regional and state-based parties. From 1991 to 1998, the Congress was unable to fully comprehend the deep-seated change in the politics of the country. The combined blow of Mandal–Mandir politics reduced its footprints. Pointing to the post-Rajiv Gandhi years till the installation of UPA in office as 'some of the most difficult moments in our party's history', Sonia Gandhi acknowledged that the Congress had to struggle to 'overcome doubts over its very existence'.[1] In terms of leadership, ideology, and policy, the Congress was at the crossroads. It confronted a multi-dimensional crisis—of political identity, mobilization strategy, and organizational coherence. Central to the crisis was the inability of its leadership to articulate a paradigm which had broad appeal, and yet address the social, economic, and political issues facing society and polity in India, especially the underprivileged who formed a major chunk of its support base.[2]

Two factors had a long-lasting effect on Congress fortunes. One was the politics of social cleavages (especially the politics of caste) and the other was the changing nature of the economy (unequal effects of neo-liberal economic policies noted in Chapter 2). Thanks to V.P. Singh's decision to implement the Report of the Mandal Commission recommending reservations in government employment for the OBCs, they emerged as a major force in national politics (Mandal 1).[3] The policy pronouncement prompted widespread disturbances and violence in several parts of the country, with members of the upper castes taking to the streets in protest. Despite the violent protests, the National Front government did not backtrack on 27 per cent reservation for OBCs in central government jobs. This had far-reaching implications in changing the balance of power between castes and represented a major victory for the OBCs and parties advocating the interests of the upwardly mobile backward castes. The Congress was placed on the back foot while the BJP faced a challenge to its attempts to forge Hindu unity.

When the Mandal Commission submitted its report in 1980, the Congress party was in power but Indira Gandhi did not do anything to implement it. Rajiv Gandhi did nothing either, telling his aides: 'It's a can of worms; I won't touch it.'[4] The CWC criticized V.P. Singh for his 'cynical opportunism, intellectual dishonesty, and political malfeasance'.[5] Objections to Mandal ranged from concerns that economic backwardness was being obscured to the fact that politicization of caste was a conscious ploy by caste-based parties to weaken and hurt the Congress. Eventually, the party did not oppose Mandal reservations but nevertheless favoured exclusion of the economically privileged sections of OBCs.[6] As for the BJP, it was emboldened to stoke up communal tensions to deflect the threat that the Mandal decision was posing to their principal constituency, the upper castes. Incensed by the possibility that reservations would heighten caste consciousness and thereby erode Hindu unity, the BJP–RSS–VHP combine intensified its Ayodhya campaign.[7]

Disillusioned with the Congress's reluctance to openly support reservations in central government employment, the OBCs in north India rallied behind backward caste formations that forged an alliance of OBCs, Dalits, and Muslims to counter both the BJP and Congress. The rising power of backward castes in the wake of the Mandal decision signalled a profound shift in India's democratic politics which swept the Congress out of power from Uttar Pradesh and Bihar for the next two decades and more. The threat posed by the failure to accommodate backward caste aspirations was particularly acute in these two states where it had problems in accepting the rising influence of these groups, which was not the case in other states such as Andhra Pradesh, Tamil Nadu, Karnataka, Kerala, Goa, Maharashtra, Gujarat, Madhya Pradesh, Chhattisgarh, Rajasthan, and Orissa, where their group interests were seriously addressed and accommodated.[8] The lower caste parties took full advantage of their numbers and mobilized their caste identities as a way of taking over power in the north Indian states.[9] By 1990, it was left with no core vote in these parts; it was transformed into the residue of every social grouping. Its inclusive ethos, which had attracted the socially disadvantaged to its fold, became the very reason why each community sought an exclusivist communitarian destiny elsewhere. The loss of power in the north increased its electoral dependence on the southern states. From this point onwards, its power was concentrated in south and western India, and it was increasingly difficult to stage a comeback in these two states which had for so long been the citadels of the party.

The great challenge faced by the Congress at the national level came from the rise of the BJP as an alternate pole. During this period it went through a crisis marked by vacillation on policy issues, lack of trust in the leadership, and factional feuds.[10] There was open expression of discontent from all sections within the party which had been plagued by a series of splits, conflicts, and factional disputes that had seen various key figures abandon it. In particular, the defection of Arjun Singh and N.D. Tiwari in May 1995 to form the All India Indira Congress (Tiwari) party underscored the divisions within.[11] The party was hard-pressed to control its internal bickering with several leaders charge-sheeted in the *hawala* case and senior bureaucrats accused of receiving payments from the Jain brothers for party and political expenses in return for favours in getting commissions and contracts for their steel fabrication company and for middle men they assisted in getting contracts for MNCs.[12] According to Madhav Rao Scindia, the 'party organization has failed, the CWC hardly ever meets. The AICC meets after long intervals. The Congress party's politics has become isolated from the grassroots.'[13] The state of the party organization was particularly abysmal in Bihar and Uttar Pradesh, as well as in Maharashtra and West Bengal.

The Congress went into the 1996 elections discredited by charges of corruption against its leaders and a pervasive feeling that large sections of the electorate were turning against it. The leadership downplayed the effects of economic liberalization but in the end this issue proved critical in turning the tide against the party. Rao led the Congress to its worst ever electoral defeat, with party leaders blaming the poor result in 1996 parliamentary elections on the unpopularity of Rao and the factionalism that had dogged the party. The middle classes, which had stuck with the Congress as the natural party of governance through most of the post-Independence period, began to cast around for alternatives. Popular support appeared to have declined at the all-India level, with the erosion being significantly higher in the key states of Uttar Pradesh, Bihar, West Bengal, and Tamil Nadu.

Following this, the pressure on Rao to resign from the presidentship gained momentum, especially as the slide of the party continued unabated. He did so from the leadership of the Congress Parliamentary Party (CPP) in September 1996 and was replaced by Sitaram Kesri for a short period. In May 1996, a BJP government was formed which lasted 13 days. Later, the Congress with 140 seats provided outside support to a United Front government led by H.D. Deve Gowda and later by I.K. Gujral to avert elections and counter the BJP. However, neither of these goals was achieved. Kesri pulled the rug from beneath the feet of the United Front government led by Deve Gowda in March 1997, charging that the prime minister was eagerly pursuing corruption cases against Congress leaders.[14] The removal of Deve Gowda did not, however, lead to the formation of a Congress government. The United Front leaders regrouped and rallied behind I.K. Gujral to prop up a successor government and it again agreed to support it from outside. It, however, fell out with I.K. Gujral over the report of the Jain Commission probing Rajiv Gandhi's assassination.[15] It indicted the Dravida Munnetra Kazhagam (DMK) in the assassination of Rajiv Gandhi and therefore sought its removal from the ministry, with which the government refused to comply.[16] On 28 November 1998, the Congress withdrew support to the United Front government. When the minority United Front government fell for the second time as a consequence of the Congress's withdrawal of support, there was every indication that the BJP would benefit from this instability and win sufficient seats in the next elections to form a government at the Centre.

In 1998, the NDA, a coalition of 16 parties led by the BJP, formed a government in New Delhi. This marked a crucial turning point as for the first time the BJP formed a government at the Centre ending decades of erstwhile political isolation. Before the 1998 elections, Sonia Gandhi emerged from seclusion to campaign for the Congress 'to save the country from those who use religion and caste to divide the country', as she put it.[17] Travelling in jet aircraft and helicopter, she visited 138 constituencies across the length and breadth of India in 34 days. *India Today* declared that her campaign was 'unparalleled in electoral history' and claimed that she had virtually 'hijacked the party'.[18] More than ever before, the Congress was totally identified with a single person. However, when the votes were counted, the BJP emerged as the single largest party with 171 seats while the Congress tally remained low at 141, the party posting its lowest ever vote share of 25.4 per cent.[19] Sonia Gandhi's campaign clearly did not reverse the party's decline but it succeeded in checking further erosion of social support and contributed to the collapse of the United Front. Moreover, it curbed factionalism and defections from the party. Congress leaders admitted that minus the Nehru–Gandhi family, the party would have been worse off. Referring to the improved performance in the 1998 elections, the CWC declared: 'The Congress party owes its electoral gains [of] 28 more seats than in the 1996 elections to her alone.'[20]

The Congress tried to bring down the BJP-led NDA government formed in 1998 with the help of the AIADMK leader, J. Jayalalitha, who withdrew support from the government in 1999. Jayalalitha's defection and her party's 18 votes were crucial in hastening the end of the NDA government. After this, Sonia Gandhi was led to believe that Mulayam Singh Yadav would support the Congress claim to form an alternative government. But she failed to cobble together the majority figure of 272 Members of Parliament (MPs) in the Lok Sabha to form the government when he refused to support her claims. This left Atal Bihari Vajpayee as caretaker prime minister and the BJP the frontrunner in the 1999 elections. Voters were dismayed by the Congress role in pulling down the United Front and the Vajpayee governments. In the 1999 elections, Sonia Gandhi's projection as prime minister provoked a fierce opposition to her foreign origins. In May 1999, questioning the decision to promote her as the Congress's candidate for prime-ministership on the grounds of her not being 'of this earth' and her lack of 'experience and understanding of public life', Sharad Pawar, P.A. Sangma, and Tariq Anwar raised the banner of revolt against her leadership.[21] Their letter to the party president stated that the 'personalized campaign started by the BJP against you is reprehensible and needs to be opposed strongly. At the same time we would again state that the issue ... is real ... and cannot be wished away.'[22] They demanded that the Constitution should be amended to ensure that only 'natural born' citizens can become president, vice-president, and prime minister. In response, she resigned from the post of party president. The CWC rejected these claims and reiterated its faith in her party leadership. The focus on Sonia Gandhi's foreign origins was misplaced, distracting from the basic issue that had been at the centre of opposition to Congress politics, which was the tendency towards dynastic rule which means that membership of the 'family' overwhelmed all other considerations.

In the 1999 election, the Congress slumped to its worst ever electoral performance: it had won just 112 seats, a decline of 29 from its 1998 tally, which in itself was among the poorest showing ever by the country's oldest party.[23] In fact, the Congress and its alliance partners, the AIADMK, Rashtriya Janata Dal (RJD), Indian Union Muslim League (IUML), and the Rashtriya Lok Dal (RLD), could together muster only 134 seats. The party won fewer seats than the BJP in three elections in a row—in 1996, 1998, and 1999. It ruled 17 states in 1985, but by early 1990 it governed only 9 states and only 3 of these—Karnataka, Andhra Pradesh, and Maharashtra—were sufficiently large to be considered important. It lost the two key southern states of Andhra Pradesh and Karnataka to regional parties in late 1994 and lost control of all the state governments in the Hindi heartland, most notably the state of Uttar Pradesh which was the fulcrum around which its politics had turned since Independence. It was relegated to the third place in the assemblies of Uttar Pradesh, Bihar, and Karnataka. In Gujarat, the BJP had slowly built its base among the OBCs, tribals, and Dalits at the expense of the Congress.

The fate of the Congress, out of power since 1996, depended crucially on its attitude towards the BJP, and by extension the role of religion in politics. The most difficult question confronting it was the ideological positioning over secularism. Since the emergence of the BJP as a formidable political force claiming to represent all Hindus, it sometimes found it difficult to draw the line between majoritarian and secular politics, especially as it tried to appropriate the positions of the BJP to assuage majoritarian religious sentiment. In terms of principle, it had no difficulty in projecting its support for secularism which it differentiated from the principles of Hindutva.[24] In practice, it lacked the political will to take a firm stand against the practitioners and purveyors of polarization and violence without fearing that it will alienate the majority community. The central event which dominated this period was the pogrom against Muslims in Gujarat which followed the burning of a train compartment of the Sabarmati Express in February 2002. Violence swept across Gujarat in an orchestrated series of 'revenge' massacres. In the days and weeks that followed, further waves of violence swept through the state and the victims were almost all Muslims. Reports of numerous fact-finding missions provide the broad outline of events leading to one of the most brutal carnages in the history of Independent India. Though it was not in power at the Centre or state it could not ignore the meaning and implications of such mass violence with state complicity for the future of communal harmony and national integration. It was a crucial test for the Congress, not only in terms of its response to the mass violence, but in how to deal with Hindutva politics.

Another significant moment for the Congress was the changes in the National Curriculum Framework (NCF) introduced by the NDA government. Under Murli Manohar Joshi, a BJP politician with close links to the RSS/VHP, the Human Resources Development Ministry of the NDA government, launched a campaign to 'saffronize' (Hinduize) all levels of education by revising textbooks, instituting regulatory changes, and appointing sympathetic officials to important positions in educational institutions. A key issue was the changes in textbooks issued by the National Council for Educational Research and Training (NCERT), particularly those in history and social sciences. The new textbooks published in 2002–3 immediately became the subject of criticism for their numerous distortions of history and, above all, the Hindutva perspective embedded in the NCF 2000 for primary and secondary education which was also the basis of the new school textbooks.[25] From this point onwards Sonia Gandhi adopted a much clearer position against the BJP and its communal agenda.[26] At a mammoth rally at Delhi's Ramlila grounds on 30 March 2003, Sonia Gandhi attacked the government for endorsing the RSS and its divisive agenda.[27] It was the first forthright attempt to regain secular space. She campaigned strongly on the issue of pluralism and reiterated the commitment that Congress would preserve the secular identity of the state. Exhorting the people to throw out 'this communal government' and restore Congress rule again, she said, the forces of *firka-parasti* (disruptionist forces) 'today were seeking to undo everything that had been achieved under the Congress'.[28] 'We reject the politics of hate. We will go to the people with politics that unites, not divides, politics that heals, not wounds,' she stated.[29] The 14-point charter adopted at a three-day meeting in Shimla in July 2003 highlighted the party's new willingness to take on the BJP frontally on the ground of its communal politics. For the first time in the post-Indira Gandhi period, the Congress campaigned on an unambiguous separation of religion and state and reaped dividends from this.

COALITION AS A PATHWAY TO POWER

Facing repeated electoral setbacks, there began a discernible change in the Congress strategy after being consigned to a long spell in the opposition. This was the recognition of coalitions as a necessary pathway to regain power and contain the further expansion of the BJP, regional parties, and lower caste politics. The period from 1989 to 2004 created a distinct strategic configuration resulting in a dispersal of power from one party to many competing ones and from New Delhi to the states. The reconfiguration of the party system saw Congress dominance giving way to a multi-party system.[30] It was difficult to form a government or hope that it would last without the induction of powerful regional parties in the government. In 1996, regional parties dominated the United Front comprising 'democratic and secular forces', playing a key role in the selection of Deve Gowda as the prime minister. The installation of the BJP-led government in 1998 could never have happened without the support of regional parties.[31] This was in sharp contrast to the past when regional and state parties held office in the states at the pleasure of the Congress-controlled Centre. These developments made formation of electoral alliances and post-poll coalitions necessary.

While the Congress had lost its dominant position, it clung to the idea that one party could speak for India in its entirety, while its premier rival, the BJP, had factored in the inevitability of coalitions in its strategy. It thus appeared to be out of tune with the new developments in the political process although it had a long history of coalition-building in the states. It had adjusted itself to power-sharing and coalitions quite early in Kerala and West Bengal, indicating an ability to come to terms with the political realities which give rise to multiple parties. It had accepted the coalition logic in Tamil Nadu, Jharkhand, Uttar Pradesh, Jammu and Kashmir, Bihar, and Maharashtra. Thus, in the states it was prepared to form an alliance to win power. The problem was its unwillingness to countenance a coalition as an option at the national level, equating it with instability. In his presidential address in 1997, Sitaram Kesri dismissed the insistence that 'coalitions are here to stay', claiming that '[t]he Congress itself has been the most successful coalition'. Rejecting the inevitability of coalitions, Kesri spoke of the achievability of single-party government at the Kolkata plenary session in August 1997.[32] The political resolution underlined that 'the Congress Party has the will and capacity to ensure and acquire the support of the people of this country for a viable and stable one-party government in the country'.[33]

Having enjoyed the fruits of office for so long, Congress politicians were averse to sharing power with other parties. It had, however, to reckon with the fragmentation of the party system and the rise of regional alternatives, which made it impossible for it to win a majority on its own. By refusing to form a pre-electoral coalition, it failed to translate its higher percentage of votes spread across the country into seats. It is important to remember that while coalitions were possibly the only means of coming to power, this option was harder for it to follow because it was in direct competition with many of the regional parties. For example, Chandrababu Naidu in Andhra Pradesh has an ideological affinity with secular parties but the rivalry at the state level logically hinders an adjustment with the Congress at the Centre. It could not coalesce with these regional parties except in states where the Congress itself had been reduced to a third or fourth position, such as in Tamil Nadu. By comparison, the BJP, with a concentration of support in the north and north-western regions, could more easily find allies in southern and eastern India where it posed no threat to its prospective allies.

With very little prospect of winning a single-party majority in the foreseeable future, the Congress had to accept the reality that it was a residual force in several key states. The game changer was the sobering experience of April 1999 when Sonia Gandhi failed to marshal the support of 272 MPs to form a government. This failure compelled the leadership to reappraise and rework its electoral strategy to form a coalition. In March 2001 in Bengaluru, it resolved 'to wage every war, fight every battle, make every sacrifice, to remove the BJP-led NDA government at the centre'.[34] Sonia Gandhi gave indications of the shift when she stated at the chief ministers' conclave at Mount Abu in 2002 that: 'Our main aim is to strengthen the party. The ideal situation would be to have our own governments but we do not have a closed mind on the issue of coalitions.'[35] The rationale was to unify all secular forces to combat communalism and ensure the defeat of the BJP. By 2002, it had moved away from the fixation with one-party dominance to adjust to working a coalition with other parties 'principally to continue being the primary reference point in the polity'.[36] Sonia Gandhi quietly began the process of reaching out to non-Congress parties to break the entrenched tradition of anti-

Congressism in the party system and this facilitated the way for the party's return to power at the Centre. Her principal contribution was in making a dent in the politics of anti-Congressism that had put her party out of reckoning for a fairly long time.

In 2004, it proceeded to build a broad coalition of secular political parties across the country, now making an all-out effort to forge alliances. For a start, it was agreed that coalition partners would collectively decide on the leadership in the event of a victory for the alliance in 2004. A high-level committee was set up to reach a pre-poll alliance with secular parties. This followed close on the heels of the report of the Pranab Mukherjee committee (December 2003), which concluded that the Congress could win only with alliances. This reinforced the new thinking of the party.[37] Sonia Gandhi reached out to parties like the DMK even though Congressmen had accused DMK of being hand-in-glove with the assassins of Rajiv Gandhi.[38] She made peace with Sharad Pawar despite the fact that he had split from the Congress over the issue of her foreign origin and poor leadership abilities and established the Nationalist Congress Party (NCP). Most importantly, the long spell of the NDA government opened up space for cooperation with the Left, a major break from past hostility that had characterized the CPI (M)–Congress relationship. Indeed, the UPA could not have come to power without building bridges and forging relationships, especially with the Left parties.

The series of state-specific alliances enabled the UPA to get ahead of the NDA in the 2004 polls. The Congress was able to form better alliances owing to the widespread concern over the BJP's sectarian agenda after the Gujarat pogrom of 2002. The actual difference between the vote shares of the two alliances was less than 1 per cent of the popular vote.[39] However, overall, the electoral coalition scored a major success, winning 222 seats against 188 for the NDA. If the UPA overtook the NDA in 2004, it was because its allies brought in fresh support.[40] It, however, allowed the Congress to break out of the kind of isolation it had encountered in previous polls where it had as many or even more seats but was bereft of friends. Its pre-electoral coalition paid rich electoral dividends in Maharashtra, Bihar, Tamil Nadu, Andhra Pradesh, and Jharkhand. It won 145 seats; its share of the votes was 26.8 per cent, followed by the BJP at 22.2 per cent. The BJP's tally dropped to 138, down from the 182 seats it won in 1999, while the Congress increased its tally from 114 to 145.[41] The allies contributed 74 seats and 9.1 per cent of the vote to the combined tally.[42] It won only 54 seats in the absence of allies, which was a little more than a third of its total strength of 145 seats.[43] Of the larger states, it swept only one, Andhra Pradesh, without a major regional ally.[44] Overall, coalitions were extremely important in the Congress alliance's victory, just as it was for the BJP alliance in 1998 and 1999 elections.[45]

INDIA SHINING AND *AAM AADMI*

There was, however, much more to the defeat of the NDA than the success in forging astute alliances. Good alliances are important but they alone cannot explain the stunning ouster of the NDA.[46] Basically, what helped the Congress was its changed political approach as the party positioned itself as a champion of the aam aadmi (the common man) against the 'India Shining' campaign supported by the NDA.[47] Proud of the NDA government's performance, the BJP decided to broadcast its achievements under the slogan 'India Shining' through an expensive media blitz.[48] The central message was that 'India never had it so good'.[49] Impressed by the expanding economy which witnessed high growth which went up to 8.2 per cent in 2003, the BJP decided to showcase its achievements. It espoused the 'feel good' theory largely on the record of one year, which was supposed to indicate a great future ahead.[50] It, however, discovered to its discomfiture that India was shining only for the elite and middle classes, and this too restricted to some regions and cities, and most of the issues that mattered to them had little relevance for the majority of voters who remained poor and dependent upon agriculture for employment. Agriculture, where over 60 per cent of the population works, fared very poorly in these years and manufacturing did not fare much better, with most of the high growth occurring in the services sector. The benefits of high growth did not trickle down to the masses, especially the rural masses who were reeling under a severe agricultural crisis. India may well have been shining for the elite and urban middle classes, but when an entire country was asked to endorse that proposition, the response was overwhelmingly in the negative.

When the BJP launched the 'India Shining' campaign, very few predicted that the event would signal the beginning of a quiet but strong challenge to economic reforms. It proved to be suicidal as it showed the BJP was far removed from the people. Occurring in the midst of an agrarian crisis that brought hardship to millions, it caught the public imagination because it summed up deep-seated insensitivity to vulnerabilities that define the lives of many people: high rates of unemployment, precarious livelihoods, limited social protection, and lack of redress when governments ignore citizen demands. 'India Shining' campaign seemed to have wholly ignored the big livelihoods issue and, above all, the blot on the government's image for its perceived inaction during the communal violence in Gujarat in 2002. Even though the central issue behind the defeat was economic, rejection of the politics of religious division and conflict also played an important role. For all these reasons, the 'feel good' factor was far from pervasive and the NDA government's decision to call an election on this ground earlier than necessary proved to be a big mistake. The 'India Shining' slogan backfired sharply and was largely responsible for the defeat of the NDA. As an editorial in *Frontline* put it: 'India Shining deserves an award for the worst advertising campaign of the past quarter century: by seeming to mock the deprivations of the mass of voters in rural as well as urban areas, it opened up a huge credibility gap for the ruling party.'[51]

Moreover, the BJP's core constituency did not require a propaganda blitz to be reminded about the improvement in their comfort levels during the NDA years. By contrast, these slogans actually angered the vast majority of the population, serving only to remind them that the benefits of high growth had not reached them.[52] The party later admitted its 'India Shining' publicity offensive had been harmful in the election.[53] Newspaper reports and editorials conceded that it was a major cause for the defeat of the BJP, particularly in urban areas, the target audience of the campaign. Advani, who described it as 'valid' but 'inappropriate for our election campaign', echoed the negative assessment of the campaign after the election. 'By making them verbal icons of our election campaign, we gave our political opponents an opportunity to highlight other aspects of India's contemporary reality ... which questioned our claim,' he said.[54]

On the other hand, the 'India Shining' slogan prompted the Congress to make aam aadmi the central plank of its campaign against the BJP-led government and its elitist orientation.[55] Its advertisements challenged the claims of India Shining with the simple question: '*Aam aadmi ko kya mila?*' ('What did the common man gain?')The poor in the slogan '*Congress ka haath garibon ke saath*' ('Congress's hand [the party's electoral symbol] is with the poor') was replaced by '*Congress ka haath, aam aadmi ke saath*' ('Congress's hand is with the common man').[56] The focus on the aam aadmi symbolized the politics of the 'new Congress' which evidently was keen to move away from excessive stress on the word *garib* which its strategists felt vindicated the charge that the 'Congress was happiest pedalling poverty'. One thing was clear, however—at least at the level of concept, if not practice—the aam aadmi focus frontally challenged the basically divisive and exclusivist premises of the BJP's governance of India.[57]

The result was an unexpected electoral defeat of the NDA as voters wanted not just a change in government but a radical change in economic policy. The NDA's defeat was a surprise for the Congress too, which had probably not counted on returning to power in 2004. Its leaders claimed that the party had altered the public debate by focusing on the day-to-day concerns of the people. The verdict was an expression of frustration with the existing order and a vote for regime change, as Sonia Gandhi put it. The people expressed their resentment against divisive politics of the BJP that had damaged social harmony and its elitist economic policies, that had neglected weaker sections of society, she said.[58]

The election results underscored the mass resentment against rising social inequalities amongst groups, which was a crucial factor in the defeat of the NDA. In the face of growing expectations coupled with widespread disaffection with the middle classes and elite cornering the benefits of high growth, the strategists concluded that the party needed to modify its approach to economic reforms and distributional issues more generally. Two of its biggest initiatives—the National Rural Employment Guaranteee Act (NREGA; see Chapter 6) and the extension of reservations to backward castes in higher education in 2006—were part of this modification, both anti-market, based on the perception that it had to mobilize those excluded from the market and government jobs.[59]

WORKING THE UPA COALITION

The UPA was a complex coalition for several reasons. The most powerful person in the Congress was outside of the government, and in precisely the same way, the CPI (M), a key political player, was not part of the government, extending outside support.[60] The Congress and its pre-poll allies came together to form the UPA, which consisted of 19 parties, including the Congress.[61] The UPA's coming to power was a major shift for both the Congress and its allies. The party's dependence on regional parties and the direct participation of these parties in a Congress-dominated coalition gave the UPA government a distinct character different from all Congress ministries in the past.[62] Though led by the Congress, the governing coalition was underpinned by a working relationship with the Left parties. The UPA, which had won 222 seats, was well short of a majority needed to form the government. The Left Front, in this context, emerged as the pivotal bloc in the Fourteenth Lok Sabha, for without the support of the 61-member Left Front, the UPA would not have been able to garner a parliamentary majority. The CPI (M) with 43 seats was the third largest party in the Parliament and the second largest in the coalition among its outside supporters. The Left's softening towards the Congress came in the wake of the ascendancy of the BJP to the status of the single largest party in the 1996, 1998, and 1999 elections. These parties pledged support to the UPA so long as communalism represented by the BJP remained a threat to national unity and communal harmony. Sonia Gandhi's strong attacks on the BJP and Hindutva forces after the Gujarat violence of 2002 reinforced their resolve to go with the Congress.

But the UPA, from the very outset, faced major political challenges both with regard to survival and the stability and governance of the coalition.[63] The Congress, as the single largest party with only 145 seats, managed to dominate the coalition. Governing such a coalition was going to be no easy task, however. Although the regional parties were rarely consulted regarding policy decisions, the Congress did not run into major problems with them because their primary interest was to increase their influence at the Centre and obtain important cabinet posts. The ruling party was quite willing to oblige and accommodate such demands.[64] The bargaining was so intense that it delayed the announcement of portfolios for several days in May when the government assumed office. The Congress was, however, unwilling to concede space on policy matters.

The UPA, unlike many coalitions which are formed on the basis of a minimalist agenda mutually beneficial to the partners, was driven by a maximalist agenda to facilitate a progressive, secular, and activist state. It was not a typical office-seeking alliance, the outside support of the Left lending it a distinct ideological dimension. This entailed reconciling major differences in perspectives and policies between the Congress and Left parties in areas of food security, the public distribution system, labour reforms, disinvestment and privatization, and the like. The implementation of this ambitious agenda depended upon the political will and readiness to go slow on further economic reforms. Even so, the government's approach to economic reforms remained more or less unchanged even though it did not push ahead full speed in this area.

Despite the opposition of the Left parties, the UPA continued the policy of economic liberalization, albeit with a human face. The Congress backed economic reforms, while also announcing through the National Common Minimum Programme (commonly known as NCMP), which was positioned as an alternative to the 'India Shining' rhetoric of the NDA, that it had a democratic and political commitment to equity through redistribution. Although the corporate sector was quick to express its apprehensions that the two goals were incompatible, and that the UPA government must give priority to economic growth over redistribution, it was clear that economic growth must go hand-in-hand with a measure of redistribution.[65]

The Congress–Left relationship, more than the internal dynamics of the UPA coalition, shaped the priorities and orientation of the UPA government. The CPI (M) leadership was determined to keep the BJP out of power to prevent it from undermining the secular–democratic framework.[66] Having drawn a distinction between the secular Congress and communal BJP, the CPI (M) supported the Congress to mobilize maximum political forces to protect secularism.[67] This marked a great shift in the CPI (M)'s position, unlike in the past when it indirectly joined hands with the BJP to make sure that the Congress remained out of power. Jyoti Basu was the architect of this shift and the ensuing alliance;[68] it could not have been formed without a leader of his stature lending weight to the idea and persuading the CPI (M) leadership to accept it. In consequence, the Congress under Sonia Gandhi enjoyed closer and better relations with the two Left parties than at any time since Indira Gandhi's leftward turn in 1969.[69]

Despite constructive engagement, there were a range of issues, especially in economic and foreign policies, where the perceptions and policies of the Congress and Left differed. The Left Front, especially the CPI (M), was clear that they did not want to join the UPA government despite pressure to do so because of its long-standing policy of avoiding being placed in a subordinate position. The Left's 'outside' support meant that though they did not take on the responsibilities of governance, they would exert substantial influence on central government policies on the basis of a negotiated NCMP to guide policy and governance. The NCMP acknowledged: 'The people of India have voted decisively in the 14th Lok Sabha election for secular, progressive forces, for parties wedded to the welfare of farmers, agricultural labour, weavers and weaker sections of society, for parties irrevocably committed to the daily well-being of the common man across the country.'[70]

The NCMP was a minimum starting point for making economic growth socially inclusive and regionally balanced. While the Left played an important role in shaping the NCMP, the Congress claimed that: 'This NCMP is based predominantly on the Congress's own election manifesto. So, it should be clearly understood by all of us that when we fulfill a NCMP pledge, we are fulfilling a commitment of our manifesto itself.'[71] It enunciated six basic principles of governance, which, inter alia, constituted the objectives of the UPA. To quote two of its basic principles: '[T]o preserve, protect and promote social harmony and to enforce the law without fear or favour to deal with all obscurantist and fundamentalist elements who seek to disturb social amity and peace' and 'to provide for full equality of opportunity, particularly in education and employment, for SCs, STs, OBCs, and religious minorities'.[72] It identified seven priority sectors for focused attention: agriculture, water, education, health care, employment, urban renewal, and infrastructure.[73]

The NCMP represented an advance in at least two ways: first, it accepted the need for provision of some immediate relief to the people rather than the earlier reliance on a 'trickle-down' effect of higher growth; second, it clearly held the state responsible for providing such relief. On several issues, ranging from employment guarantee to social sector expenditure, it had a very different thrust from that of the liberalization agenda. Perceiving the popular mood, it envisaged a more active role for the state in promoting employment and welfare. Its strength was its recognition of the progressive powers of the state and democratic process, and an acceptance of the proposition that improving the living conditions of the overwhelming majority was the responsibility of the state, which it must discharge. A noteworthy feature was the position on the question of distribution. It recognized that rapid economic growth was a necessary but insufficient condition for poverty reduction, and that this required the creation of an appropriate enabling environment for the underprivileged which can make it possible for them to reap the benefits of more rapid economic growth through an expansion in employment.[74]

COALITION POLITICS AND THE PARTY'S SOCIAL BASE

Overall, the 2004 elections had witnessed the emergence of a Congress-led multi-party alliance system alongside a strategy targeted at the lower social orders. The Congress adjusted to the changed reality of running a large multi-party government without too much difficulty. Sonia Gandhi acknowledged: 'For all of us, a coalition at the Centre is a new experience. We have adjusted easily, proving our opponents and critics wrong.'[75] It ran a fairly cohesive coalition as no major party walked out of the coalition until 2008 when the Left parties departed. However, the AICC resolution (2007) stated explicitly that such a coalition cannot be at the cost of the revival of the Congress, particularly in the states where its base had eroded.[76] In other words, in the long run there was no alternative to a revived Congress coming to power on its own.

Therefore, the real problem was not the management of political equations and differences with coalition partners but rebuilding support in some of the large states which had been annexed by its regional rivals. Both in the north as well as south, for long periods the Congress has been in the opposition. It was difficult to regain power it had lost in Uttar Pradesh, Bihar, West Bengal, and Tamil Nadu. It was conscious that in some of these states its principal political opponents were parties that were supporting it at the Centre. The 2006 Hyderabad plenary resolution noted that 'even in a coalition political parties do not have to give up the expectation or aspiration of securing larger political space for themselves'.[77] While there was no contradiction between coalitions and party rebuilding, the fact was that alliances with regional parties in several states had come at the expense of the party setting aside its own growth potential owing to the compulsions of coalition politics. A peculiar conundrum confronted the Congress: so long as the state units remained anchored to fulfilling the larger objectives of the high command's emphasis on parliamentary elections, the organizational base in the states remained shallow and prevented its spread as a political force.

More germane to the restoration and revival of the Congress was the social character of the constituency, the underclass, which once again formed the pillar of its political support. The move to extend 27 per cent reservations to OBCs in higher education institutions was part of a plan to demonstrate the backward caste and social justice credentials of the Congress Party.[78] This party had traditionally supported the reservation principle, starting with Nehru, who pushed the constitutional amendment in 1951 guaranteeing reservations for SCs and STs. However, the Congress leadership was ambivalent on the issue of extending the same to the OBCs after Rajiv Gandhi questioned the scientific basis of OBC quotas in his Lok Sabha speech in September 1990 and argued for a comprehensive action plan for the disadvantaged groups. He had criticized the V.P. Singh government for thinking only 'around caste' and 'vested interests in particular castes'.[79] Reservations in higher education institutions were an attempt to counterbalance this approach which had contributed to the long-standing distrust of the backward castes, which was seen as generally an upper-caste-friendly party. Against this perception, the quota gamble was a crucial element of the political strategy to wean away the OBCs from regional and state-based parties which have been the preferred choice of the backward-caste voters. Even though the party's top leadership was indifferent to it and there was strong disagreement within the Congress with regard to the timing of the quota proposal (and more so with Arjun Singh for trying to take credit for it),[80] it could hardly afford to disown the issue. On the other hand, open support would alienate the upper castes. If, however, the Congress stuck firmly to its pro-quota stand, it could hope to win some OBC support and offset the lower-caste advantage enjoyed by regional parties like the Samajwadi Party and the BSP that claimed to be the champions of the disadvantaged.

Propelled by the pressures and counter-pressures, the Congress was keen to strike a balance between the competing claims of the disadvantaged and the advantaged. Sonia Gandhi underscored the point that extension of OBC quotas to central educational institutions would go hand in hand with an increase in seats for general category students. This combined approach of instituting OBC quotas and increasing seats at the same time found approval in the Cabinet. The final decision reflected three main concerns of the Congress and the prime minister in particular. Nothing should be done to damage the knowledge base of the economy; hence (*a*) there should be no dilution in the existing seats and opportunities available in the 'non-reserved' categories; (*b*) the extension of the 27 per cent reservation for the OBCs should be staggered to ensure that the requisite infrastructure was in place; and (*c*) certain institutions of 'national/strategic' importance were kept out of the reservation regime.[81]

The Lok Sabha unanimously approved the legislation for reservations for OBCs in central educational institutions by a voice vote in December 2006. Cross-party support marked the debate on the Bill as virtually every speaker lauded the UPA government's initiative to introduce reservations for OBCs in higher education, which they argued was long overdue. The support for the legislation cut across parties except the BJP which opposed the provision on the exclusion of minority educational institutions. Inspired by key provisions in the Constitution, namely, Article 46 and Article 15(5), the new legislation was one of the UPA's most significant measures, as it was the first time that the Parliament through laws recognized reservation of seats in educational institutions as a necessary measure to give effect to the constitutional provisions of equality. The policies of NREGA and OBC reservation reflected the need to focus programmes on the lower echelons of society to regain the support of these sections which were once the party's principal constituency.[82]

Historically, the success of the Congress was built upon its capacity to draw together a broad spectrum of social groups across the country under its commodius structure. It tried to be the broadest church possible, the 'coalition' before coalitions became the norm. As a big tent party, its strength lay in its ability to reach out to the rainbow coalition, and above all to the bottom of the social heap. This consistency and spread of support helped the party to occupy the dominant space in the political spectrum for close to four decades. However, this picture changed significantly after economic liberalization. Between 1996 and 1999, its voter profile underwent sharp erosion among the middle classes, while the poor, the slum dwellers, the unemployed, and minorities continued to swell the ranks of the party. During this period, the upper and middle classes, as also the upper castes, drifted away towards the BJP.[83] The 2004 elections reinforced this trend: the higher the class, the greater the vote for the NDA. The class slope was the opposite in the case of the UPA and the Congress.[84] Over two-thirds of about 25,433 respondents in the 2004 National Election Study (NES) election survey of political attitudes on economic reform said that these benefit only the rich or none at all.[85] Most of these people voted for the Congress and UPA while those who thought reforms had benefited the entire country voted for the BJP-led NDA.[86] As mentioned earlier, the Congress did not fail to notice the economic dissatisfaction behind the NDA's defeat.

The turnaround in Congress fortunes came about after its reinvention as a party of the aam aadmi. It was, therefore, no surprise that it endorsed the NCMP and accepted a programme of targeted state interventions for the poor and deprived.[87] It was at the same time keen to win back the middle classes under its umbrella and sought to find a workable middle path to reconcile the interests of its electoral base among the poor and its desire to gain the approbation and approval of the upper and middle segments of society. Three issues needed to be addressed if the 2004 election result was to have a lasting and positive impact. These were equity-based growth strategies, social protection for all, and inclusive pluralist politics, which are discussed at length in Chapters 5, 6, and 7, respectively.

NOTES

1.   'Post-Rajiv Years Most Difficult for Congress: Sonia Gandhi', *The Times of India*, 28 December 2009.
2.   Interview with Digvijay Singh, 2 October 2008.
3.   In 1979, the Janata Party government appointed the Second Backward Classes Commission under the chairmanship of B.P. Mandal, an MP, in terms of Article 340 of the Indian Constitution, to investigate and identify the socially and educationally backward classes and examine the question of reservation for them. The Committee, in its report submitted in 1980, recommended reservation of 27 per cent in government employment for the OBCs. After 10 years, the V.P. Singh government implemented the mandate of reservation of 27 per cent government employment for the OBCs. This was challenged in the *Indra Sawhney* v. *Union of India* (1992). In a majority judgement, the apex court expanded the scope of Article 16(4) of the Constitution and upheld reservation for the OBCs. *Indra Sawhney* v. *Union of India* AIR 1993 SC 477: 1992 Supp (3) SCC 217.
4.   Quoted in Inder Malhotra, 'Genie Is on the Table', *The Indian Express*, 18 May 2006.
5.   CWC Resolution quoted in 'Congress Succumbs', Editorial, *The Times of India*, 1 September 1990.
6.   The Narasimha Rao government added a notification for reservation of 10 per cent for 'other economically backward sections of people' who were not covered by existing schemes of reservations, but this was struck down by the Supreme Court in its 1994 verdict in the Indra Sawhney case.
7.   Peter van der Veer (1996), 'The Ruined Centre: Religion and Mass Politics in India', *Journal of International Affairs*, vol. 50, no. 1, Summer, pp. 255–77.
8.   Francine Frankel (1990), 'India's Democracy in Transition', *World Policy Journal*, vol. 7, no. 3, Summer, pp. 521–55, esp. p. 539.

9. Stuart Corbridge and John Harriss (2000), *Reinventing India: Hindu Nationalism and Popular Democracy*, Oxford University Press, New Delhi, p. 221.

10. See Yubraj Ghimre, 'Search for New Power Centres', *Outlook*, 1 January 1997.

11. Arjun Singh and other rebels quit the Congress alleging the Rao government of trying to scuttle the probe into the assassination of Rajiv Gandhi. There were reports of the missing file from the PMO which gave credence to the charge. The government filed a Special Leave Petition (SLP) before the Supreme Court on 22 December 1996, seeking to restrain the Jain Commission from inquiring into any aspect dealing with the role of the LTTE. Rajesh Joshi, 'End of the Jain Commission', *Outlook*, 19 January 1996. Available at www.outlookindia.com/article.aspx?200578 (accessed on 19 March 2012).

12. Frankel (2005), *India's Political Economy: 1947–2004, The Gradual Revolution*, 2nd edition, Oxford University Press, New Delhi, p. 690.

13. Madhav Rao Scindia, interview published in *Outlook*, 1 May 1996.

14. Sitaram Kesri claimed: 'Even now, we are the party which can make or unmake a prime minister. If we have extended our support to Deve Gowda, it's with the hope that he would pursue our policies, mainly on foreign and economic affairs. And, of course, the Government's secular credentials should not come under a cloud.' Kesri quoted in 'Kesri Declares War', *Outlook*, 16 April 1997.

15. Ibid.

16. For the findings of the report on the indictment of the DMK, see Praveen Swami, 'The Jain Commission', *Frontline*, vol. 14, no. 23, 15–28 November 1997. Also see Manoj Joshi, 'Reckless Revelations', Cover Story, *India Today*, 8 December 1997.

17. *India Today*, 16 March 1998.

18. Ibid.

19. Yogendra Yadav (1999a), 'Electoral Politics in the Time of Change: India's Third Electoral System, 1989–99', *Economic and Political Weekly*, vol. 34, nos 34 and 35, 21–8 August, pp. 2393–9, esp. p. 2394.

20. CWC resolution cited in *India Today*, 16 March 1998.

21. Three senior members of the CWC—Sharad Pawar, P.A. Sangma, and Tariq Anwar—questioned the projection of Sonia Gandhi as the Congress (I) prime-ministerial candidate and expressed their concern over her foreign origin and inexperience in politics in a letter dated 15 May 1999. The joint letter stated, 'It is not possible that a country of 980 million, with a wealth of education, competence and ability, can have anyone other than an Indian, born of Indian soil, to head its government.' It went on to say: 'Our inspiration, our soul, our honour, our pride, our dignity, is rooted in our soil. It has to be of this earth.' Letter quoted in Venkitesh Ramakrishnan, 'Revolt in Congress (I)', *Frontline*, vol. 16, no. 11, 22 May–4 June 1999.

22. Ibid.

23. Sonia Gandhi set up a committee headed by Antony in 1999 to introspect into the reverses in the electoral performance of the Congress. Antony

Committee's analysis of the 1999 general elections found that the party had lost most seats by margins of 6 per cent or less. This committee proposed a series of measures to bring about structural changes in the organizational set-up of the Congress. *Congress Sandesh* (2000), 'Antony Committee Report', January. Available at www.congresssandesh.com/dec_jan_issue/cwc.html.

24.   Aiyar (2003), 'Can the Congress Find a Future?' *Seminar*, no. 526, June, pp. 14–22.

25.   Both the NCF and textbooks were subsequently withdrawn by the UPA government within a few months of coming to power in 2004.

26.   Interview with Abhishek Singhvi, MP, Rajya Sabha, 2006–2012, 2012–present, New Delhi, 16 November 2010.

27.   Sonia Gandhi's speech at the convention of the Block Congress Committee and District Congress Committee presidents at the Ramlila Maidan, New Delhi. *Congress Sandesh* (2003), 'Nation Suffered Enough under the BJP: Sonia Gandhi', April. Available at www.congresssandesh.com/april-2003/report/2.html.

28.   *Congress Sandesh*, 'Nation Suffered Enough under the BJP'.

29.   Ibid.

30.   See articles in Zoya Hasan (2008), *Parties and Party Politics in India*, 5th impression, Oxford University Press, New Delhi.

31.   The most powerful regional parties, which include the Telugu Desam Party, the DMK, AIDMK, the Trinamool Congress, the Akali Dal, the Samata Party, and the Biju Janata Dal, extended support to the NDA.

32.   Political Resolution of the 80th Plenary Session of the Congress held at Kolkata on 9–10 August 1997. Available at www.wbpcc.org/plenary.htm (accessed on 17 November 2009).

33.   Ibid.

34.   Bengaluru resolution quoted in Congress President's Speech at the 82nd Plenary Session, Hyderabad, 21–3 January 2006, *Congress Sandesh*. Available at www.congresssandesh.com/feb-2006/cp_address.html (accessed on 10 February 2010).

35.   Editorial, 'The Message from Mount Abu', *The Hindu*, 12 November 2002.

36.   Interview with Aiyar, 26 September 2010.

37.   'Pranab Mukherjee Committee Report', *Asian Age*, 31 December 2009. Available at http://www.asianage.com/main.asp?layout=2&cat1=5&cat2=154& newsid=83475&RF=DefaultMain(accessed on 27 Janaury 2012).

38.   Mahesh Rangarajan (2005b), 'Polity in Transition: India after the 2004 General Elections', *Economic and Political Weekly*, vol. 40, no. 32, 6 August.

39.   Ibid.

40.   E. Sridharan (2004b), 'Electoral Coalitions in 2004 General Elections: Theory and Evidence', *Economic and Political Weekly*, vol. XXXIX, no. 51, 18–24 December 2004, pp. 5418–25, esp. p. 5420.

41.   Alistair McMillan, 'Alliances Did the Trick for the Congress', *The Hindu*, 20 May 2004.

42.   Ibid.

43.   Rangarajan (2005a), 'Congress in Coalition', *Seminar*, no. 545, January, pp. 30–4.

44.   Yadav (2004), 'The Elusive Mandate of 2004', *Economic and Political Weekly*, vol. 39, no. 51, 18 December, pp. 5383–98, esp. p. 5388 .

45.   Sridharan, 'Electoral Coalitions in 2004', p. 5420.

46.   Arun Swamy (2004), 'Back to the Future: The Congress Party's Upset Victory in India's 14th General Elections', Occasional Paper Series, June, Asia Pacific Center for Security Studies, Honolulu. Available at http//www.dtic/mil.tr/fulltext/u2/a446094.pdf.

47.   'The aam aadmi in India is that person who does not have a connection to the system. Whether he is poor or rich, Hindu, Muslim, Sikh or Christian, educated or uneducated, if he is not connected to the system, he is an aam aadmi.' This definition of aam aadmi is given by the Congress president. Available at www.congress.org.in/new/sonia-speeches.php (accessed on 9 January 2012).

48.   The Comptroller and Auditor General of India later criticized the NDA government for diversion of funds and incurring unauthorized expenditure of Rs 63.23 crore for the 'India Shining' campaign without parliamentary approval. 'Now, CAG Decides to Dig into NDA History', *The Times of India*, 26 May 2005.

49.   Baldev Raj Nayar (2005), 'India in 2004: Regime Change in a Divided Democracy', *Asian Survey*, vol. 45, no. 1, pp. 71–82.

50.   Rammanohar Reddy, 'India Shines through Verdict 2004', *The Hindu*, 14 May 2004.

51.   Editorial, 'India Shines', *Frontline*, vol. 21, no. 11, 22 May–4 June 2004.

52.   K.C. Suri, 'Reform: The Elites Want It, the Masses Don't', *The Hindu*, 20 May 2004.

53.   L.K. Advani said the two catchphrases 'Feel Good' and 'India Shining' had hurt the BJP. He said it was 'not wrong … but not appropriate'. Reported in *BBC News*, 'BJP Admits "India Shining" Error', 28 May 2004. Available at www.news.bbc.co.uk/2/hi/south_asia/3756387.stm.

54.   Ibid.

55.   Janardhan Dwivedi, Secretary, Congress party, is credited with introducing the idea of aam aadmi in the Congress election campaign in 2004. Aam aadmi has its equivalent in American and British English. The nearest is probably the 'Average Joe' or common man.

56.   V.R. Narayanaswami, 'Aam Aadmi and the Average Joe: Names that Signify Group Identity', *Live Mint.com*, 14 March 2010.

57.   On some of these arguments, see Zoya Hasan (2006), 'Bridging the Divide: Indian National Congress and Indian Democracy', *Contemporary South Asia*, vol. 1, no. 15, December, pp. 473–88.

58.   Congress president's opening address at the AICC Session, New Delhi, 21 August 2004. Available at www.congress.org.in/new/sonia-speeches.php (accessed on 17 November 2009).

59.   The discussion on reservations for OBCs is based on Chapter 4 in Zoya Hasan (2009), *Politics of Inclusion: Castes, Minorities, and Affirmative Action*, 2nd edition, Oxford University Press, New Delhi.

60.   The forerunner to the 2006 political controversy was the decision of the Supreme Court in August 2005 which made it clear that it was impermissible to introduce quotas in unaided private educational institutions that do not receive financial support from the state. This meant that educational opportunities in the private institutions would remain outside the purview of the affirmative action policies of the state for disadvantaged groups.

61.   Rajiv Gandhi's speech on the Mandal Commission in the Lok Sabha, published in *The Indian Express*, 9 June 2006.

62.   Interview with Arjun Singh, 20 November 2009.

63.   Ibid.

64.   Ashutosh Varshney (2007b), 'India's Democratic Challenge', *Foreign Affairs*, vol. 86, no. 2, March–April, pp. 93–106, esp. p. 103.

65.   Rangarajan (2007), 'Reviving the Congress', *Seminar*, no. 569, January, pp. 34–7.

66.   Pre-poll allies included the RJD, DMK, NCP, PMK, TRS, JMM, LJP, MDMK, AIMIM, PDP, IUML, RPI (A), RPI (G), and KC (J). For details of the Congress allies see E. Sridharan, 'Electoral Coalitions in 2004', p. 5419.

67.   Rangarajan, 'Reviving the Congress'.

68.   Krishna K. Tummala (2004), 'The 2004 Election in India and Its Aftermath', *Asian Journal of Political Science*, vol. 12, no. 2, December, pp. 31–58.

69.   Tummala (2009), 'Coalition Politics in India: 2004–2009', *Asian Journal of Political Science*, vol. 17, no. 3, December, pp. 323–48.

70.   Sections of the media poured scorn on the UPA's effort to formulate the NCMP, and on its contents, branding it the 'Crash Markets Programme'. See Praful Bidwai, 'Welcome UPA, without Illusions', *Frontline*, vol. 21, no. 12, 5–18 June 2004.

71.   Interview with Brinda Karat, CPI (M) Rajya Sabha MP, 2006–12, and Member of the Politburo of CPI (M), 10 July 2010.

72.   Prakash Karat, Interview, *Rediff.com*, 5 June 2008. Available at www.rediff.com/news/2008/jun/17sld1.htm (accessed on 16 January 2012).

73.   Finance Minister Mukherjee acknowledged Jyoti Basu's contribution to building the Congress–Left alliance in his tribute to Basu after his death and said in fact he was an architect of the UPA government in 2004. Repeated in *India Today*, 17 January 2010.

74.   Rangarajan, 'In a Difficult Phase', *The Telegraph*, 6 February 2006.

75.   'National Common Minimum Programme of the Congress-led United Progressive Alliance', May 2004. Available at http://pmindia.nic.in/cmp.pdf (accessed on 20 May 2009).

76.   Sonia Gandhi's speech at the AICC Plenary, Rajiv Nagar, Hyderabad, 21–3 January 2006, *Congress Sandesh*. Available at www.congresssandesh.com/feb-2006/cp_address.html (accessed on 10 February 2010).

77.   'National Common Minimum Programme of the Congress-led United Progressive Alliance'.

78.   Ibid.

79.   Editorial, 'On the Right Track', *The Hindu*, 8 July 2004.

80.   Speech cited in D.K. Singh, 'Old Politics for New Times', *The Indian Express*, 20 November 2007.

81.   Ibid.

82.   Resolution on Political Affairs. Available at www.rediff.com/news/2006/jan/22cong1.htm (accessed on 22 July 2011).

83.   Yogendra Yadav, Sanjay Kumar, and Oliver Heath, 'The BJP's New Social Bloc', *Frontline*, vol. 16, no. 23, 6–19 November 1999, pp. 32–3.

84.   Yadav (2004), 'The Elusive Mandate of 2004', *Economic and Political Weekly*, vol. 39, no. 51, 18 December, pp. 5383–98.

85.   'National Election Study 2004: An Introduction', *Economic and Political Weekly*, vol. 39, no. 51, 18–24 December 2004.

86.   NES 2004 finding on political attitudes to economic reforms reported in Suri, 'Reform: The Elites Want It, the Masses Don't'.

87.   Varshney, 'India's Democratic Challenge'.

4 Two Power Centres and Government–Party Relations

The success of the Congress after years of 'terminal decline' marked a critical juncture in its history. The 2004 elections provided the Congress-led coalition with a mandate to govern but also afforded the party an opportunity to renew the idea of the Congress which assumed a stronger role in the government–party relationship.[1] What took place in 2004 was not just a return of the party to power but also its significance in the governing process. Rajni Kothari points out that

it is the Congress as a party rather than as a governing structure that has been assigned the role of providing a new institutional framework. This is a distinctive challenge, in which the focus is on the party, beginning with the way Sonia Gandhi has laid it out and hopefully to be continued by the party, rather than merely as a governing structure.[2]

Under the new institutional framework, Manmohan Singh, a person with no political support base of his own, headed the coalition government. While Sonia Gandhi, the person with a support base, stayed out of it. The very fact that she eschewed a government post tilted the balance in favour of the party.

The Congress in this period was, however, different from what it had been in the earlier phase. It did not exercise the kind of dominance it had during the first few decades after Independence, and ran, for the first time, a coalition government at the Centre. Under these circumstances, two important issues need to be considered. One relates to the party's new relationship with the government and the emergence of two power centres after the UPA came to power; the other issue relates to organizational regeneration given the greater salience the ruling party enjoyed under a new arrangement. The critical issue was whether the new situation would lead to the renewal of the party and party building or would the Congress as a party be overtaken by the pragmatism of power.

THE CONGRESS PRESIDENT AND THE
PRIME MINISTER

Two approaches to the government–party relationship have prevailed under Congress governments since 1947. Jawaharlal Nehru treated 'the party as a vital and valuable instrument for gaining power and building a nation'.[3] During his tenure, the Congress formed a partnership with the prime minister and both gained from the 'relationship of mutuality'.[4] He was expected to hold regular consultations and discussions with party leaders, which he did for the most part. Nonetheless, the party leaders frequently criticized their ministerial colleagues for not consulting them or the chief ministers for getting too much of their own way because Nehru was aware of their importance in the states.[5] The fact remains that Nehru, as indeed all his ministers, drew their organizational identity and political legitimacy from being members of the Congress.[6]

This 'model of mutuality' was supplanted during the Indira Gandhi era by 'prime-ministerial domination'. Starting with the split in the Congress in 1969, the subordination of the party to the government and the domination of the prime minister was absolute. She came to control all key government and party matters and the party became a compliant and acquiescent instrument. She more or less dispensed with the party's organizational apparatus which had acquired salience only during elections.[7] This became particularly so after its triumph in the 1971 election. Thereafter, she did not countenance any challenge to her leadership and actually made the party organization superfluous and powerless.[8] This produced a 'new political process' which centralized decision-making, weakened institutionalization, and made for an overtly personalized form of governance.[9] Once the Congress returned to office in 1980, she retained the office of party president. As the offices of the prime minister and Congress president were combined in one individual, the party tended to become an extension of the government and administrative apparatus. Prime ministers Rajiv Gandhi and Rao had followed this pattern of amalgamating the two offices.[10]

The relationship between the government and party underwent a major redefinition with the UPA government in 2004. It was necessitated by the new circumstances. Sonia Gandhi had built the UPA and also helped it to win the election. She was therefore the obvious choice to head the government. The new government was not even fully in place when the BJP campaigned against a foreign-born citizen holding the office of prime minister and threatened to launch nation-wide agitation should she become prime minister. This campaign the BJP had initiated way back in 1999 when L.K. Advani stated: 'There is no question of handing over this country to anyone other than those who belong to it.'[11] The BJP, then and later, harped on the foreign origin of the Congress president and demanded a national debate on the issue. The NDA promised to introduce legislation barring anyone born on foreign soil from holding the office of president, vice-president, prime minister, and chief justice of India. 'It was in effect a promise to change the rules of the electoral game in a way that would disqualify the principal rival.'[12] Exit polls showed that this issue was not much of a factor in the 2004 elections, but it still did not dissuade the BJP from persisting with it after its defeat in the elections.

BJP leader Sushma Swaraj threatened to shave her head if Sonia Gandhi was sworn in as prime minister. Several of the Congress party's allies too had opposed her candidacy for the office on the same grounds in 1999. In the negotiations prior to the 2004 elections, they obliged the Congress to agree that the prime minister would be chosen by a consensus after the election. However, after the surprise win of the UPA which she led, a sufficient number of parties were willing to accept her as prime minister, and she could therefore have assumed that position had she been inclined to do so.[13] Throughout this period, the Left parties defended her right, as an equal citizen, to hold the highest public office.

Faced with the BJP's xenophobic attack and the divisiveness it was certain to generate, Sonia Gandhi decided to decline the post of prime minister even though she had the support of over 300 MPs. Because of her foreign origins 'she was concerned about becoming a divisive prime minister, rather than one who unites the country'.[14] On 19 May 2004, she told Congress legislators in the central hall of Parliament:

[O]ne thing has always been clear to me—and that is, as I have often stated, that the post of prime minister has not been my aim. I was always certain that if I ever found myself in the position I am in today, I would follow my inner voice. Today that voice tells me that I must humbly decline this post.[15]

Sonia Gandhi's decision was immediately hailed as Gandhian in scope: the idea of renunciation; that is, spurning power when you have it in your grasp. *The Hindu* implored that Sonia Gandhi's 'stunning act of self-denial' should not 'be allowed to be seen as an endorsement of the vicious campaign that the Sushma Swarajs, the Uma Bhartis, the Govindacharyas [all BJP stalwarts], and the rest in the Sangh Parivar have launched to block and subvert the electoral verdict.... In no democracy are losers in an election entitled to overrule the umpire on who won and lost.'[16]

By renouncing power, she took the wind out of the sails of the BJP/RSS campaign. It was a political masterstroke that put paid to the hysterical opposition to her Italian and Roman Catholic origins.[17] It unsettled the BJP which had predicated its entire strategy on the assumption that she would become prime minister. They would then exploit the middle-class unease with her foreign origin to de-legitimize the government. In the event, her refusal to assume power upset their calculations.[18] Even after she declined the prime-ministership, the BJP conjured up an image of Sonia Gandhi as the extra-constitutional boss and criticized Manmohan Singh's performance on the ground that he was her 'puppet'. It relentlessly attacked him as a 'weak' prime minister, who 'allowed his high office to be "devalued" by making 7 Race Course Road [the prime minister's official residence] subservient to 10 Janpath [Sonia Gandhi's official residence]'.[19]

TWO POWER CENTRES

A basic premise of a parliamentary democracy is that the office of the prime minister is held by the leader of the dominant party: in other words, executive and political powers are vested in the same person. The UPA changed this by instituting a division of powers between the prime minister and party president. For the first time, a leader who was not the prime minister was more powerful than the executive head of the government. Though it was Sonia Gandhi who won the political mandate, she nominated Manmohan Singh to the post of prime minister. *Newsweek* described him as 'one of the 10 most influential world leaders' for ushering in India's transition 'from stagnant socialism to a spectacular takeoff in the global economy' and he played a 'key role in India's emergence as one of the rising powers of the 21st century'.[20] She chose him despite his strong association with neo-liberal policies at a time when the Congress was seeking to lessen its significance. He was not a conventional mass politician but enjoyed a reputation for personal integrity.[21] It was, however, clear from the very outset that he was nominated prime minister not because of his intellectual eminence or economic acumen or his reputation for integrity but because Sonia Gandhi wanted to make the point that she did not covet the top job and apparently Singh too did not. He was, however, the only Congress prime minister never to have won a Lok Sabha election, having taken the Rajya Sabha route to Parliament since 1991.[22]

As the president and the lead campaigner for her party in the 2004 elections, Sonia Gandhi was pre-eminent in the political scheme of the Congress. She had taken the party from 114 seats in 1999 to 145 seats in 2004 and more importantly, forged a pre-poll and post-poll coalition with Left support which helped the UPA to form a government at the Centre. Her political primacy was indisputable; she enjoyed a hegemonic position throughout the five years of the UPA even though the Congress had less than 150 Lok Sabha seats.[23] Given this situation, it is hardly surprising that a division of power came about which formalized a distribution in which the head of the government and head of the party would respectively focus on executive and party affairs. Indeed, political power was itself structured in such a way as to divorce it from the executive. To complicate matters further, the prime minister had to operate under a coalition more complex than any preceding coalition government. Under the UPA, Manmohan Singh had to run a coalition government that was constrained by the party, his own ministers, and allies, and also by the NCMP, the Congress–Left Coordination Committee, and the National Advisory Council (NAC), all these factors operating concurrently.

Even while Sonia Gandhi was formally outside the government, it was patently clear from the outset that she would have a role in the government.[24] Indeed, one of the first things the UPA government did was to define an official role for her, and one that would legitimize her involvement in policymaking though not in the day-to-day functioning of the government.[25] The NAC was the mechanism through which this was achieved. A statutory body headed by Sonia Gandhi and composed of civil society activists, the NAC was created to enable her, and through her the party to have a say in policy matters.[26] It was intended to give her the authority to interact with government officials and at the same time give the UPA a pro-people image. Its brief was to act as a watchdog of the government and oversee the implementation of the NCMP, and operate as an interface between the government and civil society to 'provide inputs for the formulation of policy by the government and support to the government in its legislative business'.[27] It was expected to exert pressure on the government to fast-track the implementation of the NCMP.[28] The NAC was decried as unconstitutional, undemocratic, and a super-cabinet but it remained essentially an influential advisory body providing policy inputs into the deliberative process of the executive.[29]

The decision to separate governance from political leadership, two equally important tasks, and placing each of them in a separate sphere ended the fusion of two often competing imperatives of governance and political stewardship, which the centrally driven Congress was prone to allow. At the first AICC session (August 2004) after the UPA came to power, Sonia Gandhi stated that 'after many years we now have both a prime minister and a Congress president. It is a new experience but I have no doubt that both party and government will emerge stronger.'[30]

One positive consequence of the division of powers was the return of the Congress Party to the centre stage. Sonia Gandhi's decision to retain the party presidency enhanced the party's prestige and value. Its new profile reversed not only the trend of the later years of Indira Gandhi but also the long-established tradition of strong heads of government being the pivot of the political system. This was unusual for the Congress because under its dispensation power had hitherto flowed from the government to the party, and not the other way round. Nehru onwards, prime ministers have had the upper hand in relations with Congress presidents, and the prime minister, when not president of the party, nominates the party president.[31] Under the UPA, there was a crucial shift in the government-party relationship but this did not result in the domination of the party over the government. Party leadership provided the ideological foundations for some of the government policies in important areas that directly affect people. While it would be an overstatement to say that the Congress's ideology shaped the framework of government policy, Sonia Gandhi pushed two ideas that clearly helped the party immensely: the NREG and increased social sector expenditure; and pluralism and secularism. This was a novel experience for the Congress, although it was the established pattern in most parliamentary systems, including India prior to 1971, in which the party sets out the broad directives to the government which acts on them. It may be worth recalling that in 1955, addressing a conference of chief ministers and

Pradesh Congress presidents on the theme of coordination between the Congress organization and the administration in the context of worsening relationship between the organizational and governmental wing, Nehru stated the unmistakable fact that a parliamentary system of government was essentially party government.

> In India it is the Congress session or the All India Congress Committee which gives broad directives. We have to act up to them.... If the AICC lays down a certain policy, either we will have to follow it or if we cannot do so we will have to go and place our difficulties before the organization. The AICC gives us a basic approach. Within that, the government has a large measure of freedom.[32]

While a central role for the party is a characteristic of most parliamentary systems of government, it is unusual for the party president to be more powerful than the prime minister. In the event, the division of power engendered fears of the party and government acting as competing and rival power centres during the UPA rule. It periodically provoked friction, especially because in policy matters, the party and the government did not see eye-to-eye on some crucial economic and social policy issues and often pulled in opposite directions. Some of the prime minister's economic or foreign policy decisions did not receive the immediate support of his party because he remained 'the outsider in the party'.[33] The divergence in policies gave rise to a perception that Manmohan Singh lacked authority and legitimacy. It generated uneasiness in business and media circles with regard to its impact on economic reforms. According to its critics, the dual power structure was standing in the way of economic reforms because it prevented the prime minister from giving the 'desired policy direction' to the government. The expectation was that Manmohan Singh, who as finance minister oversaw the liberalization of the economy, would as prime minister open the economy further and improve India's governance only if he was unhindered by politics. This hope led many analysts to contend that if the UPA government was not constrained by the politics of two power centres, it would be better able to implement economic policy 'rationally'. However, given the complex nature of coalition politics, it was unlikely that the prime minister could move forward with economic reforms without the coalition's support regardless of two power centres.

The dualist model was criticized primarily because Sonia Gandhi had enjoyed a great deal of power and legitimacy which her critics blamed for diminishing the PMO.[34] There was, however, no getting away from the fact that as the elected leader of the Congress Party in the Lok Sabha, she was likely to be more powerful than the prime minister handpicked by her. Besides, Manmohan Singh was not a professional politician, a limitation compounded by his reluctance to seek election to the Lok Sabha. After his nomination as prime minister, there was no dearth of safe seats from where he could have contested the elections and would, in all probability, have won because his appeal was not that of a mass leader but his economic expertise in terms of understanding the policy process and specific knowledge and management of the economy, which, in the party's perception, was an important factor in the Congress government's success.[35] In the end, much of the criticism was directed at Sonia Gandhi who had taken on an active pro-people agenda which was in many respects at variance with the government's economic reforms agenda. In the five years of the UPA, she reportedly wrote and forwarded 98 letters to the prime minister.[36] These letters related primarily to the social sector and a few related to policy issues such as rehabilitation and disaster management. In an overwhelmingly large number of cases the government acted upon these requests, underlining her influence on the UPA government. Some of the policies which she pressed the central government to adopt helped the party to rebuild its social base among the poor. There was therefore no reason to be defensive about the party's assertive approach towards the government but the Congress allowed itself to be pushed on the back foot on the issue of the party's role in the government. It did not affirm the primacy of the ruling party in the parliamentary system or that it could reasonably be expected to exert influence on government's policy.[37]

Be that as it may, both Sonia Gandhi and Manmohan Singh readily acknowledged the imperatives of two power centres and deferred to each other.[38] Abhishek Singhvi notes that unlike the media hype about Sonia Gandhi engaging in backseat driving in the UPA, she was quite deferential towards the prime minister 'who has had his way on most issues'.[39] She had to give way because she was clear that governance and economic policymaking were his prerogative. Vir Sanghvi wrote in a similar vein: 'It is fashionable to portray the prime minister as her cipher, but the truth is that she seems in awe of him, always defers to his intellect and experience, and rarely involves herself in administrative matters.'[40] Asked at the *Hindustan Times* Leadership Summit whether there was any tension between her and Manmohan Singh, she seemed to indicate there was none. She stated that 'those who have doubts about the prime minister and I working together obviously do not know either the prime minister or me'.[41] On the perceived government–party disconnect, she categorically stated: 'The Prime Minister has taken a close personal interest in each of them [welfare goals]. And I know it has not been easy for him to balance different considerations.'[42] The inference: there may be differences in our approaches but party and government are not in conflict. Manmohan Singh also agreed that 'as chairperson of the UPA, she had a legitimate influence in the functioning of our government' and that she 'was a source of strength, not weakness' to him.[43]

Overall, the dual power centre model worked under UPA-1 for two important reasons. One was the aura surrounding Sonia Gandhi's renunciation; second, the Left's outside support and the NCMP which provided a measure of cohesion to the UPA. In the final analysis, what held the government and party together was the mutual understanding at the top. There was no public discord between the two leaders; in fact 'there was much greater harmony between the prime minister and [the] party president than under previous dispensations', noted a senior Left leader.[44] In the longer run, however, the division between executive and political power was not a viable system of governance.

'THE CONGRESS PARTY IS ALIVE, THE ORGANIZATION IS DEAD'

Owing to Sonia Gandhi's decision to decline the post of prime minister, the party acquired greater power and influence than earlier when the two offices were combined in one person and it was the office of the prime minister that bestowed authority on the office of the party president. In the event, there was great expectation that she would use her moral authority to reshape and reorganize the party. An editorial in *The Indian Express* noted: 'The hope was that she would bring a new focus towards reviving a party that, despite its somewhat fortuitous victory at the hustings, was in dire need of being put back together again.'[45] The continuing challenge that confronted her leadership was how to reorganize the party. A handful of senior leaders dominated the cabinet and the CWC, and a mutually beneficial relationship between the leader and the 'leaders' flourished at the expense of organizational vitality.[46]

For much of its history the Congress was a democratic, decentralized party, with strong state units and dedicated party workers. Because of its strong organization, its influence penetrated downwards quite effectively, at least to the sub-district level and sometimes further down to the taluka level. This influence had, however, been seriously eroded because the party machinery was in shambles. Although the party existed throughout the country and the Congress flag was still said to be flying in every village, town, and district, the organization was, for the most part, dysfunctional. In brief, the organization was non-existent, but the Congress was alive. Most leaders lacked a mass base or grassroots support, and their influence was dependent entirely on their proximity to the party president. The party did not have a membership register, it had no properly institutionalized norms of recruitment and membership, its cadre had virtually disappeared, and the once powerful political machine had all but ceased to exist. The rules of political advancement were arbitrary and did not depend upon legislative or political performance or some measure of competence and ability.[47] There were major barriers to entry because the organization was controlled by powerful elites at the local level. The party had no institutional mechanisms for incorporating new groups or recruiting leaders with some popular base.[48]

Until the early 1970s, the Congress used to have regular elections 'even if they were sometimes stage-managed. No elections were held after Indira Gandhi felt let down by the Congress organization leaders.'[49] Elections which had been promised early in Rajiv Gandhi's tenure were never conducted during his term as party president.[50] After his untimely death, the party realized the importance of a strong party organization to meet the challenges of cadre-based parties. Rao proved equally unable to stem the decay of the party organization. He did even less to reorganize the party though he recognized that the party organization was extremely weak and plagued by factionalism and dissidence at all levels. Election to the CWC was held in 1992 after a gap of 20 years.[51] The elections, however, proved to be messy, with an embarrassing number of irregularities, squabbles, and indeed violent clashes between factions across the country.[52] The election turned into a farce when Rao decided to nominate members who had actually been elected to reinforce his primacy in the party. He pulled out Sharad Pawar and Arjun Singh from the elected group and nominated them. His own defence was that 'the party leaders in the states have got so used to old habits that they have forgotten the process of election, compelling him to nominate PCC [Pradesh Congress Committee] and CWC leaders'.[53]

Sonia Gandhi was elected unopposed as the president of the Congress for the fourth time in September 2010. She has been the longest-serving president, having steered the party since April 1998, surpassing Indira Gandhi's record of eight years.[54] She was challenged only once by Jitendra Prasada in 2000 and he was resoundingly defeated. Her presidentship saw the induction of her son Rahul Gandhi into the Congress organization, as a general secretary, in September 2007.

Organizational failings were apparent by the time Sonia Gandhi first took over as party president in 1998. By this time, the party as an institution had collapsed and served primarily as a vehicle for individual ambition and self-advancement. When she took over the reins of the party, she held out the hope of reorganizing it on democratic lines. She was aware of the organizational atrophy and the risks this posed to the Congress capacity to engage in mass politics. The failure to translate massive turnouts at election meetings into electoral victories had given rise to the perception that the fundamental malady was organizational decline and therefore the emphasis on revamping it. Sonia Gandhi repeatedly called for strengthening of the organization, particularly in those states which had been annexed by political rivals.

Notwithstanding her recognition of the importance of the party, Sonia Gandhi did not succeed in finding ways of strengthening the party in the states. The organization did not undergo any restructuring even though her stated preference was to focus on party building, which was one reason she had advanced for not accepting the post of prime minister.[55] While she periodically highlighted the need for organizational renewal, she was unable to shake up the dilapidated organization even though the situation demanded it. It is true that it is not easy to reorganize the Congress and the difficulties of holding elections or sorting out the problem of bogus membership were immense in a large and loosely organized mass-based party like the Congress, but even so, internal party elections were essential for intraparty democracy.

THE PERSISTENCE OF THE 'TOP-DOWN MODEL'

The Congress has shied away from holding elections to the AICC or the CWC or PCCs. Elections to the CWC were promised and the party's top decision-making body was reconstituted in 2004, and renamed the Congress Steering Committee. However, again the leadership fell back on the old 'top-down' device of recasting the CWC through nominations.[56] It is clear that the Congress prefers nomination to the election route. Unsurprisingly, nominated PCCs, the CWC, and the Congress parliamentary board can hardly function as effective forums of decision-making, policy debate, and conflict resolution.

Sonia Gandhi set up at least three major committees to review and reorganize the party. The first was the task force headed by P.A. Sangma and the second major one was the A.K. Antony Committee entrusted with looking into the reasons for the worst ever Congress performance in the 1998 elections. The latter concluded that organizational weaknesses contributed immensely to its election fiasco. It recommended decentralization of ticket distribution and the need to announce the list of nominees sufficiently in advance. As part of the democratization process from the grassroots, it proposed a process of secret balloting by active members of the party. Making a case for 'a federalization in the work and decision-making processes within the party',[57] it recommended that the nomination of PCC chiefs must end. The CWC discussed these structural deficiencies in the light of the Antony Committee report. The report was adopted but none of the recommendations were ever implemented.[58] One CWC member said: 'We deliberated on it for nine hours. Yet, when the time for reorganization came, all the PCC chiefs were retained and the AICC posts were filled up by ageing leaders.'[59] All the recommendations were given the go-by, in preference to the crucial criterion of winnability.[60]

When the UPA came to power in 2004, Sonia Gandhi set up a third committee known as 'The Group to Look into Future Challenges' headed by Veerappa Moily to examine the same issues: party reorganization and intraparty reforms. In line with the reports of previous committees, this Group identified the lack of internal democracy as one of the reasons for the growing disillusionment with the organization.[61] Like its predecessors, it recommended organizational democratization and election to district units to usher in internal democracy. As earlier, no progress was achieved because the top leadership remained divided on holding elections to the various decision-making bodies of the party. While a section favoured elections at all levels and doing away with the nomination culture which stunted the regional and local growth of the party, another section of leaders sounded a note of caution, apprehending that moneybags could seize control over the organization.

All these committee reports were shelved for fear of upsetting the status quo. If implemented, these recommendations could facilitate the party's reorganization. In principle, Sonia Gandhi may well support party elections to all posts, but was probably advised against it by the core group on grounds that it was unrealistic to hold elections to party posts. This was indeed the case as the 'people who surround Sonia Gandhi are themselves rootless and have no interest in democratic processes'.[62] Hence, there was the persisting belief 'that it [the party] can be rebuilt, in a top-down fashion, once again as a dominant "national" party'.[63] As a consequence, the party organization was not reformed and the concept of 'high command' remained entrenched. There was no change in this principle even though Sonia Gandhi was disinclined to exercise absolutist control over the party. However, decision-making and the execution of programmes continued to be the responsibility of a core group of leaders close to the Congress president. As a senior leader argued:

It was not the selfish lust of power at the summit which stands in the way of elected leadership, but the narrow self-interest of the coterie around the president that prevents democratization. It is the pervasive fear of the upper echelons that the consequences might be undesirable for both leaders and the party, that is to say, instability and dissidence in the party would be fuelled by those defeated in the election and many in the coterie might find themselves booted out, because they are all nominees, and few of them have any measure of support.[64]

Rahul Gandhi admitted that democracy within political parties was non-existent and this was true of his own party; that it was important to democratize entry to modernize the party set-up. He called himself a 'symptom' of the ills of Indian politics: 'dynasty, patronage, and money'.[65] Furthermore, he conceded that people cannot enter politics unless they are well-connected. He told a group of students that politics is a closed system, and said:

If I had not come from my family, I wouldn't be here. You can enter politics either through family or friends or money.... My father was in politics. My grandmother and great grandfather were in politics. So it was easy for me to enter politics. This is the problem. I am the symptom of the problem. I want to change it.[66]

He said he wanted to use his 'unfair advantage to prise open the world of politics for the young. Ironically, he wants to weild dynasty to strengthen democracy.'[67]

After he took over as a general secretary of the Congress in 2007, Rahul Gandhi started to take a keen interest in restoring internal democracy, beginning with the party's student body, the National Students' Union of India (NSUI) and the Youth Congress.[68] Arguably, 'the Congress cannot remain untouched; it cannot escape this process', observed one of his colleagues.[69] Elections in the Youth Congress can generate a 'culture of democracy' and lead to competitive elections higher up in the Congress.[70] But his efforts were limited to the Youth Congress and the NSUI and that too to a few states. He hoped that the Youth Congress rejuvenation would feed into the parent party but that has not happened. Rahul Gandhi's democracy drive made very little impact on the Youth Congress and even less on the Congress party.

FAMILY AND PARTY

The nature of political leadership has changed significantly since the death of Rajiv Gandhi even though the Congress functioned as a centralized party. It has had two full terms in office (1991–6 and 2004–9, not counting the UPA's second term from 2009 onwards) with non-Nehru–Gandhi prime ministers in Rao and Manmohan Singh. The latter is the only prime minister to have had two terms and has been the longest serving one, with the exception of Nehru and Indira Gandhi. This has been a significant change for a party that prides itself in being led by the Nehru–Gandhis. Significantly, the Congress returned to power in 2004 but it did not revert to a model of absolute dominance that characterized it until 1989. Most leaders observed that Sonia Gandhi's leadership style was very different: decision-making was not arbitrary or subjective but noticeably consultative. Her control over the party apparatus was not as tight as earlier and individual leaders were sometimes able to have their way and still remain in the party.[71] There has been a de-concentration of power with greater latitude being given to chief ministers. No chief minister has been abruptly removed or dismissed. There is much greater tolerance of popular leaders like Y.S. Rajshekar Reddy (Andhra Pradesh), Digvijay Singh (Madhya Pradesh), Sheila Dixit (Delhi), Tarun Gogoi (Assam), and Ashok Gehlot (Rajasthan), all of whom have led their respective states to victory in the elections at least twice.[72] Clearly, the party has begun realizing the limits of their distrust of state leaders and state politics 'because it is suffering in states where it has no regional leaders'.[73] It however, remains anchored in the model of personality-oriented leadership, a trademark of the party.

Political parties in India are frequently controlled by political dynasties, none more famous than the Nehru–Gandhi clan. The party's top leadership has remained with the family with Jawaharlal Nehru, Indira Gandhi, Rajiv Gandhi, and Sonia Gandhi heading the Congress. There was a brief interruption after the assassination of Rajiv Gandhi in 1991 which was the second tragedy to strike the family within a decade. Dynastic politics had taken root following the seamless succession of Rajiv Gandhi into the party leadership in the aftermath of his mother's assassination. His success in leading the party to a spectacular victory in 1984 lent, so to speak, further legitimacy to the succession. The elevation of Sonia Gandhi on the same principle was an acknowledgment of the family's importance to the Congress and its charismatic appeal. She emerged as a major influence on the party a few years after Rajiv Gandhi's assassination even though the Congress had offered the leadership to her in 1991. But she was reluctant to join politics and had in fact opposed Indira Gandhi's decision to induct Rajiv Gandhi into the Congress and 'when in 1984, he told her that he was going to accept the prime ministership, she begged him to refuse'.[74] She overcame her inhibitions, as she explained in a later interview because

Many of my senior colleagues asked me to come and help the Congress … there was a conflict within me.… I have photographs of my husband and my mother-in-law in my office … each time I walked past those photographs, I felt I wasn't responding to my duty, the duty to this family and to the country. I felt I was just being cowardly to just sit and watch things deteriorate in the Congress for which my mother-in-law and the whole family lived and died.[75]

She had told senior party members and allies that she wanted to revive the ramshackle and decaying party and defeat the BJP, which she saw as a threat to the secular India defined by Nehru. She emphasised that '[a]t that time there was a trend … that was 1998 and the BJP was gaining. And that was the main reason for me taking that decision.'[76] After a precipitous decline, the Congress experienced a major revival under her leadership.

Leaders in the Congress readily recognize that the major factor behind the party's longevity has been the leadership of this family even though sizeable sections of the urban middle classes were clearly uneasy with the dynastic principle. Aiyar notes that the Nehru–Gandhi family provides 'the Congress the comfort of continuity'. He further points out:

'Their greatest contribution to the Congress is in keeping it together, situating it as a natural party of governance, and providing it continuous leadership, and most important, legitimate leadership.'[77] The Congress always claims that as a broad tent party it represents everyone: it is the pan-Indian appeal of the family that lends credence to this claim. Though their original stronghold was Uttar Pradesh, they were seen to belong everywhere. This lack of narrow political base, coupled with the Gandhi name, lends the party broad appeal.[78]

Arguably, the family is not a straightforward dynasty. 'It is a succession of people who have adhered to policies that serve the poor', observed Aiyar.[79] From Indira Gandhi's garibi hatao to Sonia Gandhi's NREGA, the Nehru–Gandhi family has been identified with a pro-people approach to development. 'It is a dynasty which is endorsed by the party overwhelmingly for the mundane reason that members of the family are vote catchers. The significance of the family is principally connected to electoral success.'[80] 'The dynasty has delivered', as Vinod Mehta expressed it in an interview.[81] Party leaders credit Indira Gandhi for the Congress's return to power in 1980; Rajiv Gandhi was posthumously given credit for stemming the tide against the Congress in 1991, and Sonia Gandhi for two consecutive victories of the Congress-led UPA in the 2004 and 2009 elections. As a party, the Congress has never been quite the same without the Nehru family at the helm, as 'the experience of Congress party workers had been that only a member of the Nehru–Gandhi family led the Congress to victory or had been able to reverse a Congress defeat'.[82] 'The party needed the Nehru–Gandhi family as much as the family needed the party.'[83] The party's reliance on the family failed it in Gujarat (2002, 2007) just as it failed it in Uttar Pradesh (2004, 2009), Bihar (2010), Orissa (2004, 2009), West Bengal (2006), and Tamil Nadu (2011). The Congress failed to dislodge incumbent governments, and it lost Punjab and Himachal Pradesh (both in 2007). This has, however, not lessened their influence or the dependence of the party on them. Although Rajiv Gandhi presided over a massive erosion of the Congress vote base in the Hindi heartland, the legitimacy and authority of his leadership were not seriously questioned within the party even after it was pushed irrevocably into political marginalization due to some of his fatal mistakes. Sonia Gandhi's dominance was not challenged by anyone except Sharad Pawar when he questioned her leadership on the issue of her foreign origins and left the party to form the NCP.

As a leader, Sonia Gandhi enjoys unparalleled authority and influence; perhaps greater than that exercised by any other leader since 1984 when the party won 400 plus seats. There is, however, little doubt that the over-dependence on the Nehru–Gandhi family has resulted in the party withering from within. It has weakened its capacity to develop organizational cohesion.[84] These practices and tendencies that are responsible for party atrophy persist because, as James Manor suggests, 'there is a systemic need within the Congress for them'.[85] The 'dynasty' has become the organizing principle of the Congress, structurally justified by 'the dynasty's standing as an arbiter; standing above the country's many and often adversarial, diversities'.[86] Infighting and factional conflict are rampant in the organization, which therefore needs a neutral arbiter to keep the peace. The 'dynasty', though inimical to a democratic system, has played a very important role as a mechanism for internal party conflict resolution. The Congress has numerous differences on ideology, strategy, and policy, but these differences cease after Sonia Gandhi takes a decision after which 'the squabbling leaders accept her ruling and follow the leader'.[87] The party cannot, however, overlook the contradiction between the primacy of the Nehru–Gandhi family and the need to revitalize the organization through internal democracy.[88] The irony is that the party does not have to choose between the Nehru–Gandhi family's charismatic appeal and widening the base of the party's leadership necessary to strengthen it in the states 'but there is a misperception that these two patterns are mutually exclusive'.[89]

The over-dependence on the Nehru–Gandhi family to mobilize support has discouraged the emergence of a strong and credible second-tier leadership capable of mounting effective state-wide mobilizations in crucial states like Uttar Pradesh, Bihar, West Bengal, Gujarat, and Karnataka. Second-level leaders who do rise belong to influential political families.[90] Many of them are the products of a privileged upbringing and have a head start and an unfair advantage in electoral management.[91] Patrick French estimates that 37 per cent of Congress MPs in 2009 had reached the Lok Sabha through a family connection.[92] Most of the high-flying young MPs inherited their seats because of their family background.[93] For the middle and senior ranks of Congress leaders, 'this situation was highly frustrating'.[94] It encouraged a tendency to turn politics into a family business, and once politics becomes a family business, it will become even more disconnected from the people,[95] with legislators nominating children and spouses.[96]

With many party MPs and leaders running family fiefdoms of their own, there is hardly any pressure to democratize the party. When parties get centred on families, 'structured families replace merit',[97] and this has an impact on both access to power and mobilization.[98] Instead of the CWC, the core group, which comprises the top echelons of the party and the government, takes all important policy decisions. This no doubt indicates a broadening of the apex of power, in the sense that a single leader does not take all the decisions, but the rest of the party is excluded and remains in the dark about the rationale for the decisions taken by the party and government.[99] The greater the discretionary power vested with a core group of leaders, the more it depends solely on a select group of leaders for ideas on politics and policies. Not surprisingly, there are perfunctory discussions in the Congress on most issues.

At the level of local units, the party remains in the hands of individuals who have greater access than others to the higher echelons than knowledge about voters' needs. This gulf is deep and is aggravated by the tendency to marginalize leaders who have at least some vestiges of grassroots links for fear of upsetting the status quo. At a meeting organized to deliberate on the party's shrinking base, one Congress leader said '[p]eople who could not win a single election were the decision makers', rather than mass leaders.[100] There has been a tendency to induct 'non-Congress people in the party', observed Arjun Singh.[101] He lamented that people who have nothing to do with the Congress are occupying important positions. With the exception of a few, the party leadership is far removed from the grassroots and has more in common with the elite and middle classes than with the poor who vote the party to power. The primacy given to personal loyalty places a premium on Delhi-based strategists, rather than mass politics. Consequently, it lacks a critical mass of leaders who enjoy political support of their own. Few leaders have a political base outside their constituency. Most of them show an unwillingness to take up and agitate on economic issues as individual and immediate interests are paramount. Very often, party workers who join the party do so for economic reasons. 'For them, party work is a business proposition and they enter the party to earn money.'[102]

Sonia Gandhi has a feel for mass politics and a talent for working the crowd. She has mass appeal but most of her close aides and advisors do not. Like her husband, she too is surrounded by people who lack a feel for the hustle and bustle of local or state politics. Some of her key advisors are from the Rajya Sabha. The list of party office-bearers is made up 'almost wholly of backroom specialists'.[103] Of the 19 members of the CWC in 2006, only 1 was a Lok Sabha member. Of the rest, 13 were Rajya Sabha members, 2 lost the 2004 Lok Sabha election, 1 lost the 2003 Madhya Pradesh Assembly election, and 2 others were former chief ministers.[104] Of the 7 party general secretaries, 3 were Rajya Sabha members, 2 lost the 2004 Lok Sabha election, and 2 were former chief ministers. Of the 5 who held independent charge, 2 were Rajya Sabha members while the other 3 lost the 2004 general election. A rising number of powerful cabinet ministers also belong to the Rajya Sabha, whereas during the Nehru era and after, most important cabinet posts went to Lok Sabha members. In the process, the Lok Sabha, which is directly elected and answerable to the people, has been devalued as several influential politicians prefer to enter the Parliament through the Rajya Sabha route. The Rajya Sabha, Mukherjee concedes,[105] is not the ideal abode of 'real political activists' as this reflects 'a growing disinclination to engage with the risks of mass politics'.[106]

Ignoring mass leaders has enfeebled the organizational fibre of the party. It has directly affected its ability to retrieve large chunks of its erstwhile base that have been sliced away by other formations. Although the party is important in relation to the government, the response of the Congress to most fundamental issues is to think in terms of new policies and schemes; it is 'governmental rather than political.... This failure to distinguish between modes of governmental action and possible responses of a party apparatus is obvious. It sees filing of affidavits, creation of inquiry commissions, or budgets and policies as instruments of political action.'[107] As Prithviraj Chavan, minister of state in the UPA government, said in an interview:

[W]e are becoming too minister-centric in the states and even at the centre. Nobody will trade a ministerial position for a party position. The power that a minister enjoys of dispensing favours, of amassing wealth and patronage is so huge that people take up party responsibility only to see that they will get ministerial berth later. This is something we have to introspect: how to reorganize the party.[108]

Organizationally, the Congress's biggest challenge has been its inability to connect to local realities in politics. A top-down political structure has hampered this task and led to organizational degeneration. It has not been able to find a way to fuse its various policies and connect different economic and political programmes under a central overarching idea or set of ideas. The real disjuncture is not between the government and party, but between economic and political programmes and the leadership, which often cannot deliver on promises and initiatives. Despite its efforts to broaden its social base and make it more in sync with India's diverse society, it continues to function as an expedient political patronage machine. The designated party spokesmen or group of ministers (GoMs) articulate the party's position on television channels and thus allow the media to dictate the political discourse, which is deemed to be a sufficient alternative to the mobilization of the masses in any form. Other activities include holding periodic demonstrations, workshops, and seminars in auditoriums.

During the UPA rule, power rested with the party president, but the lack of progress in party building and democratization was palpable despite the party's new importance and the much better equation between the party and government. It still did not function as a properly institutionalized political party, with even apex decision-making bodies such as the CWC not meeting sufficiently frequently. In 2009, the CWC met just thrice, demonstrating a disregard for broad-basing leadership and decision-making processes. Party elections are necessary even though 'elections alone will not reduce the centralization and concentration of power in the Congress'.[109] The structure of decision-making in the Congress needs to change to make it more democratic and accountable. Both intraparty democracy and leadership contests are important as they can provide the party the benefit of a range of options in reconfiguring its tactical and strategic response. In the absence of these two processes, power brokers and rootless leaders hold sway and deny members the right to decide who is best equipped to lead them at different levels of the polity. This in turn discourages new faces and new ideas even as it dampens the substantive policy discussion necessary to invigorate and rejuvenate any political party.

NOTES

1.   Rajni Kothari, 'The Idea of the Congress', *The Indian Express*, 14 June 2004.
2.   Ibid.
3.   Robin Jeffrey (1994), 'Prime Minister and the Ruling Party', in James Manor (ed.), *Nehru to the Nineties: The Changing Office of the Prime Minister in India*, Hurst & Co., London, p. 160.
4.   On the relationship of mutuality between party and government during the Nehru era, see ibid., pp. 164–7.
5.   Ibid., p. 161.
6.   Harish Khare, 'Sonia, Manmohan, Party, Government', *The Hindu*, 18 June 2005.

7.   Interview with Inder Malhotra, senior journalist, columnist, and former Editor of *The Times of India*, New Delhi, 18 October 2010.

8.   M.V.R. Gowda and E. Sridharan (2009), 'Parties and the Party System, 1947–2006', in Sumit Ganguly, Larry Diamond, and Marc Plattner (eds), *The State of India's Democracy*, Oxford University Press, New Delhi.

9.   Stanley Kochanek (1976), 'Mrs. Gandhi's Pyramid: The New Congress', in Henry Hart (ed.), *Indira Gandhi's India: A Political System Reappraised*, Westview Press, Boulder, Colorado, pp. 104–5.

10.   Harish Khare (2004), 'The Indian National Congress: Problems of Survival and Re-Invention', in Subrata Mitra, Mike Enskat, and Clemens Spieb (eds), *Political Parties in South Asia*, Praeger, London.

11.   'The L.K. Advani Chat'. Available at www.rediff.com/chat/lkchat.htm (accessed on 28 December 2011).

12.   Khare, 'Sonia Gandhi, the BJP and the Foreigner Issue', *The Hindu*, 30 April 2004.

13.   Khare, 'Colours of Sonia's Foreignness', *The Hindu*, 19 May 1999.

14.   Interview with Mani Shankar Aiyar, 26 September 2010.

15.   Full text of Sonia Gandhi's speech to the CPP published in *The Times of India*, 18 May 2004.

16.   Editorial, 'Sonia Gandhi's Stunning Political Sacrifice', *The Hindu*, 19 May 2004.

17.   Abhishek Singhvi pointed out that Sonia Gandhi was accompanied by Manmohan Singh when she went to see the president in 1999. She may well have nominated him as the prime minister had the Congress formed the government at that stage. Interview, 16 November 2010. Vir Sanghvi makes the same point in his assessment. See Vir Sanghvi, 'The Quiet Italian', *Outlook*, 16 October 2006.

18.   Khare, 'Strengths of a Weak Prime Minister', *The Hindu*, 11 May 2005.

19.   Ibid.

20.   *Newsweek* article cited in 'Manmohan Tops Newsweek's List of 10 World Leaders', *The Hindu*, 18 August 2010.

21.   There were several leaders senior to Manmohan Singh and with much longer political experience. For example, when Mukherjee was Indira Gandhi's finance minister, he appointed Manmohan Singh as the governor of the RBI. There was Arjun Singh who had held every important political position barring that of the prime minister.

22.   Manmohan Singh contested and lost the Lok Sabha election from South Delhi in 1991. He is not the only prime minister to take the Rajya Sabha route. Prime ministers Deve Gowda and I.K. Gujral were Rajya Sabha members. But Deve Gowda had won a Lok Sabha election earlier, while Gujral had never won a Lok Sabha election.

23.   Neerja Chowdhury, 'UPA's Power-Sharing Dilemma', *The Indian Express*, 26 July 2004.

24.   Aarti Jerath, 'The Political Triangle', *The Times of India: Crest Edition*, 22 October 2011.

25.   Interview with Nikhil Dey, Co-Convenor, National Campaign for People's Right to Information (NCPRI), New Delhi, 9 December 2010.

26.   NAC-1 was given statutory powers by an executive order issued by the cabinet secretariat. Sonia Gandhi as the chairperson of the NAC was given cabinet rank. For an analysis of NAC mandate and functioning, see Ruchi Gupta (2011b), 'Deconstructing the NAC', *Seminar*, no. 624, August, pp. 82–5.

27.   Ibid., p. 83. The members of the NAC are nominated by the prime minister in consultation with the chairperson of the Council. The funds for the functioning of this council are provided from the budgetary allocation for the PMO. Composition, functions, membership of NAC, available at http://nac.nic.in/ (accessed on 26 December 2011).

28.   A petition was filed with President A.P.J. Abdul Kalam against all MPs including Sonia Gandhi in February 2006 who were holding several offices concurrently. On 23 March 2006, Sonia Gandhi resigned as MP and from the post of chairperson of the NAC. In May 2006 she won a by-election by more than 400,000 votes from the same Rae Bareli constituency. The NAC was revived on 29 March 2010 with Sonia Gandhi as chairperson after she was given a clean chit by the Joint Parliamentary Committee (JPC) in 2008 which stated that Sonia Gandhi had not violated the norms of 'office of profit' law by holding the chair of the NAC. The clarification regarding the law came when the JPC defined 'Advisory Office' as '[a]ny office that is associated with purely giving counsel or recommendation on any particular subject/policy, in respect of any matter of public importance/interest and for with there is no procedure of salary or remuneration except compensatory allowance is known as "Advisory Office" or with different name.' In short, Sonia Gandhi had not held the office of profits in any way, the JPC stated.

29.   Gupta, 'Deconstructing the NAC', p. 83.

30.   'Opening Address by the Congress President at the AICC Session on 21 August 2004, New Delhi'. Available at www.congress.org.in/new/sonia-speeches.php (accessed on 15 August 2009).

31.   Khare, 'Obligations of the New Mandate', *The Hindu*, 18 May 2009.

32.   Nehru's speech cited in Khare, 'Finding New Rhythms of Coordination', *The Hindu*, 5 July 2006.

33.   Vidya Subrahmaniam, 'A Government and a Party in Combat Mode', *The Hindu*, 16 June 2006. According to her: 'Manmohan Singh remains an outsider in a party that is congenitally attached to the Nehru–Gandhi family and is unable to accept a division of labour between a non-Gandhi prime minister and a Gandhi party president.'

34.   See, for example, Shekhar Gupta, 'Handicap at 7, Race Course', *The Indian Express*, 8 July 2006; Neerja Chowdhury, 'The Doctor Needs a Shot in the Arm', *The Indian Express*, 18 May 2006; and Khare, 'Recouping the Central Authority', *The Hindu*, 20 June 2008.

35.   Indira Gandhi was the first prime minister to become a Rajya Sabha member but within a year she fought and won an election from Rae Bareli and was a Lok Sabha member for the rest of her political life. Rao, when he became the prime minister in 1991, was not a member of either the Lok Sabha or Rajya Sabha but soon contested and won an election. Rajiv Gandhi as well as Sonia Gandhi and their son Rahul Gandhi have been Lok Sabha members.

36.   In response to a Right to Information (RTI) application filed by television news channel CNN-IBN, the PMO revealed that Sonia Gandhi sent 25 letters to Manmohan Singh in 2004, 34 in 2005, 25 in 2006, 8 in 2007, and 6 in 2008. Available at ibnlive.in.com/.../whose-upa-98-letters-show-sonias...boss/70334-37.html (accessed on 5 July 2011).

37.   Khare, 'Finding New Rhythms of Coordination'.

38.   In UPA-2, the two power centres were not on the same page on a number of issues. See Rajeev Deshpande and Diwakar, 'Will They Go the Distance?' *The Times of India Crest*, 10 April 2010.

39.   Interview with Abhishek Singhvi.

40.   Sanghvi, '10 Years on, Sonia Gandhi Is a Little Less of an Enigma', 14 March 2008. Available at www.livemint.com/2008/03/.../10-years-on-Sonia-Gandhi-is-a.html (accessed on 28 December 2011).

41.   Sonia Gandhi's comments at the *Hindustan Times* Leadership Summit, in 'I Didn't Want Rajiv To Be a Politician: Sonia', *DNA*, Mumbai, 12 October 2007.

42.   Ibid.

43.   Quoted in Smita Gupta, 'Shall We Tell the PM', *Outlook*, 13 February 2006.

44.   Interview with Sitaram Yechury, Politburo Member, CPI (M) and Rajya Sabha MP, 2006–12, 2012–present, New Delhi, 15 July 2010.

45.   Editorial, *The Indian Express*, 24 January.

46.   Khare, 'Let the Party Begin', *The Hindu*, 2 February 2005.

47.   Ibid.

48.   Pratap Bhanu Mehta (2001), 'Reform Political Parties First', *Seminar*, no. 497, January, pp. 16–19.

49.   Interview with Digvijay Singh, 19 December 2009.

50.   Sukumar Muralidharan, 'A Difficult Legacy', *Frontline*, vol. 15, no. 2, 24 January–6 February 1998.

51.   Rao, cited in James Manor (2011a), 'The Congress Party and the "Great Transformation"', in Sanjay Ruparelia, Sanjay Reddy, John Harriss, and Stuart Corbridge (eds), *Understanding India's New Political Economy: A Great Transformation?* Routledge, London.

52.   Manor (2003), 'Organizational Renewal', *Seminar*, no. 526, June, pp. 23–6.

53.   Ibid., p. 24.

54.   The electoral college for the election of the party president comprises 7,946 PCC delegates. Kay Benedict, 'Process for Reelecting Sonia as Cong President Set in Motion', *India Today*, 3 September 2010. Available at

http://indiatoday.intoday.in/story/process-for-reelecting-sonia-as-cong-
president-set-in-motion/1/111183.html (accessed on 27 March 2012).

55.   Interview with Singhvi.

56.   In September 2010, the PCCs passed a 'unanimous resolution' authorizing
Sonia Gandhi to nominate the PCC president in state after state. By October that
year, Sonia Gandhi had re-nominated most of the PCC presidents. During 'the
organizational election in the Congress, delegates from booth to block, district to
state level committees, were "allotted" to influential leaders at different levels and
then "elected unanimously"'. See D.K. Singh, 'The Hand that Clutches Tight',
The Indian Express, 18 September 2010. Elections to the CWC too did not take
place and, instead, the AICC meeting held in Delhi in November 2010 authorized
the Congress president to nominate the 25-member CWC. According to a report
in *The Indian Express*, 18 September 2010, Digvijay Singh was present at the
Uttar Pradesh Congress Committee (UPCC) meeting in September 2010 to ensure
a unanimous resolution asking the Congress president to nominate the UPCC.

57.   The committee headed by Antony in 1999 to introspect into the reverses
in electoral performance of the Congress in 1999 proposed a series of measures
to bring about structural changes in the organizational set-up of the Congress.
Congress Sandesh (2000), 'Antony Committee Report', January. Available at www.
congresssandesh.com/dec_jan_issue/cwc.html. Aiyar, member of the Committee,
stated that such recommendations were to bring the party back to its 'position of
primacy in Indian politics'. Interview with Aiyar, New Delhi, 17 December 2009.

58.   Bhavdeep Kang, 'Mark Antony's Word', *Outlook*, 13 December 1999.

59.   Quoted in *India Today*, 6 March 2000.

60.   The CWC meeting on 5 June 2008, a week after the party's defeat in
Karnataka, decided to set up yet another committee headed by Antony to help
it overcome the slump of successive assembly election defeats.

61.   The panel chaired by Veerappa Moily included Rahul Gandhi,
Jairam Ramesh, Sachin Pilot, Digvijay Singh, Jagdish Tytler, Salman Khurshid,
and Anand Sharma.

62.   Interview with Digvijay Singh, 12 October 2008.

63.   Kothari, 'The Congress and Its Nemesis', *Frontline*, vol. 15, no. 10,
9–22 May 1998.

64.   Interview, Aiyar, 26 September 2010.

65.   D.K. Singh, 'Rahul: If I'd Not Come from Gandhi Family, I Wouldn't Be
Here', *The Indian Express*, 1 October 2008.

66.   Ibid.

67.   Shoma Chowdhary, 'Rahul Gandhi', *Tehelka*, 30 May 2009.

68.   Towards this end, he hired a firm run by J.M. Lyngdoh and K.J. Rao,
former election commissioners, to oversee intra-party elections for the Youth
Congress and the NSUI. For report on elections in Youth Congress and NSUI,
see Akshaya Mukul, 'For the First Time I've Seen a Politician Who Is Totally
Clear about What He Wants', *The Times of India Crest*, 13 February 2010.

69. Interview with Singhvi.

70. Ibid.

71. Report on CWC meeting in *Frontline*, vol. 22, no. 12, 4–17 June 2005.

72. Interview with D.P. Tripathi, General Secretary and Chief Spokesman, Nationalist Congress Party, New Delhi, 28 December 2010.

73. Ibid.

74. Sanghvi, 'The Quiet Italian'.

75. Interview of Sonia Gandhi by Shekhar Gupta, editor-in-chief, *Indian Express* on 'Walk the Talk', NDTV, 15 May 2004. Available at www.aicc.org. in/new/walk-the-talk.php.

76. Ibid.

77. Interview with Aiyar, 4 December 2009.

78. Interview with Dileep Padgoankar, New Delhi, 7 March 2009.

79. Interview with Arjun Singh, 20 November 2009.

80. Interview with Aiyar, 13 November 2009.

81. Interview with Vinod Mehta, New Delhi, 27 December 2010.

82. Francine Frankel (1990), 'India's Democracy in Transition', *World Policy Journal*, vol. 7, no. 3, Summer, p. 521–55.

83. Interview with P. Sainath, Rural Affairs Editor of *The Hindu*, Mumbai, 20 December 2009.

84. Manor, 'The Congress Party and the Great Transformation'.

85. Ibid., p. 216.

86. Baldev Raj Nayar (2005), 'India in 2004: Regime Change in a Divided Democracy', *Asian Survey*, vol. 45, no. 1, pp. 71–82, esp. p. 77.

87. This comment is based on interviews with Congress leaders close to Sonia Gandhi.

88. Malini Parthasarathy, 'Critical Choices for the Congress (I)', *The Hindu*, 18 March 1998.

89. Ibid.

90. Patrick French has estimated that 28.6 per cent of MPs in the Fifteenth Lok Sabha had a hereditary connection. He calls them 'hereditary MPs'. See Patrick French, 'The Princely State of India', *Outlook*, 17 January 2011.

91. With regard to the growing importance of dynastic politics, Saba Naqvi and Debarshi Dasgupta note that 'the process is not just about promoting one's children but also about protecting interests. Politics now involves the collection and spending of huge sums of money. Leaders consider it prudent to keep it all in the family. Increasingly, only the offspring or spouse is trusted as the guardian of the family fortune. This is one of the main reasons for the proliferation of family rule across the land.' Saba Naqvi and Debarshi Dasgupta, 'Surname Does a Victory Lap', *Outlook*, 8 June 2009.

92. Sanghvi, 'Politics of Inheritance', *Hindustan Times*, 31 May 2009.

93. French, 'The Princely State of India'.

94. Ibid.

95.   Ibid.

96.   Although 60 per cent arrived on some alternative merit, it is evident that family politics was strongly entrenched, especially in northern India.

97.   The leader of the opposition in the Rajya Sabha, Arun Jaitley, said at the *Hindustan Times* Leadership Summit in November 2010 that '[s]tructured political parties being centred around families.... Structured families and dynasties replacing the criteria of merit. This is one challenge if actually we are able to address, it may impinge on the kind of thought process we have and the kind of perspective we have to issues.' 'Political Families Replacing Merit a Challenge: Jaitley', *The Hindu*, 21 November 2010.

98.   Mehta, 'Reform Political Parties First'.

99.   Interview with Arjun Singh, 20 November 2009.

100. D.K. Singh, 'Congress Leaders against Outsourcing Party Base', *The Indian Express*, 23 May 2008.

101. Interview with Arjun Singh, 10 October 2009.

102. Interview with Sheila Dixit, Chief Minister of Delhi, 1998–2003, 2003–2008, 2008–present, 8 January 2010.

103. Subrahmaniam, 'Mass Leadership and Backroom Politics', *The Hindu*, 8 April 2008.

104. Ibid.

105. Mukherjee was the first Rajya Sabha member to be appointed finance minister by Indira Gandhi in 1982. Indira Gandhi encouraged him to contest elections which he did twice, in 1977 and 1980, but lost both times, finally making it to the Lok Sabha in 2004 and again in 2009.

106. Manini Chatterjee, 'Upper House, Upper Hand', *The Indian Express*, 1 April 2006.

107. Tridib Suhrud, 'Is Congress a Political Party', *The Indian Express*, 11 March 2008.

108. Prithviraj Chavan, Interview, 'Ideas Exchange', *The Indian Express*, 1 June 2008.

109. Interview with Arjun Singh, 20 November 2009.

5 Coping with Inequalities

Reconciling the welfare of the people at large with economic liberalization alongside political pressures for distribution was the greatest challenge confronted by the Congress after it returned to power in 2004. The overall failures of successive governments were manifest in areas such as employment, education, health, child nutrition, and the provision and maintenance of infrastructure. The principal question was the contrast between annual macroeconomic growth rates and average growth rates in the indices of social/human development of the aam aadmi, the slogan and constituency that brought the Congress-led UPA to power. It is well known that the process of economic liberalization has had negligible impact on the well-being of the people at large; it has created eddies of discontentment across India and this has threatened the party's social base. The need for the Congress to forge a political balance was unmistakable as the levels of inequality and disparity in society, already epitomized by hierarchy and privilege, had increased markedly after economic liberalization. This was the central political issue confronting the Congress which depended on the lower social orders for its political support even as it wanted to push ahead with its 9 per cent economic growth strategy which primarily benefited the upper and middle classes in terms of better opportunities, jobs, and income but whose support was insufficient for electoral success and on which it could scarcely rely.

The basic question is this: Could the Congress government pursue high economic growth while reducing poverty and inequality? This question would be addressed not generally but with reference to the political response of the UPA government. Against the background of the sharp recovery staged by the Congress in the 2004 parliamentary elections, the chapter examines, on the one hand, the change in the approach to state intervention and, on the other, its emphasis on social policy through centrally sponsored schemes to rebuild political support.

Without renewing the organizational strength on the ground, the Congress's political advance was very greatly dependent upon its deft use of social policies and centrally sponsored schemes to build a powerful counterbloc against the BJP and also the Left, although the latter were to play a critical part in goading the UPA to adopt these policies. Yet, it was not easy for the Congress to deliver on promises to promote growth with equity, to reconcile the interests and aspirations of the poor with elite and middle class pressures to encourage private investment and deliver high GDP growth.

'GROWTH FIRST'

The dominant paradigm of the Congress since Independence rested upon the role of the state in industrialization and development. For decades, change with continuity was the overriding theme of its ideology. During the last two decades, the 1980s and 1990s, economic change had been given precedence over continuity, whereas earlier continuity in outlook, values, and principles tended to be given precedence. In comparison to the past, when the Congress was not expressly committed to high growth as an economic strategy, post 1991 it was strongly committed to the strategy of rapid growth; it embarked on a policy course that fundamentally altered the development path. As a consequence, the state's role as the prime driver of economic growth, a regulator of private investors, and, above all, an agent working to reduce inequalities was altered. Emphasis shifted from distributive justice to encouraging private initiative to achieve high growth and this contributed to a shift in the distribution of income in favour of the elite and upper middle classes.[1] The cumulative effect of these changes was profound as it became clear that the policy establishment and a powerful section of the Congress favoured such policies. Henceforth, Congress leaders began to temper their anti-capitalist rhetoric and commitment to redistribution. Economic liberalization since then has seen the puncturing of the state's centrality, resulting in a change in the balance of forces between public and private sector with a much greater role for the capitalist sector. Government interest had to be limited to areas which have to do with the social sector: health, education, and to some extent agriculture and rural development.

Over time, the state shifted from being a reluctant capitalist state to a strongly pro-capitalist one with a clear and conspicuous dominance of the corporate sector.[2] This dominance was achieved through an alliance of the corporate sector with the government and bureaucracy. It operates on a scale that far exceeds anything that existed before, and as a result, the locus of power has moved away from New Delhi to the corporate towers of Mumbai.[3] Although the state continues to negotiate between conflicting interests, its autonomy has declined as it has become increasingly involved in promoting primarily the corporate sector.[4] The relationship between corporate lobby associations—such as the CII, FICCI, and National Association of Software and Services Companies (NASSCOM)—and various ministries at the Centre has become closer under the UPA, and new businesses have forged powerful links with the state-level bureaucracy.[5] As a consequence, 'where there was a muted presence of leading lights of the business community in the Congress party and its projection of itself—the role of the captains of industry in national life as well as their association with the party is no longer disavowed or hidden, but is in fact asserted,' notes Aiyar.[6] With the shift to a market-based economy, attention drifted from poverty alleviation to increasing growth. Of course, 'this thesis', he says, 'has been challenged by the leadership on grounds that the only shift that has been made is from garibi hatao to aam aadmi. Where garib was the paradigm, now it is aam aadmi.'[7]

Manmohan Singh indisputably favoured the high growth strategy. He emphasized a strong commitment to the goals of poverty alleviation but according to him economic growth was a prior condition to wage a war on poverty. Singh stressed on a growth target of 10 per cent per annum as the key to inclusive development. For him, this was essential because 'we will be able to invest more resources in the social sector, in education and in health'.[8] Under his dispensation, sustained high growth was seen as a solution to meet important needs and help maintain pro-poor expenditures. Hence, nothing should be done to hinder growth as without growth there can be no equity.[9] He was, of course, not the only one to focus on market-based, growth enhancing policies, even though his emphasis on it was the most consistent and thus contributed to wider application and acceptance of this conceptual approach and paradigm in practical discussions in the Congress.

Many social scientists and economists have written powerfully on the limits of growth as a measure of progress and the need to shed the obsession with high GDP growth as currently defined which has nothing to do with human development. Sustained and rapid growth was obviously a central component of any poverty-reduction strategy, but economic growth was only a means, not an end. However, policymakers justified high growth on grounds that everyone benefits from it in the long run. Besides, the argument goes that economic growth and equitable development were both important but prioritizing distribution leads to the distribution of poverty and there was no point in doing that. Therefore, in a trade-off between rapid growth and distributive justice, rapid growth had to be accorded priority on the ground that equity at the expense of growth leads only to the redistribution of poverty.[10] The promotion of prosperity even if it means delaying distributive justice must be encouraged so as to redistribute prosperity rather than poverty.[11]

Several senior leaders were however apprehensive that the gains of growth have been uneven and that social and economic conflicts were increasing. Therefore, it was critical that rapid growth translate into opportunities and outcomes for a greater number of people than had so far been possible. Influential voices in the party were uneasy about the failure to make growth more inclusive despite massive human deprivation. Many of them, notably Sonia Gandhi, were keen that the party give greater weight to redistributive justice and equity; the poor needed to be shielded from the vagaries of the market and must be given the benefits of prosperity that the market refused to share with them. Involved as most of them were in electoral politics rather than only policymaking, they were more concerned about rising income inequalities and the loss of popular credibility as a consequence of the government's active role as a promoter of private capital rather than public interest. Sonia Gandhi, in her 2007 Nexus lecture in The Hague, reiterated her faith in the importance of equity with growth:

I am aware that the market in many quarters is seen as the new ruling deity, but our experience shows that there is still a critical role for the state and its institutions. Market-led growth is necessary, but it is not sufficient. In the context of 'inequality', which is 'very visible', she reiterated 'the goal of the Congress party remains one of equity and growth'.[12]

The BJP's defeat on the slogan of 'India Shining' in the 2004 parliamentary elections and the economic discontent which lay behind it encouraged a change of strategy.

HIGH GROWTH, RISING INEQUALITY

The Indian economy has been on a 'growth expressway' since 2003–4. The rate of economic growth has gone up steadily, and from 2005 to 2008 it exceeded 7 per cent, making India among the fastest growing economies in the world, growing at a rate no one would have remotely imagined in the late 1990s. The momentum was interrupted by the global economic crisis in 2008 when growth slowed down to 6.7 per cent in 2008–9.[13]

In consequence, India now receives a great deal of international attention as a rising economic and political power, even as the majority of its citizens are poor and impoverished. For the middle class eager to bask in the still notional prestige of an 'emergent' power, scarcely a day passed without someone saying that India is emerging or has emerged. It was common to read reports and commentaries with titles like the 'The Rise of India' or 'India Awakens' or 'New Dawn', indicative of a major change in the country's self-image.[14] 'India is a roaring capitalist success story', exclaimed the journal *Foreign Affairs* in 2006 when Lakshmi Mittal, the fifth richest man in the world, succeeded in his takeover of the Luxembourg-based steel company Arcelor.[15] Mittal thereafter monopolized the front page of every newspaper in France and Europe for several months. This was in part because leaders of Western economies looked upon India as one of the major drivers of economic growth.[16] The affluent sections of society support this theory to serve notice that we have arrived on the world stage of powerful nations.

No doubt the proportion of the population that is rich has significantly increased, and a substantial middle class has emerged. The top 20 per cent has fared extremely well; but this kind of economic growth is disequalizing to say the least. High GDP growth has produced an increasing concentration of wealth and inequality with the private corporate sector the chief beneficiary of the economic boom. Profits of the corporate sector have grown at 25 per cent and more per annum, and profits-to-sales were running in the region of 12–14 per cent, which is among the highest in the world.[17] Even more dramatically, the ratio of billionaire wealth rose from less than 1 per cent of GDP in the mid-1990s to 23 per cent in 2008, and was 14 per cent in early 2010, after a fall and recovery.[18] The increase in the number of billionaires who epitomize 'emergent India' indicates the increasing divide between the rich and the poor.

If economic growth was the sole criterion for judging performance, India, or one might say Indian business, has done remarkably well. However, such a 'business-centric view of India suppresses more facts than it reveals'.[19] It conceals, for example, that the 'great power' on the world stage was also a 'republic of hunger'.[20] According to one estimate, about 320 million of its citizens reportedly go to bed without food every night, representing over a third of the estimated 840 million hungry people across the world.[21] High-growth India is a country of immense poverty and inequalities where the numbers of poor, unhealthy, and illiterate are unacceptably high.[22] It is now widely accepted that urban–rural imbalances and income inequality have grown since economic reforms began. Apart from regular stories in newspapers of farmers' suicides in Maharashtra, Andhra Pradesh, and Punjab, appalling stagnation in health, nutrition, and education indicators, declining public spending, hideously skewed growth distribution, and, above all, growing unemployment expose India's reality and the overstated talk about its emergence as a global power. This has given a sharper edge to the long-standing fracture between the 'Two Indias'. An editorial in the *Economic and Political Weekly* expresses this succinctly: 'There is now the thriving India—mainly urban, skilled and entrepreneurial, with close links to the globalized world and acts as though the other India does not exist. This other India—mainly rural but also the underbelly of the cities—has been left behind because it has neither assets nor skills.'[23]

These disparities and inequalities have been intensified by large-scale corruption.[24] Corruption and using the state as a means of accumulation have always existed, but the scale and ubiquity of corruption have intensified since the 1990s, giving rise to fears of the growth of crony capitalism becoming an integral part of India's growth trajectory. The numbers of scams and scandals have been growing as hundreds of billions of rupees are extracted in a variety of ways. Rampant discretionary powers enjoyed by the political class which they use to favour certain large private players has resulted in the gratuitous takeover and handing over of resources ranging from mining rights to sale of telecom spectrum and the mobilization and/or disposal of often illegal and inadequately compensated expropriation of land for industrial and real estate projects. The belief that surplus accumulation among state personnel and business groups has been occurring at a rapid pace was strengthened also by individual politicians elected to the Parliament and state legislatures reporting huge increases in their asset holding over time.[25]

One important reason for this was the ability of the private sector to acquire scarce resources cheaply by paying off politicians in power. The other was the government incentives to the corporate sector through tax concessions and a significant reduction in the corporate income tax rate.[26] In successive budgets, the UPA government handed huge concessions to the corporate sector. Between 2007 and 2009, tax revenue foregone on account of exemptions amounted to over Rs 131,000 crores.[27] Most of these exemptions benefit the corporate sector, and if these concessions were eliminated, the additional revenue would be 8 per cent of the GDP.[28] If this legitimate revenue were collected and utilized for public investments, government could commit much larger sums of money to official programmes for the eradication of poverty and would be able to build much-needed infrastructure and generate significant employment.

Inequalities also arise from a basic asymmetry between growth of the national product and the source of income of the majority, which is agriculture.[29] Agriculture has stagnated, per capita food consumption has fallen, and thousands of 'farmers have committed suicide between 1995 and 2010'[30] (see Chapter 6). Industry has grown sluggishly and forms only about one-fourth of the GDP. The labour-intensive manufacturing boom of the kind that powered the economic growth of almost every developed and developing country in the world has not occurred in India. The service sector was growing much faster and fuelling a large proportion of the growth rate. It accounted for half the economy in 2006, with agriculture and industry accounting for roughly equal shares of the rest. The share of the tertiary sector had risen from about 41 per cent in 1991 to around 54 per cent in 2005–6. This sector grew by 34.4 per cent over the past two decades and now accounts for over 50 per cent of India's annual GDP. Most of the job growth was in hotels, restaurants, finance, and insurance. Services, which account for 55 per cent of GDP, formally employ just 2 million people or less than 0.5 per cent of the country's labour force.[31] This growth model has left behind large numbers of citizens who are unorganized, unskilled, and without knowledge of English; services-based growth is primarily for the middle classes and elite.

India's growth process is for the most part jobless, 'employment is not keeping step with growth';[32] it is not geared to creating sufficient opportunities for work and employment to meet the needs of the growing labour force.[33] The rise in employment was much below the rate of output growth.[34] Large-scale employment was the key to poverty alleviation but this had not happened under the service-led growth model. Employment in the organized sector had actually shrunk despite high rates of growth while employment in the unorganized sector increased significantly. In 2004–5, less than 7 per cent of the large labour force was employed in the formal economy.[35] The remainder of the workforce was employed in the unorganized sector. Of the 35 million or so with formal sector jobs, 21 million were government employees. This leaves only 14 million working in the private sector. Insufficient numbers of people have moved from the low-wage and low-income agricultural sector to the higher growing manufacturing and service sectors.[36]

In 2010, India was one of the world's top economies in terms of income growth, but it was outperformed by much poorer countries in terms of human development.[37] Even nations which have much less growth numbers have done better on this count.[38] Moreover, spectacular growth has not reduced poverty sufficiently quickly;[39] in fact, it has proved rather difficult to reduce the incidence of poverty or uplift the number of poor at a comparably rapid pace. India is home to half of the world's poor and destitute, even the most optimistic estimates holding that the number was 300 million in 2004–5.[40] The percentage of the population below the poverty line was declining but, as the Planning Commission acknowledges, 'at a pace which is no longer acceptable given the minimalist level at which the poverty line is fixed'.[41] Progress is not commensurate with growth when the surpluses available to tackle this problem have increased substantially.

It is clear from the aforementioned account that overall economic growth rates do not capture India's social reality and do not give an indication of the social development of poorer sections. Yet, GDP had been elevated to being the sole criterion for judging the country's economic achievement even though India had patently failed to meet the basic needs of the majority of the population that continued to live in acute poverty and deplorable conditions. Economic development cannot be disengaged from social development since such growth would neither be possible nor sustainable in the long run unless it translates into an improvement in the quality of life for the poor.

CHALLENGE OF RECONCILING DISTRIBUTION
WITH GROWTH

From the standpoint of distribution, the formation of the UPA government was a turning point. After losing several crucial state assembly elections between 2002 and 2004, the Congress was well aware that it could not regain power without a stronger emphasis on social welfare and redistributive measures as a very large segment of the population felt ignored by economic reform policies. Ever since it embraced high growth as a state goal and promoted the private sector to achieve it, the Congress has struggled to come up with platforms that can marshal the support of the economic majority while not alienating the middle classes and the elite. It was particularly conscious of the need to differentiate itself from the BJP, which feels less constrained by the demands of mass politics. One of the significant distinctions between the two relates to the weight given to the distributive agenda and social welfare measures necessary to alleviate poverty. To drive home the difference against the backdrop of 'India Shining', the top leaders after assuming office in 2004 constantly emphasized the idea of inclusion. Prime Minister Manmohan Singh said at different forums, notably at the National Development Council meeting in 2006, that India cannot develop without 'economic inclusion'.[42] The two tracks were clear: high growth, but make it more inclusive through social policy and distributive measures.[43] It pointed to a willingness to increase government interventions outside the growth process to improve opportunities for those excluded from it.[44] This did not indicate a rejection of economic liberalization but greater emphasis on 'calibrated liberalization'.

In this regard, some Congress leaders criticized the dominant growth model, but even they did not seek a radical change in the economic strategy. There was therefore no criticism of the growth strategy per se; in truth they were extremely proud of the high growth achieved under the Congress-led UPA. Even those committed to redistribution appeared to be convinced that it was important to maintain the high growth rate, otherwise, they asked, how can the government garner the resources to do 'good things' such as increase public expenditure on education, nutrition, health care, roads, and infrastructure.[45] The core issue was quite simply this: continue to produce growth of 9 to 10 per cent and then use the proceeds of that growth to build a more inclusive society. In short, most leaders had bought into the Planning Commission's line that 'high growth will deliver taxes, taxes will deliver money, money can be spent on government schemes, and then MPs can go to their constituencies and claim that the UPA government has done so much development work'.[46] For the most part, they were happy to go along with this 'grow and spend' approach.[47] Basically, inclusive growth means growth plus inclusiveness; it does not mean growth which is inclusive. The trouble with such a framework is that it does not adequately recognize that equity is a political issue; it is not outside the growth process.

The 2004 election results provided the context for the re-emergence of a strong opinion within the Congress that accommodation of the poor through a politics of redistribution was crucial to winning elections. Although the business-driven growth model underpinning policymaking saw no change, it shifted the emphasis of public policy from growth to inclusive growth as the centrepiece of several of its interventions. This necessitated a change in the balance between market and state in favour of a better mix between the goals of accumulation and redistribution. Therefore, within a few months of assuming office, the UPA government crafted a number of centrally sponsored government schemes designed to improve opportunities for those excluded from India's growth story, especially the rural poor and minorities, reflecting as an editorial in *The Hindu* noted, a 'refreshing change of emphasis'.[48]

The Congress was not about to give up economic liberalization and the economic reform agenda. It was keen to assure both domestic and foreign capital that its social policy commitments would not be at the expense of private business. It is well known that the defeat of the NDA was a source of disquiet and dismay in these circles. The *Wall Street Journal* had declared Manmohan Singh as 'the most reassuring candidate'. It warned that 'if India truly wants to become an economic power it has to pay heed to the global voters known as investors, in addition to its own voters at home. India now attracts attention as well as capital, and the same market forces that have helped to promote an economic revival will ruthlessly punish policy mistakes.'[49] To reassure investors, Finance Minister P. Chidambaram had to miss the first session of the Fourteenth Lok Sabha for a few days during which he made a trip to Mumbai to restore confidence among the leading lights of the stock market regarding the UPA government's adherence to economic reforms. This was in response to a massive fall in the sensex as investors were worried that a

Left-supported UPA would pursue policies that would hurt growth and business. The consternation was also because, on a number of issues, ranging from employment guarantee to social sector expenditure, the Congress party's manifesto was fairly radical and its thrust was very different from the liberalization agenda, and the NCMP was a great cause of concern for private investors. Most notably, the Congress and the NCMP it endorsed were in deference to the public mood which visualized an active role for the state in promoting employment and welfare.[50] This went against the Washington consensus[51] and the basic interests of business and finance capital which was interested not in the retreat of the state, as is commonly argued, but in a change in the role of the state so that it could become an instrument for promoting its own exclusive interests.

Manmohan Singh, supported by P. Chidambaram, and Deputy Chairman of the Planning Commission Montek Singh Ahluwalia, the three persons most closely associated with the induction of the economic reform policies, were in charge of policymaking under the UPA. Sonia Gandhi seemed to have given Manmohan Singh a free hand in economic policymaking. The prime minister and his inner circle remained committed to accelerated economic reforms while the critics of liberalization were more or less kept out of the government or any important economic ministry. Although Sonia Gandhi did force the government's hand on some issues like the NREGA, important economic policy decisions were the prerogative of the prime minister and his government colleagues. The tilt in the balance of economic decision-making in the government in favour of the neo-liberal policies led to disquiet and uneasiness among sections of the Congress which felt that it went against the thrust of the 2004 verdict. This unease did not, however, coalesce into a visible opposition because Sonia Gandhi did not allow a counterpoint to develop against Manmohan Singh, even though she herself was committed to a broadly progressive agenda. This concern regarding the fiscal conservatives controlling policymaking was even more acute among the Left parties which had extended outside support to the UPA regime on the express understanding that the Congress would promote genuinely inclusive growth through a strong push for the social sector.[52]

For four years the Left functioned as a brake on the government's bid to speed up economic reforms, notwithstanding the Left Front's own pursuit of liberalization in the states it ruled: it blocked the privatization of profitable public sector companies and prevented the wholesale privatization of telecommunications, civil aviation, and the retail trade, and held back the entry of speculative finance capital in the pension schemes and in the insurance sector. For example, when the government mooted the idea of disinvesting a 10 per cent stake in Bharat Heavy Electricals Limited (BHEL), the Left parties decided to stay away from the UPA Coordination Committee meetings and returned only when an assurance was given by the UPA chairperson that BHEL would not be privatized.[53] They lamented that the government failed to meets its obligations under the NCMP.

The five years of UPA witnessed an ideological contestation between fiscal conservatives who wanted to reduce spending and those who favour it, and a backward and forward movement on the twin goals of growth and equity. In particular, policies and issues relating to the social equity agenda led to a public battle between the Left parties and the NAC, on one hand, and the PMO and Planning Commission on the other which would often use arguments similar to what the corporate sector had been using to criticize policies like NREGA. Significantly, the NAC rather than the Congress was the source of important ideas such as the RTI and the right to employment. The Congress had virtually outsourced the equity agenda to the NAC while the party contributed little in terms of either generating radical ideas or sending any concrete proposals to the government.[54] The NAC, however, had to negotiate with the government which looked upon equity as a question of finance or fiscal prudence or at best as a by-product of some good policies.

FOCUSING ON SOCIAL POLICY

From 2004, there was a sharp focus on inclusive policies overall. The high growth model saw no change but the serious imbalances between growth and distribution were addressed through a substantial increase in social sector allocations.[55] This idea found its way into the NCMP which was interpreted as a 'charter for increased social spending' to implement social welfare measures.[56]

The political insignia of the Congress government was inclusive growth, an idea that was projected as the key to politically sustainable economic development. High on the government's agenda of greater inclusiveness were actions to address disparities in access to education, health care, water, and other public services that are necessary for people's well-being. Congress leaders set about constructing massive public programmes which would make their inclusive intentions clear. Moreover, the central government had serious money at its disposal to spend on these programmes. In the past, governments faced severe fiscal constraints and could not spend substantial money on poverty-reducing initiatives which often diminished its impact. The acceleration of economic growth from around 6 per cent to 9 per cent between 2004 and 2009 combined with major tax reforms resulted in an exponential increase in government revenues, providing headroom to the state to spend on social sector and anti-poverty programmes. No period since Independence had produced such high levels of sustained growth and generated such large revenues that could be pumped into the welfare of people as under the UPA which witnessed a major change in spending patterns. The total tax revenue has increased by 31 per cent per year since 2003, so that by 2009, the government had four times more money to spend than in 2003.[57] Before 1991, the central government had spent only 30 per cent of the plan budget on social sectors and rural development. But since 2004, that figure went up roughly to 70 per cent.[58] However, even at the present level, the tax revenue falls far short of revenue collected in several other countries, and is not enough for the scale of public investment required by the country. Nonetheless the total budget allocation for social sector registered a sharp increase from 2005–6.[59]

Thanks to the revenue windfalls, the UPA was able to unveil the biggest ever post-Independence expansion of government expenditure to address social deficits in ways that directly have an impact on the lives of people.[60] This enabled the government to launch several centrally sponsored schemes and a series of initiatives since 2004 that have a bearing on poverty alleviation. These initiatives were aimed at investing in rural and urban infrastructure and maximizing the generation of employment. Taken together, over a hundred centrally sponsored odd government schemes and rights-based social legislations mark a significant departure in policymaking and indicate an attempt to reconcile growth and equity.

Articulating the party's philosophy, Mukherjee claimed that the Congress's development strategy had changed radically with the RTI Act,[61] provision of employment, education, and food for a large section of its people.[62] 'I don't know [of] any [other] country in the world which has given the legal right to food to its people,' Mukherjee said, while referring to the right to food legislation.[63] Such a strategy it hoped would address the issues of development and, in reality, usher in all-round development. Despite his opposition to a rights-based approach and his own preference for empowerment,[64] Manmohan Singh also highlighted the role of his government which had 'put in place a framework which makes it possible, as never before in India's history, to implement [a] rights approach to the realization of basic human rights'.[65] These legally mandated rights went counter to the global consensus on market-led growth which overrides political and ethical concerns about inequality.[66] Shaped in response to the pressures of democratic politics, this was, in effect, a 'reform of the reform programme'.[67]

The centrally sponsored schemes had come to constitute two-thirds of the central financial assistance from about one-third 20 years ago. The spending on the nine flagship programmes established by the UPA government was Rs 271,840 crores.[68] These schemes entail fiscal transfers from the central government to the states and are intended to address human development and infrastructural requirements in sectors for which the states are responsible.[69]

The budgetary allocations for the social sector were increased in comparison to the previous years. According to the *Economic Survey 2009*, the combined social sector expenditure by the central and state governments increased from Rs 141,740 crores in 2002–3 to Rs 294,412 crores in 2007–8,[70] as a percentage of GDP, it increased from 5.6 per cent in 2004–5 to 6.6 per cent in 2008–9.[71] In absolute terms, social sector spending rose from Rs 36,000 crores in 2003–4 (the last year of the NDA government) to Rs 120,000 crores in 2008–9 (the last year of the UPA-1 government).[72] Since 2004, the central government expenditures created a number of new poverty-reducing programmes such as Bharat Nirman (a cluster of six infrastructure programmes), Sarva Shiksha Abhiyan, Mid-day Meals Scheme, NREGS, Total Sanitation Campaign, National Rural Health Mission (NRHM), Integrated Child Development Services, Jawaharlal Nehru National Urban Renewal Mission (JNNURM) and Polio Eradication, and spent Rs 271,840 crores.

Although social welfare spending had nearly doubled, it was still among the world's lowest levels of such expenditure and was much less than what was necessary and feasible, given the growing revenues with the government.[73] Despite strong growth, India lags far behind other BRIC (Brazil, Russia, India, and China) countries in social sector achievements, spending the lowest on education and health, according to a study by Assocham.[74] The funds allocated fell far short of what the UPA promised on just health and education, which was 3 per cent and 6 per cent, respectively, of GDP. An even greater increase in public investment was required to bridge the shortfalls in the social provisioning of public goods. Nonetheless, even with less investment than required, it was substantially more than the social expenditure in the Ninth and Tenth plans.

THE PERSISTENCE OF DEPRIVATION

The UPA's officially proclaimed goal of ensuring that high growth rates were also inclusive proved to be highly inadequate for meeting the challenge to redress poverty. The Eleventh Plan strategy was to combine high growth with critical interventions in the social sector but this may not have yielded the desired results, as is evident from the Mid-Term Appraisal which noted that the progress on inclusiveness was below expectations.[75] Inclusive growth did not produce commensurate improvements in human development that is to say it had not succeeded in translating accelerated growth into inclusive development.[76] Even with increasing outlays on the social sector, low levels of human development persist. The performance of the programmes/schemes was unsatisfactory as utilization was poor in many states and progress on the targets set was tardy. In any case, the centrally sponsored schemes have their limitations. The central government can devise schemes, issue guidelines for implementation, and allocate funds but the implementation is in the hands of states. The cutting edge of implementation, the delivery of public services, the interface between government and the people, is at the state level. Social sectors such as education, health, and agriculture and rural development, which account for the bulk of central resources are all sectors which are basically in the sphere of state governments and most of these funds need to be transferred to states for them to spend. Although each centrally sponsored scheme is formulated in close consultation with state governments, for example, the Sarva Shiksha Abhiyan, the Mid-day Meal Scheme, the NREGA, the NRHM, ICDS, and Pradhan Mantri Gram Sadak Yojana (PMGSY), most of these schemes are either specifically state government subjects or are concurrently under both the state and central governments. Much depends upon the capacity of the states to utilize these funds. Beyond the quantum of money spent, little attention was paid to delivery mechanisms which consume 75 per cent to 85 per cent of the expenditure on poverty alleviation schemes.[77]

It is clear that reducing income poverty in India is a task that will require systemic change, rather than simply better delivery of services or better targeting of existing systems to the poor.[78] Under the existing policy regime, the scope for hastening deliberate redistribution is limited, in part because the state lacks the commitment to do so and its capacity to implement pro-poor policies has always been limited.[79] Despite inclusive economic and social development being a high-priority national goal reiterated in successive AICC and National Development Council (NDC) meetings and the speeches of the prime minister and the Congress president, distributive policies and their implementation did not receive the attention they deserve. This was starkly evident from the UPA government's silence on the recommendations of the National Commission for Enterprises in the Unorganized Sector (NCEUS) 2009, which made major recommendations which, if implemented, could accelerate inclusiveness and social security.[80] The silence has much to do with the Commission's approach which did not confine its analysis to enterprises but went on to focus on the entitlements of the unorganized sector workers and obligations of employers within a rights framework. This set the Commission on a collision course with the government which was not convinced of the need to move beyond a business-oriented approach to the social security framework. It also has to do with the evidence produced, which was that the bulk of India's unorganized sector was steeped in poverty and deprivation, and that their situation has not improved markedly over the past decade. Its finding that 77 per cent people in India live on Rs 20 a day was picked upon by critics, which further annoyed the government because it dented the UPA's and India's image.[81] Unemployment was the most important problem and therefore the Commission's report emphasized the urgent need to expand employment for those in the lower echelons of the economy. This was, however, not acted upon because recognition of the rights of the unorganized sector would have changed the growth process, and this was a source of annoyance for the government.

Taken as a whole, the balance of policies remained in favour of a business-centred model of growth but India's democratic politics reinforced pressures for redistribution. Plebeian pressures found some resonance and space in the Congress because the poor form an important voting bloc for the party, and therefore it has to focus on winning their support by addressing popular concerns. Since the days of garibi hatao, it has developed the knack of formulating public policies and taking political advantage of them.[82] In view of the persistence of mass deprivation, Congress politicians have had to walk a tightrope to calibrate the pace of economic change.[83] The desire to achieve 9 per cent growth remains undiminished but high growth cannot win elections and so they had to pay attention to redistribution and welfare correctives that go against the mainstream of market orthodoxy. The dualism was explicitly endorsed by the Congress plenary resolution in 2010: 'Economic growth and social justice are two sides of the same coin and must go hand in hand.'[84]

The repertoire of social policies built up by the UPA government had not fully impacted on the people but it was a sign that mass perceptions do matter in democratic politics. The UPA's experience shows that there was room for government policies to provide direct benefits to people who were unable to meet their basic needs. This could be in the form of anti-poverty programmes or guaranteed employment in public works or subsidized food under the public distribution system (PDS). All these can be regarded as direct interventions to contain inequalities. Public pressure was able to force the crafting of public policies that can work in the interests of urban and rural poor. Greater political participation has led to a sharper sense of inequity and an attempt to use politics to rectify it. The need for the Congress to change course and accommodate the broader social interests of the poor to secure their political support was the strongest indication yet of these pressures. The importance of social policy and public programmes which delivered benefits to people cannot be overstated. It was clear that policy performance not only mattered but also helped to determine the outcome of the election in favour of the Congress and the UPA in 2009.

NOTES

1.   C.P. Chandrasekhar, 'Free Right Turn', *Frontline*, vol. 27, no. 12, 5–18 June 2010.

2.   See Atul Kohli (2009c), *Democracy and Development in India: From Socialism to Pro-Business*, Oxford University Press, New Delhi, esp. 'Introduction', pp. 1–22.

3.   Amitav Ghosh, 'Grand Illusion', *Hindustan Times*, 30 August 2011.

4.   Partha Chatterjee (2008), 'Democracy and Economic Transformation in India', *Economic and Political Weekly*, vol. 43, no. 16, 19–25 April, pp. 53–62, esp. p. 56.

5.   Pranab Bardhan (2009), 'Notes on the Political Economy of India's Tortuous Transition', *Economic and Political Weekly*, vol. XLIV, no. 49, pp. 31–36.

6.   Interview with Mani Shankar Aiyar, 13 November 2009.

7.   Ibid.

8.   Prime Minister's Speech, 83rd AICC Plenary Session, Speeches, Prime Minister's Office. Available at http://pmindia.nic.in/speeches.htm (accessed on 24 April 2011).

9.   Interview with Harsh Mander, Member, NAC, 16 December 2010.

10.   Aiyar (2010), 'Dilemma of Development and Democracy', 24 November. Available at www.cmsindia.org/ManiShankarAiyar24Nov2010.pdf.

11.   Ibid.

12.   Nexus lecture by Sonia Gandhi, 'Living Politics: What India Has Taught Me', 9 June 2007, Nexus Institute, The Hague. Available at www.congress.org. in/new/sonia-speeches.php (accessed on 29 December 2011).

13.   'Mid-Term Appraisal of the Eleventh Five Year Plan: An Overview.' Available at planningcommission.nic.in/plans/mta/11th_mta/.../chap1_overview.pdf (accessed on 14 January 2012).

14.   See the use of titles: 'The Rise of India', *Business Week*, 8 December 2003; 'India Awakens', *Time*, 18 June 2008.

15.   Pankaj Mishra, 'The Myth of the New India', *The New York Times*, 10 July 2006.

16.   Baldev Raj Nayar and Samuel Paul (2003), *India in the World Order*, Cambridge University Press, Cambridge.

17.   T.N. Ninan (2008), 'Boom and Gloom', *Seminar*, no. 581, January, pp. 1–7, esp. p. 5.

18.   As a share of GDP, social sector investment is close to that of Russia and Saudi Arabia, even while India's level of per capita income is much lower than in those countries. Sunil Khilnani, 'The Blurred Horizon', *Outlook*, 10 January 2011.

19.   Mishra, 'The Myth of the New India'.

20.   Phrase used by Utsa Patnaik (2010), *The Republic of Hunger*, Three Essays Collective, New Delhi.

21.   Ammu Joseph, 'Covering the Republic of Hunger', *India Together*, 30 January 2006.

22.   Kohli (2006a), 'Politics and Redistribution in India'. Available at http://www.princeton.edu/~kohli/Politics%20and%20Redistribution%20in%20India.pdf.

23.   Editorial, 'Can There Be Any Hope', *Economic and Political Weekly*, vol. XLV, no. 17, 24–30 April 2010.

24.   Jayati Ghosh (2002), *Social Policy in Indian Development*, Report prepared for the UNRISD project on 'Social Policy in A Development Context', November, UNRISD, Geneva.

25. Chandrasekhar, 'Capital Gains', *Frontline*, vol. 27, no. 26, 4–17 December 2010.

26. Tax concessions increased from Rs 104,471 crores in 2008–9 to Rs 120, 483 crores in 2009–10. Sitaram Yechury, 'Governing by Wealth', *Hindustan Times*, 7 March 2011.

27. Venkatesh Athreya, 'Seductive Sophistry', *Frontline*, vol. 27, no. 6, 13–26 March 2010.

28. Subrat Das and Yamini Mishra (2010), 'What Does Budget 2010 Imply for the Social Sector', *Economic and Political Weekly*, vol. XLV, no. 13, 27 March, pp. 64–8, esp. p. 68.

29. Aseema Sinha, 'Globalisation, Rising Inequality, and the New Insecurities in India'. Available at www.apsanet.org/imgtest/TaskForceDiffIneqDevSinha.pdf (accessed on 25 January 2011).

30. P. Sainath, 'In 16 Years, Farm Suicides Cross a Quarter Million', *The Hindu*, 29 October 2011.

31. Saikat Datta, Anuradha Raman, and Arindam Mukherjee, 'A Ten Foot Trench, Rs. 14.50', *Outlook*, 9 April 2007.

32. Kaushik Basu, 'Let the Cream Percolate', *Outlook*, 9 April 2007.

33. Chandrasekhar and Ghosh (2007), 'Recent Trends in Employment in India and China: An Unfortunate Convergence?' *MacroScan*, 5 April. Available at www.macroscan.org/anl/apr07/pdf/india_china.pdf.

34. Chandrasekhar, 'Unemployed in a Thriving Economy', *Frontline*, vol. 23, no. 5, 11–24 March 2006.

35. Edward Luce (2007), *In Spite of the Gods: The Strange Rise of Modern India*, Little Brown, Paperback edition, Abacus, London, p. 48.

36. Sinha, 'Globalization, Rising Inequality, and New Insecurities in India'.

37. Sainath, 'HDI Oscars: Slumdogs versus Millionaires', *The Hindu*, 18 March 2009.

38. Sainath, 'India 2007: High Growth, Low Development', *The Hindu*, 24 December 2007.

39. By contrast, China has been able to move people out of extreme poverty within just a generation, which is more than what any other country in world history has achieved. Bardhan (2010), *Awakening Giants, Feet of Clay: Assessing the Economic Rise of China and India*, Oxford University Press, New Delhi, pp. 90–103.

40. The Expert Group Report, known as the Tendulkar Report, estimates aggregate poverty to be 37.2 per cent. See Government of India (2009a), 'Report of the Expert Group to Review the Methodology for Estimation of Poverty', Planning Commission, Government of India, November. Available at www.planningcommission.nic.in/reports/genrep/ rep_pov.pdf. Another committee headed by N.C. Saxena found 50 per cent people to be poor. See Government of India, Ministry of Rural Development, Economic and Monitoring Wing, September 2009. Available at www.scribd.com/.../Saxena-Committee-Report-on-Poverty-Estimates-in-India

(accessed on 23 November 2010). The NCEUS estimates that 77 per cent of the population in the unorganized sector is vulnerable and works under deplorable conditions.

41.   Government of India (2006c), '*Towards Faster and More Inclusive Growth. An Approach to the 11th Five Year Plan*', Planning Commission, Government of India, June. Available at planningcommission.nic.in/plans/planrel/apppap_11.pdf.

42.   See the Prime Minister's Closing Remarks at the 54th Meeting of the National Development Council, 19 December 2007. Available at pib.nic.in/release/release.asp?relid=34145 (accessed on 24 December 2011).

43.   Ashutosh Varshney (2007), 'India's Democratic Challenge', *Foreign Affairs*, vol. 86, no. 2, March–April, pp. 93–106, esp. p. 100.

44.   Muchkund Dubey and S.N. Jha (2002), *Social Development in India: The Policy Canvas: An Overview of the Last Fifty Years & Emerging Issues for the Twenty-First Century*, Council of Social Development, New Delhi.

45.   Jairam Ramesh, 'Limits to Growth Revisited', Convocation Speech, Tata Institute of Social Sciences (TISS), Mumbai, 11 May 2011. Available at moef.nic.in/downloads/public-information/Limits%20to%20growth.pdf (accessed on 25 May 2011).

46.   Interview with Abhijit Sen, Member, Planning Commission, New Delhi, 2 November 2010.

47.   Ibid.

48.   Editorial, 'On the Right Track', *The Hindu*, 8 July 2008.

49.   Editorial, *The Wall Street Journal*, 19 May 2004. The *Wall Street Journal* even asked editorially '[w]hy should developing countries like India have such frequent elections?' and it went on to add that if a country like India does have elections, then surely the outcome cannot be left entirely to the Indian people; 'foreign investors' too must have a say since they have a 'stake' in the Indian economy.

50.   The rise of neo-liberalism in India can be dated to the beginning of economic reforms in 1991. As elsewhere, it means the rule of the market, privatization, deregulation, and a cut back on public spending on social services such as health and education. Prabhat Patnaik underlined the strong opposition faced by neo-liberalism in India which made it difficult for it to hold sway in the country. In his words:

The triumph of neoliberalism in India was never complete. The nationalised banks continued to remain state-owned; key public sector companies were not privatised; pension funds were not handed over to speculative finance capital; the currency was not made fully convertible; and the financial sector's holding of foreign assets, other than the foreign exchange reserves of the Reserve Bank of India (RBI), continued to remain minuscule. In short, the two interlinked and mutually reinforcing processes underlying neoliberalism, namely, the dismantling of the public sector and integration with global finance, remained arrested. [Prabhat Patnaik (2009a), 'Time for Change', *Frontline*, vol. 26, no. 7, 28 March–10 April]

51.   The term 'Washington consensus' was proposed in 1990 by economist John Williamson to describe a set of specific policy prescriptions that constitute the economic reform package promoted by the IMF, World Bank, and US Treasury Department in the developing countries. These policies include macroeconomic stability, opening up the economy with regard to trade and investment and expansion of market forces in the domestic economy.

52.   The CPI (M) regularly presented notes to the UPA government on various policy issues. See *Policy Issues: Left Alternatives. Notes Submitted by the Left to the UPA Government on Some Important Policy Issues*, CPI (M) Publication, New Delhi, October 2006.

53.   Cited in K.V. Prasad, 'The Election Results and Coalition Politics', *The Hindu*, 12 May 2006.

54.   Interview with Mander.

55.   Social sector spending in India includes poverty reduction interventions; expenditures in the fields of health, education, and nutrition; and social assistance and social welfare. Most departments of government are in some way responsible for expenditure under this broad head. It also includes the PDS, ICDS, the Mid Day Meal Scheme, and other social security measures.

56.   Smita Gupta, 'Aam or Khaas', *Outlook*, 1 August 2011.

57.   James Manor (2011b), 'Did the Central Government's Poverty Initiatives Help to Re-elect It', in Lawrence Saez and Gurharpal Singh (eds), *New Dimensions of Politics in India: The United Progressive Alliance in Power*, Routledge, London. See also Centre for Budget and Governance Accountability (CBGA) (2009), *How Did the UPA Spend Our Money: An Assessment of Expenditure Priorities and Resource Mobilisation Efforts by the UPA Government*, CBGA, New Delhi. Available at http://www.cbgaindia.org/whats_new/How%20did%20the%20UPA%20spend%20our%20money.pdf.

58.   Ibid. Also see 'The Taxman's Coffers are Overflowing', *Outlook*, 12 March 2002.

59.   Ibid.

60.   For a detailed assessment of the expenditure priorities of the UPA government and its resource mobilization efforts over its five-year term, from the perspective of the underprivileged sections of the population, see CBGA, *How Did the UPA Spend Our Money*.

61.   The RTI Act 2005 mandates timely response to citizen requests for government information. The Act provides a practical regime of right to information for citizens to secure access to information under the control of public authorities, in order to promote transparency and accountability in the working of every public authority.

62.   Mukherjee's speech at the AICC session in 2010, reported in 'National Politics: Communal Threat in Sonia Focus', *The Telegraph*, 3 November 2012.

63.   Ibid.

64.   In the first meeting of the Planning Commission after the formation of the UPA government, the prime minister expressed his scepticism about a rights-based approach; in fact, he opposed it. Interview with Sen, 23 July 2010.

65.   Prime Minister's address at the national colloquium on poverty alleviation, food security, and right to development, 9 November 2006. Available at pmindia.nic.in/speech/content.asp?id=445 (accessed on 12 April 2011).

66.   Mritiunjoy Mohanty, 'The 2009 Lok Sabha Election: a Storm in the Teacup?' *Macroscan*, 18 May. Available at www.macroscan.org/cur/may09/cur180509Lok_Sabha_Election.htm.

67.   Sinha (2007), 'Politics of Accommodation', *Journal of Democracy*, vol. 18, no. 2, April, pp. 41–54.

68.   Government schemes include the following: Bharat Nirman (a cluster of six infrastructure programmes), Rs 114,257 crores; Sarva Shiksha Abhiyan (education; figures only up to 2008), Rs 37,500 crores; Mid Day Meal Scheme (figures only up to 2008), Rs 20,625 crores; NREGA, Rs 44,480 crores; total sanitation campaign, Rs 2,550 crores; NRHM, Rs 20,000 crores; ICDS (figures only up to 2008), Rs 16,000 crores; JNNURM Rs 7,428 crores; polio eradication, Rs 9,000 crores. The total spending on poverty-reducing programmes since 2004 comes to Rs 271,840 crores. Reported in *The Times of India*, 3 June 2009.

69.   Jay Chaudhuri (2010), 'Going to the Operating Room without a Diagnostic: Reforming Centrally Sponsored Schemes', *India Review*, vol. 9, no. 2, April–June, pp. 169–203.

70.   Das and Mishra, 'What Does Budget 2010 Imply for the Social Sector'.

71.   Editorial, 'Strengthen the Social Sector', *The Hindu*, 19 June 2009.

72.   Aiyar (2009), 'Outlays for Social Sector up under UPA', *The Times of India*, 28 March.

73.   'India's Social Sector Spending Lowest among BRIC Nations', *Indo Asian News Service*. Available at sulekha.com/india-s-social-sector-spending-lowest-among-bric-nations_news_923035.htm (accessed on 4 January 2012).

74.   Ibid.

75.   The Cabinet approved the Mid-Term Appraisal of Eleventh Five Year Plan 2007–12, a report card of the government's economic performance during the Plan period, on 10 June 2010. 'Mid-Term Appraisal of Eleventh Five Year Plan 2007–12, Planning Commission: An Overview'. Available at planningcommission.nic.in/plans/mta/11th_mta/MTA.html (accessed on 10 January 2012).

76.   For an analysis of outcomes see Naresh C. Saxena (2007), 'Outlays and Outcomes', *Seminar*, no. 574, June.

77.   Aiyar, 'Dilemma of Development and Democracy'.

78.   Chaudhuri, 'Going to the Operating Room without a Diagnostic'.

79.   Jan Breman (2010), 'India's Social Question in a State of Denial', *Economic and Political Weekly*, vol. XLV, no. 23, 5 June, pp. 42–6, esp. p. 45.

80.   Government of India (2009b), 'Report of the National Commission for Enterprises in the Unorganized Sector (NCEUS), vol. 1 Main Report and vol. II Annexures', Government of India, New Delhi. Available at www.cdhr.org.in/.../ The_Challenge_of_Employment_in_India_(Vol.%20II)[1].pdf.
81.   Breman, 'India's Social Question in a State of Denial'.
82.   Interview with K.B. Saxena, Former Secretary, Rural Development, June 2010.
83.   Manor (2011a), 'The Congress Party and the "Great Transformation"', in Sanjay Ruparelia, Sanjay Reddy, John Harriss, and Stuart Corbridge (eds), *Understanding India's New Political Economy: A Great Transformation?* Routledge, London.
84.   Congress Plenary Resolution, 19 December 2010. Available at www.congress.org.in/new/125_years_of_inc_83rd_plenary_delhi.pdf (accessed on 28 December 2010).

6   Defending Livelihoods

The defeat of the NDA in the 2004 general elections represented a crucial turning point in Indian politics. It was widely interpreted as a rural revolt against rapidly rising inequalities and a rejection of Hindutva politics. This vote could not, however, be separated from the demands and concerns of the socially and economically marginalized classes and castes for an improvement in their economic condition.[1] Notwithstanding a decade of high economic growth, 300 million people remain below the poverty line. Rising inequalities were staring the Congress in the face, and more directly because the party leadership had accused the BJP of doing nothing for the poor while its policies helped the rich. Both Sonia Gandhi and Manmohan Singh blamed the NDA for the plight of the farming community and rural masses generally. The minimal challenge before them was therefore to find an economic strategy that would ensure greater equality of opportunity especially employment even while ensuring growth (see Chapter 5). The political leadership seemed to recognize the need for the state to provide livelihoods to the poor, which itself was significant given that the international discourse was moving away from state intervention and public works programmes.

THE STRUCTURE OF EMPLOYMENT

Mahatma Gandhi had once said: 'A nation may do without its millionaires and without its capitalists, but a nation can never do without its labour.'[2] India has, however, been least successful in promoting the right to work and employment, notwithstanding the promise of the Directive Principles of State Policy emphasizing that ensuring 'decent work' for all should be a crucial focus of state policy.[3] India's economic growth has not been matched by the growth of productive employment. The inability to generate employment, except in a few chosen sectors, has been the most obvious problem of the Indian development project, together with the persistence of widespread poverty and slow rate of improvement in human development. One of the major features of the neo-liberal strategy has been its failure to reverse this pattern. 'Low levels of productive employment generation in the aggregate, the persistence of poverty and low educational levels,' Jayati Ghosh points out, 'are the most significant failures of the Indian development strategy this far'.[4] The National Sample Survey (NSS) on Employment and Unemployment, held in 1999–2000, indicated a dramatic decline in the rate of employment generation. From 1994 to 2000, formal sector employment as a whole was stagnant, rising barely above half a percentage point per year throughout the latter half of the 1990s.[5]

Jobs in the informal sector have continued to proliferate at higher rates; a trend that will probably only intensify. A survey of about 1,300 manufacturing firms in 10 states and both the public and private sectors undertaken by the Institute for Human Development (sponsored by the Ministry of Statistics, Government of India) found that while total employment rose by over 2 per cent between 1991 and 1998, most of the increase came in the form of jobs offered on a temporary, casual, contract, or other flexible basis. The informal economy creates jobs, but typically the wages are low.[6] In the organized manufacturing sector, liberalization has been associated with an expanding wage gap that favours skilled over less-skilled workers. This gap, which directly contributes to the growth of income inequality, also maps on to the rising gap between the service, manufacturing, and agriculture sectors of the economy. A greater degree of labour market flexibility spurred by globalization was causing more formal sector jobs to resemble those in the precarious informal sector, in consequence, the lives of large numbers of people are characterized by vulnerability in both the urban economy and the countryside.

AGRARIAN DISTRESS AND EMPLOYMENT STAGNATION

The dichotomy between rapid economic growth and an inadequate sharing of the benefits of this was most evident in rural India, home to two-thirds of the workforce. While the growth of employment for the economy as a whole rose to 2.85 per cent per annum after 1999–2000, agricultural employment growth rates have not grown in recent years.[7] By far, the largest numbers of poor people work in agriculture, either as cultivators or as agricultural labourers. During the 1990s, agriculture ceased to employ more labour, and this was true also of the formal sector. Such employment growth as there was occurred in the informal sector or self-employment.

In his first Independence Day speech from the ramparts of the Red Fort in 2004, Prime Minister Manmohan Singh admitted that the country faced an acute agrarian crisis. He singled out the Vidarbha region in Maharashtra, stating that 'the plight of farmers made a deep impact on me'. He added: 'I am aware of the acute distress of our farmers who bear the burden of heavy debt.'[8] According to the NCRB, 100,248 farmers committed suicide between 1993 and 2003. Two-thirds of these suicides have occurred in five states—Maharashtra, Karnataka, Andhra Pradesh, Madhya Pradesh, and Chhattisgarh—which account for just about a third of the country's population.[9] Maharashtra alone accounted for over 38 per cent. In five years, from 1996 to 2001, there were 15,747 farmer suicides a year on an average.[10] The spate of farmer suicides, a chilling manifestation of agrarian distress can be traced to the economic liberalization and the reduction in prices and increasing input costs, which aggravated after 2001, by when India had embraced the World Trade Organization (WTO) recommended path for agriculture.[11] For many, the shift from food crops to cash crops worsened their plight.[12] The phenomenon of indebted farmers committing suicide in Andhra Pradesh and Punjab began in 1998 and rapidly spread to other areas where cultivation of cash and export crops was predominant. Those who have taken their lives were deep in debt. Peasant households in debt almost doubled from 26 per cent of farm households to 48.6 per cent. Nearly half the indebted farmers belong to five states: Uttar Pradesh, Andhra Pradesh, Maharashtra, West Bengal, and Madhya Pradesh. By relative share, however, Andhra Pradesh tops the list with 82 per cent of indebted farmer households, Tamil Nadu with 74.5 per cent, and Punjab with 65.4 per cent.[13] According to the RBI, the share of long-term direct institutional credit to agriculture fell from over 20 per cent in the 1970s to 12 per cent in the 1990s; short-term credit was stagnant at around 14.5 per cent. Even now, banks typically tend to give large loans, ignoring repayment capacity, and the quality of the loan.[14] The study by the TISS, at the request of the Bombay High Court, on farmer suicides in Maharashtra, notes: 'There is a general crisis of credit in the agrarian economy, reflected more in the medium and small landholdings. The debt trap is due to the inadequate credit supply to the cultivators at an affordable price and due to the rising costs of production that cannot be met.'[15]

Given low productivity and inconsistent growth, agriculture was not a viable option for the majority of the rural population, leading to a marked decline of rural employment and incomes. The Planning Commission's Approach Paper for the Eleventh Plan showed a sharp rise in unemployment among agricultural households from 9 per cent in 1993–4 to 15.3 per cent in 2004–5. Rural unemployment grew at an annual rate of 0.58 per cent between 1993–4 and 1999–2000, which was far below the growth of the rural population.[16] It is not that the government has made no attempts to solve the problem. A series of rural employment schemes, such as Jawahar Rozgar Yojana (JRY), Pradhan Mantri Rozgar Yojana, and Sampoorna Grameen Rozgar Yojana, are testimony to this.[17] However, the decline in the employment rate shows that these schemes have not succeeded in increasing employment, and therefore the growth process has been failing in terms of inclusiveness.

THE POLITICS OF GUARANTEED EMPLOYMENT

As noted earlier, in the last couple of decades the rural economy faced a serious crisis as its contribution to the national income declined sharply. Employment was at the centre of the problem. Apart from the declining reliance on this primary sector, inadequate rural infrastructure entailing lack of access to markets, inadequate provisions for health care and education, and above all, shrinking opportunities for gainful employment and stagnating agricultural growth are other significant reasons for the agrarian crisis. The UPA government took a number of policy initiatives to address the crisis.[18] These included the major initiative on rural infrastructure development, named Bharat Nirman, which covers rural housing, rural electricity connection, telephony, road connectivity, water and sanitation, expansion of irrigation capacity, and so on.[19] The total expenditure on rural development increased from 0.58 per cent of GDP in 2004–5 to 1.2 per cent of GDP in 2008–9. The bulk of this expenditure has been devoted to the generation of rural employment and beneficiary-driven programmes for rural housing.[20]

By far and away, the NREGA was the most significant programme undertaken by the government. This landmark legislation was a political game-changer. For a start, the provision of employment on demand signalled the coming into existence of the rights-based approach. Described as the 'the largest programme in the world for rural reconstruction', it found pride of place in the president's first address to the 15th Lok Sabha in June 2009.[21]

The NREGA was passed unanimously in the Lok Sabha in August 2005. This scheme came into force in February 2006 in 200 districts and was later extended to all districts. Each rural household is guaranteed access to 100 days of unskilled wage employment a year. Common work assignments include public works, small-scale road construction, water supply, flood protection, irrigation infrastructure, land development, and reforestation projects. The idea is to give a legal guarantee of employment to anyone who is willing to undertake casual labour at the legal minimum wage. Eligible applicants who do not receive work within two weeks of requesting it will receive unemployment insurance from the state. The programme seeks to tackle the urgent issue of mass deprivation and the need for employment and livelihood to prevent endemic hunger that can lead to destitution. The new law recognizes the responsibility of the state for providing a social safety net for poor households. It acknowledges the fact that the state has an obligation to protect its people from unemployment and destitution, and this was indeed a vital step towards ensuring some sort of economic and social security for the rural poor, especially as unemployment has worsened with the economic reforms in the 1990s.

MANIFESTO TO POLICY

How did the Congress zero in on a policy like the NREGA? It can be safely argued that the NREGA did not mean a reversal of economic reforms and market-oriented policies of the government but was rather an attempt to add a few redistributive measures to growth. For the Congress, the idea of an Employment Guarantee Act (EGA) and the demand for guaranteed employment were not altogether novel. It claimed that the party's attempt to provide guaranteed employment dated back to the Maharashtra Employment Guarantee Scheme (MEGS) which was introduced by the state government in 1982 and enshrined a right to unlimited employment for every adult male in rural areas. The party promised at the chief ministers' conclave in Guwahati in April 2002 that it would enact a national employment guarantee law if elected to power. Indeed, a Congress committee recommended a national act based on the MEGS. However, there was no serious debate about the merits and demerits of different social protection instruments including employment guarantee.[22] True, the 2004 election manifesto promised guaranteed employment to the rural poor but this was not in response to pressure from the rank and file of the party. It did not become a major issue in elections although livelihood and employment issues figured frequently in the Congress president's speeches. The NREGS was unique in that it was very much a top-down decision and one that was implemented quite quickly.[23] This was surprising because political parties in India make election promises, politicians get elected on the basis of these but rarely do promises get implemented, least of all with such rapidity.

However, the idea of guaranteed rural employment had been promoted by civil society activists for quite a while through public campaigns. It can be traced back to the Mazdoor Kisan Shakti Sangathan (MKSS) campaign in Rajasthan. For several years they had been campaigning on this issue and trying to persuade the Congress leadership to accept the idea in principle and at least in relation to public works for drought-affected areas like Rajasthan. This was one state which had a major employment campaign and its activists lobbied both the central and state governments on the issue, and a great deal of mobilization was undertaken to get the idea accepted. Getting it through testified to the values of activism but the movement, which was essentially limited to a single state, was not commensurate with what eventually developed into a national scheme for guaranteed employment.[24]

Three of the activists from this campaign—Jean Drèze, Aruna Roy, and Nikhil Dey—were invited by senior Congress leaders to explain the rationale of an EGA to party MPs.[25] Besides them, other civil society groups also mounted pressure for the creation of a national-level programme to alleviate the persistent deprivation. These groups drew the attention of Congress leaders to their own state government in Maharashtra which had introduced the Maharashtra Employment Guarantee Act, 1977 which came into force from 26 January 1979. In response, it was suggested that state governments should enact state-level Employment Guarantee Schemes (EGSs). But, significantly, none of the Congress governments in the states drafted an EGS; only Congress government in Karnataka did so. In Rajasthan, Ashok Gehlot was sympathetic to the idea though he did not include an EGS in the party manifesto for the December 2003 state assembly elections. At the national level, Jairam Ramesh from the very outset backed the EGA encouraged by his belief that it would benefit the party in the same way as Operation Barga helped the CPI (M) in West Bengal.[26] The leadership's receptivity to the idea of employment guarantee from the time it was mooted was reinforced by favourable Supreme Court judgements on the right to food from 2001. This emboldened activists to step up the demand for the right to work, arguing that it was politically feasible and justifiable.[27] Furthermore, the broad-based nature of the UPA coalition and its links with civil society groups created political space for these groups to lobby with the Congress, and this helped in carrying these ideas forward.[28] These links meant that these issues could not be disregarded or overlooked as they provided the UPA with a social underpinning.

Interviews with several Congress leaders confirm that Sonia Gandhi had embraced the idea of an EGS even before the 2004 election. She was convinced that rural unemployment was really a national issue and an EGS can begin to tackle it. Most importantly, she believed that it could enhance the party's rural appeal and become the answer to BJP's 'India Shining' campaign. She was advised by Left leaders such as Sitaram Yechury that NREGA was a good idea, and that by supporting it she could define her distinctive policy stance. It would help her to delineate her philosophy and ideological position as her predecessors in the Nehru–Gandhi dynasty had done. Jawaharlal Nehru, Indira Gandhi, and Rajiv Gandhi all had big ideas that distinguished their position on policy issues of significance.[29] As it transpired, the NREGA turned out to be Sonia Gandhi's big idea.

Employment guarantee would not have gone very far but for the fact that the after the 2002 communal violence in Gujarat, Congress was in search of strategies to focus attention on broader public issues.[30] It was on the lookout for a big initiative to convince people that if it were to come to power, it would introduce distributive measures for their benefit. Also, it was eager to fight the communal agenda with what it believed matters to the people, 'development rather than only anti-communalism'.[31] Moreover, the defeat in the December 2003 elections in Rajasthan and several other states indicated that it was very unlikely to win the 2004 elections unless an inclusive platform was deployed to mobilize people. There was a strong feeling that policies and promises of social legislation directed at the welfare of the rural poor might provide a positive boost to the secular agenda that had developed salience after the 2002 Gujarat riots. In brief, Congress made an attempt to corner the BJP, not so much on the ground of communalism as by shifting the ground to social welfare and distributive policies. Despite considerable convergence on economic liberalization, it has given much greater attention to social welfare and designed measures to implement it, while the BJP-led NDA during six years in power did not bring in a policy like the NREGA. Convinced of India Shining under its dispensation, it did not consider it necessary to propose such measures, even though by 2000 rural unemployment was already high and clearly the government needed to put in place measures to alleviate rural hardship. The EGS fitted well with the approach of 'economic reforms with a human face' formula and might be an astute political strategy for regaining support by appealing to the poor.[32] It could be the Congress's trump card and serve as a long-term strategy for political mobilization. Most leaders went along with it, not so much because of its employment potential but its political advantage in helping the party to regain the electoral support of the poor.[33] Also, many of them were willing to entertain radical ideas because they were in opposition and because they did not see the party as a government-in-waiting.

Most of all, the Congress was keen to rectify a growing impression that it had become a party of the wealthy because these groups had gained the most from the economic reforms. Support for employment guarantee showed a keenness to restore its distributive credentials. It was, thus, part of a larger effort to convince voters that, as in the past, it remains dedicated to its central constituency, the underprivileged masses, even as the party today spends greater energy in promoting the interests of big business and the middle classes to bolster economic growth and revenues.

In the 2004 elections, livelihood was perceived as a major concern of the poor who were looking to support parties that promised to address the problem. In the central leadership's perception, the principal reason for the NDA's defeat was a rising sense of insecurity felt by the mass of people who saw the government's claims of India Shining as the last straw. However, both the print and electronic media cautioned it against reading the 2004 election verdict as a vote against agrarian distress and rural unemployment to justify policies such as the NREGA.[34] These commentators insisted there was no evidence to prove that the Congress and its allies won due to the revolt of the rural poor against economic reforms or that the most dissatisfied sections of society had switched from the NDA to the UPA. On the other side, the Congress and Left parties had resolutely attributed the unexpected success of the UPA alliance to public dissatisfaction with the NDA's excessive zeal for economic reforms and urban-focused policies emphasized in their election campaign. This assessment was shared by civil society groups who also argued that the anxiety about economic conditions, especially unemployment, played the most significant role in the NDA's defeat. They insisted that the Congress had done better than the BJP because of the rural support it marshalled and the promises it made to the rural poor. The *Frontline* editorial on the 2004 elections summed up the position: 'In the final analysis, this election was lost by the BJP and its allies, and also by the Congress where it faced the Left, on mass livelihood issues.'[35]

Ignoring media commentary, which attributed the UPA's good performance to its smart electoral alliance, the Congress was clear that the key condition that brought them to power was the promise to tackle livelihood issues. It interpreted the BJP defeat as a sign of the agrarian crisis, which meant that they were unlikely to renege on the manifesto commitment of employment guarantee. The point at issue was not whether the BJP lost because of economic reforms but that the Congress chose to construe its defeat as a mandate for a change of policy. In effect, it was not averse to promoting the perception that the 2004 election was a national mandate for rural development in order to build support for an employment guarantee programme, while if it had gone along with the dominant media-led thinking, it would not have adopted it. Without this programme, it would not have been able to restore its popular image as a party that cared for the poor, which helped it to improve its performance in the 2009 parliamentary elections on the strength of this and other related measures. This was also seen as a way of lending credence to the idea that it was interested in developing a set of broad-based policies to tackle poverty and deprivation critical to its long-term strategy beyond 2004. This perception influenced the party's strategic thinking which put employment guarantee at the centre of the UPA government's policy agenda.[36]

RURAL DISENCHANTMENT AND EMPLOYMENT GUARANTEE

After the UPA came to power, activists began building pressure on the Congress to fulfil its promise of guaranteed employment.[37] With Sonia Gandhi not assuming the post of prime minister, she had the time as well as the need to establish her political persona. She supported NREGA which gave meaning to the pro-poor position of the party. Once she decided to lend active support, the idea of employment guarantee gained traction, encouraged further by progressive civil society groups applying pressure on key political actors to remain engaged and not to jettison their commitment to employment guarantee.[38] Employment guarantee was part of the manifesto but it did not receive much notice or scrutiny before the election, in part because the possibility of the Congress forming the government seemed so improbable and in part because election promises were rarely implemented, so there was no reason to believe that this particular promise would be any different.[39] However, after the formation of the UPA, the implementation of employment guarantee was an important key item on the government's agenda. The parliamentary standing committee on rural development described the proposed legislation as 'path-breaking' but it faced stiff opposition within and outside the Parliament.[40]

In this context, one development of significance was the creation of the NAC. The EGS was the single-most important issue for the NAC. Its influence was particularly important in the initial stages in getting the scheme off the ground. Later, individual members of the NAC, like Jean Drèze and Aruna Roy, rather than the NAC as a whole, continued to play a useful role in mobilizing party and non-party support for it, especially because the Congress did not mobilize support for it. The NAC was entrusted with the task of preparing the first draft of the NREGA. It proposed a legal guarantee of employment to every household in rural areas for 100 days for undertaking casual labour at the statutory minimum wage. Also, it provided for a phased implementation of the scheme, and the entire country was expected to be covered in five years. From the outset, the scheme was limited only to the rural areas even though the manifesto had stated it would extend to urban areas as well.

After the NAC draft was forwarded to the PMO, the Ministry of Rural Development and the Ministry of Finance were the principal institutions involved in the decision-making process. While there was a political consensus because none of the parties opposed it, the passage of the legislation was far from smooth. Even within the UPA government, individuals as well as institutions such as the Planning Commission and the Ministry of Finance expressed serious reservations about its financial implications. However, the Ministry of Rural Development headed by Raghuvansh Prasad Singh of the Janata Dal, a close ally of the Congress, strongly backed the bill, which in the end proved to be an important bulwark against the conservative opposition from the finance ministry, then headed by Chidambaram, whose central concern was to reduce the financial liability on the central government and to increase executive flexibility around the proposed scheme. They advocated targeting the scheme on 'poor' households, specifying 'productive' works and centrally notified wages to ensure that the schemes were self-selecting, removing the time-bound extension, and allowing the central government to notify the areas where the scheme would begin. However, the basic flaw inherent in the scheme was that by taking the household as the unit, it ignored the claims of all individual adults for employment guarantee, and thereby also implicitly discriminated against women. The rural development advisor to the Planning Commission argued that universalizing the scheme, although consistent with the concept of a guarantee and therefore probably legally required, would spread the resources thinly. It would repeat the experience of previous rural employment programmes where better-administrated states (with less poverty and unemployment) captured a disproportionate share of the funds.[41]

PRESSURES AND PROBLEMS

The employment guarantee proposal raised a passionate debate on the feasibility of such a constitutionally enforced right. Opinions varied, from outright rejection as a populist measure to it being hailed as the most significant step towards poverty alleviation in post-Independence India. Denounced as an 'expensive gravy train' by the corporate sector and corporate-controlled media, it aroused fierce opposition, first in the name of resource constraint, and later, when the Planning Commission stated that the total expenditure for running such a scheme would be no more than Rs 25,000 crores annually, which is not more than 1 per cent of the GDP, in the name of administrative difficulties. The hostility was not because of the scarcity of resources, but to the very idea of guaranteed employment and state activism in matters of employment and relief for the people.[42]

In this environment of scepticism, the Congress–Left alliance was a significant factor facilitating the enactment of the NREGA. Basically, it enabled the UPA to surmount the opposition within the government and outside. Not surprisingly, once it was passed, both the Congress and Left parties claimed credit for the historic legislation. According to Left leaders the two major legislations, the NREGA and the Tribal Forest Rights Act, would not have come about in their present form without the CPI (M)'s intervention.[43] They insisted that they ensured the passage of NREGA as the Congress would not have gone ahead with it unless pushed by the Left.[44] On the other hand, the prime minister and Jairam Ramesh and Aiyar, who were among its strongest proponents, asserted that the NREGA was very much a Congress idea and an essential part of its election manifesto and campaign. In his AICC speech, the prime minister maintained that 'the credit for enacting this historic legislation goes to the Congress party alone and no one else'.[45] Likewise, the Congress president underlined the point that Congress governments over the years had introduced employment programmes in the states. The EGS, therefore, built upon all these past initiatives.

Politicians, activists, and policymakers acknowledged that Sonia Gandhi's role was decisive; it was her commitment that ensured that the legislation went through. Many activists concede that even without active Left support, the Congress would not have dropped a politically winning idea because of Sonia Gandhi's commitment to it. The NREGA would have happened regardless of the Left support because this was one policy measure that she had made her own. She was determined to push it through and this helped to neutralize the latent and overt opposition within the government.[46] For Sonia Gandhi it was a 'non-negotiable', which became evident in the proceedings of a committee set up by the prime minister to work out the modalities of the scheme. Representing the UPA's position, Jairam Ramesh categorically stated in the meeting of this committee before the bill was introduced in Parliament that 'the NREGA was non-negotiable and that both the Congress high command and the Left parties were agreed on this'. This immediately brought to an end the resistance within the government to the programme.[47]

Even so, the support of the Left parties and progressive groups and was vital at crucial stages of this process, above all in maintaining pressure on the UPA not to backtrack and in pushing the Congress to remain on course. Its major involvement came in the later stages after the bill had been introduced and when it faced rough weather from the ministry of finance and to ensure that there was no dilution of key safeguards: minimum wages and universal entitlement.[48] That being the case, there is a plausible view that the dangers of watering down the legislation without pressure from Left parties in Parliament would have been greater, particularly because the Congress was willing to compromise the integrity of the bill for the short-term gain of passing it.[49]

Before the NREG Bill was introduced in the Parliament, Sonia Gandhi outlined major amendments to make it more efficacious. The amendments suggested included guaranteed employment to anyone who offered to work for the prescribed wage, rather than confining the scheme to those below the poverty line; the guarantee that, once applicable, the Bill must not be open to withdrawal at the government's discretion; the entire financial burden could be borne by the Centre with the states meeting the expenditure on unemployment allowance; and that the panchayats should play a central role in selecting the works as well as in its implementation and monitoring.

NREGA was the largest initiative on job creation in modern history,[50] given that employment as a legally enforceable right has not been granted to citizens of any other country.[51] For the first time, the Act ensures manual employment to all those who demand it in the rural areas with a provision for unemployment allowance in the event of failure to meet the demand for work. Two extreme opinions dominate response to the NREGA however. The UPA government has made exaggerated claims of success whereas the media and conservative opinion in the government and outside it have found fault with its implementation and repeatedly pointed to the corruption it has spawned and the money that has been wasted on its implementation. It took out a full-page government advertisement in newspapers in March 2007 carrying the slogan 'Let Us Make India a Republic of Work', suggesting that the right to employment had opened up huge opportunities of wage work. Such inflated claims notwithstanding, it is a legislative milestone because thanks to the NREGA, employment in public works has risen to unprecedented levels in several states, resulting in a lessening of impoverishment in many rural districts across the country.[52]

The NREGA has had an uneven record of implementation, as numerous evaluations have testified.[53] The Comptroller and Auditor General (CAG) report (2007–8) found that paltry allocations and the central government's reduced financial liability to support wage employment was one of the reasons responsible for its poor implementation.[54] Even though the scope of NREGA was extended substantially in 2007, the financial provision for the scheme was not. The actual budgetary support provided to this scheme was initially not very large and the central government was niggardly in transferring funds to the states. The financial constraints and inflexibilities prevented state governments from accessing central resources in ways that would result in more effective implementation.

Nearly 90 per cent of the funds come from the Centre and the rest from the states.[55] Expenditure capacity fluctuates: 75 per cent of available funds were spent in 2008–9, which was down from 82 per cent in the previous year. This was much below the employment and expenditure levels that would prevail had the Act been implemented in letter and spirit. It must, however, be noted that the doomsday predictions that a legal entitlement would lead to bankruptcy was not borne out. In 2010–11, the government spent Rs 40,000 crores on this programme, and this accounts for over 50 per cent of the total rural development budget.[56] 'Even 1.5 to 2 per cent of the GDP is not a high cost for such an essential programme,' avers Jean Drèze,[57] especially as he points out that the annual 'revenue foregone' on account of tax exemptions, which benefit the corporate sector, is over Rs 5 lakh crores.

NREGA AND VOTES

The Congress made it a point to claim the NREGA as a party initiative to counter the claim of the Left parties that the UPA's pro-poor thrust was due to their pressure to change the direction of economic policy. Its leaders were eager to highlight the importance of these measures in the party's scheme of policies and to point out that it was the result of a progressive emphasis in the strategy and its economic philosophy.[58] To put the party's imprimatur on the scheme, Rahul Gandhi, barely a day after assuming office as a general secretary of the party, led a delegation of office bearers to meet the prime minister and urge him to extend NREGA to all the districts in the country. Soon it was announced that the coverage of NREGA would be extended to all 596 districts (excluding urban districts) in the country by 2008–9. The Congress decision to extend the scheme to the entire country within two years of its enactment was a political decision. By then it was seen as a 'winning idea'.[59]

The budget of 2008–9 reported a quantum leap to Rs 30,000 crores for the NREGA. The Congress pitched for greater central monitoring of the scheme in the wake of opposition-ruled states taking credit for the success of the scheme where it was working and the Congress having to take the flak for its drawbacks. In October 2009, four years after it was introduced, the government decided to rename the rural employment programme after Mahatma Gandhi: Mahatma Gandhi National Rural Employment Guarantee Act (MGNREGA). The prime minister remarked that NREGA had been aptly renamed after the Father of the Nation as he had always held the concept of Gram Swaraj in high esteem. The UPA government prefixed 'Mahatma Gandhi' to NREGA to stop states from claiming the scheme as their own. Opposition-ruled states, however, devised innovative ways of appropriating credit for it by floating their own schemes from NREGA funds under the names of their states for the performance of works allowed under the job scheme like digging ponds and constructing roads and water tanks. However, the party's attitude was somewhat paradoxical. On the one hand, its political leaders claimed NREGA as one of the principal achievements of UPA, the prime minister himself describing it as 'historic and revolutionary'. Launching the massive programme, Manmohan Singh described the event as 'a landmark in our history in removing poverty from the face of the nation'.[60] On the other, the government was doing too little to ensure its proper implementation and the realization of its full potential.

Although scepticism is warranted given India's poor record of implementation of redistributive policies, the NREGA is perhaps the best embodiment of the rights framework. This (universal application, thus the beneficiary self-selects) framework is one that requires state intervention for delivery of public services and holds it accountable to the citizen.[61] The large role of the state, redistributive policies, and grassroots political activism for accountability, are not easy to sustain in the growth-driven policy environment. However, government efforts to restrain these are impeded by the immense popularity of the scheme, evident not just in the UPA's electoral triumph but also by the groundswell of mobilization for the proper implementation of the Act.[62]

The pro-poor tilt of the Congress and more particularly the NREGA was widely credited as being pivotal in returning the UPA to power for a second term. It went a long way in re-establishing the credentials of the Congress as a pro-poor party.[63] This is evident from the following account: 'When asked who she voted for, a woman returning from a polling booth in Allahabad said she voted for the hand. When asked why, she said because you labour through your hand. She believed a workers' party must be behind the hand symbol.'[64] The Congress leveraged NREGA to its advantage as it was seen to be doing something for the poor. The NES conducted by the Centre for the Study of Developing Societies (CSDS) confirmed that beneficiaries were more likely to vote for Congress than non-beneficiaries who were more likely to vote for the BJP.[65] Among beneficiaries of these policies, such as NREGA and the generous debt-waiver scheme, the Congress established a significant electoral advantage, particularly vis-à-vis the BJP.[66] Although NREGA may have been 'too limited to win an election', in terms of the numbers of people who were able to get employment, it was extremely important in sending the signal that 'the government is not only for the rich'.[67] Many in the Congress felt it was a game-changer. The demand to extend it to all districts came from the party because it created a '[feel-] good feeling' overall and persuaded voters that the UPA government had made serious efforts to provide them with a livelihood.[68] The positive support flowing from NREGA raised the prospect of a major shift in electoral politics which can be reshaped by development agendas rather than by identity politics alone.

Despite the gap between policy intention and implementation, it is important to acknowledge the critical role NREGA has played in providing a measure of inclusive growth. It has given people a right to work, to re-establish the dignity of labour, to create labour-intensive infrastructure and assets, and to build the human resource base of the country. NREGA workers across India have registered trade unions to mobilize and fight for their rights and entitlements. For the first time, both the central and state governments moved from a top-down welfare approach to a bottom-up demand-driven rights-based approach, which had the potential of ushering in structural change. Much, however, depends upon the extent to which people will fight for their rights to advance their interests. There is potential in such rights-based mobilization, which is different from traditional mobilization around issues of caste and religion. Most of this mobilization could become the building blocks of broad-based political mobilization beyond identity. Even as we recognize the significance of the central government's interventions, it is important not to overstate the achievements. A basic issue is whether a public-works-type programme is sufficient for an economy as large as India's and whether it can work in an increasingly urban economy. No less important than the NREGA would be policy interventions like greater investment in agriculture and all-round encouragement of the labour-intensive manufacturing sector.

NOTES

1. On some of these arguments, see Zoya Hasan (2006a), 'Bridging the Divide: Indian National Congress and Indian Democracy', *Contemporary South Asia*, vol. 1, no. 15, December, pp. 473–88.

2. Quoted in the Speech of the Chairman, Administrative Reforms Commission, at the national workshop on 'Strengthening the Financial Management Systems for Implementation of the National Rural Employment Guarantee Act', The National Institute of Public Finance and Policy, 19 December 2005. Available at arc.gov.in/speechnre.htm (accessed on 2 January 2012).

3. Part IV of the Indian Constitution, which deals with the Directive Principles of State Policy, enshrines principles that are fundamental in the governance of the country but which are not enforceable by the court. Article 41 provides that the state will 'make effective provision for securing the right to work' and Article 43 provides for such conditions of work that ensure a 'decent standard of life', etc. for the UNRISD project on 'Social Policy in A Development Context', November, UNRISD, Geneva.

4. Jayati Ghosh (2006), 'The Right to Work and Recent Legislation in India', *Social Scientist*, vol. 34, nos 1 and 2, January–February, pp. 88–102, esp. p. 89. Available at indiabudget.nic.in/es2003-04/chapt2004/chap104.pdf.

5. Aseema Sinha (2007), 'Economic Growth and Political Accommodation, *Journal of Democracy*, vol. 18, no. 2, April, pp. 41–54.

6. Ghosh, 'The Right to Work and Recent Legislation in India'.

7. Sheila Bhalla (2010), 'Inclusive Growth? Focus on Employment', Paper presented at 'The Challenge of Employment in India: Lessons from the Work of the NCEUS', The Institute for Human Development, 7–8 May 2010, New Delhi, mimeo.

8. PM's speech at http://pib.nic.in/newsite/erelease.aspx?relid=19870 (accessed on 4 January 2012).

9. P. Sainath, 'The Terror of Neoliberalism: The Largest Waves of Suicides in History', *CounterPunch*, 12 February 2009.

10. Sainath, '16,632 Farmer Suicides in 2007', *The Hindu*, 12 December 2008.

11. Ibid.

12. Utsa Patnaik, 'Neoliberal Roots', *Frontline*, vol. 25, no. 6, 15–28 March 2008.

13. Paromita Shastri, 'Harvest of Misery', *Outlook*, 4 July 2005.

14.   Ibid.

15.   Tata Institute of Social Sciences (TISS) (2005), 'Causes of Farmers Suicides: An Enquiry', 5 March, p. 11. Available at www.vnss-mission.gov.in/htmldocs/ Farmers_suicide_TISS_report.pdf.

16.   Planning Commission Approach Paper, Eleventh Five Year Plan, available at http://planningcommission.nic.in/plans/planrel/apppap_11.pdf (accessed on 4 January 2012).

17.   The JRY came into being by merging two other wage employment schemes, namely, National Rural Employment Programme and Rural Landless Employment Guarantee Programme, on 1 April 1989. The JRY was designed to provide additional gainful employment in rural areas and also aimed at strengthening rural infrastructure. The Pradhan Mantri Rozgar Yojana was launched on 2 October 1993. Its objective was to provide employment opportunities to poor and less educated unemployed youth through micro-level self-employment ventures. The government launched the Sampoorna Grameen Rozgar Yojana on 25 September 2001 to provide wage employment in rural areas.

18.   Patnaik, 'The Question of Employment and Livelihoods in Labour Surplus Economies', 2007. Available at www.macroscan.org/spfea/jun07/PDF/ Utsa_Patnaik.pdf (accessed on 2 January 2012).

19.   Bharat Nirman was launched as a time-bound plan for rural infrastructure by the central government in partnership with state governments and panchayati raj institutions.The plan of action entailed infrastructural development in areas like irrigation, rural roads, housing, water supply, electrification, and telecommunications connectivity.

20.   Centre for Budget and Governance Accountability (CBGA) (2009), 'How Did the UPA Spend Our Money: An Assessment of Expenditure Priorities and Resource Mobilisation Efforts by the UPA Government', CBGA, New Delhi. Available at http://www.cbgaindia.org/whats_new/How%20did%20the%20 UPA%20spend%20our%20money.pdf.

21.   President's Address to Parliament, New Delhi, 4 June 2009. Available at presidentofindia.nic.in/sp040609.html (accessed on 1 January 2012).

22.   The short-lived United Front government in 1989 had also floated such a scheme.

23.   Interview with Jean Drèze, Member, NAC, New Delhi, 16 February 2010.

24.   Interview with Nikhil Dey.

25.   Ibid.

26.   Interview with Drèze.

27.   Ian MacAuslan (2008), 'India's National Rural Employment Guarantee Act: A Case Study of How Change Happens', Oxfam. This case study was written as a contribution to *From Poverty to Power: How Active Citizens and Effective States Can Change the World*, Oxfam International. Available at http://www.oxfam. org.uk//resources/downloads/FP2P/FP2P_India_Nat520Rural_employ_gt.

28.   Ibid.

29.   Interview with Sitaram Yechury.

30.   Interview with Dey.

31.   Ibid.

32.   Jason Lakin and N. Ravishankar (2006), 'Working for Votes: The Politics of Employment Guarantee in India', paper presented to the American Political Science Association Meeting, Philadelphia, 31 August–31 September. Available at www.allacademic.com/meta/p151215_index.html.

33.   Ibid.

34.   Ibid.

35.   Editorial, 'India Shines', *Frontline*, vol. 21, no. 11, 22 May–4 June 2004.

36.   MacAuslan, 'India's National Rural Employment Guarantee Act'.

37.   Ibid. Information also drawn from interviews and newspaper accounts of the run up to the enactment of NREGA.

38.   Ibid.

39.   Ibid.

40.   Interview with N.C. Saxena, Member, NAC, 9 November 2009.

41.   Interview with Rohini Nayyar, Advisor, Planning Commission, New Delhi, 19 July 2010.

42.   Prabhat Patnaik, 'The UPA Regime and Economic Policy', *Macroscan*, 31 March 2005. Available at www.cpim.org/marxist/200404_upa_eco_pol.doc (accessed on 16 January 2010).

43.   Interview with Brinda Karat.

44.   'Left Ensured Passage of NREGA: Karat', *The Hindu*, 15 August 2009.

45.   Prime minister's speech at the AICC session, 17 November 2007. Available at pmindia.nic.in/speeches.htm (accessed on 17 November 2010).

46.   Interview with Drèze.

47.   Interview with Abhijit Sen, 23 July 2010.

48.   Interview with Yechury.

49.   Statement of Prakash Karat, General Secretary, CPI (M), *The Hindu*, 15 August 2009.

50.   Statistical evidence is available on the NREGA website launched by the Ministry of Rural Development (www.nrega.nic.in).

51.   Paranjoy Guha-Thakurta (2009), 'NREGA', *Caravan*, vol. 2, no. 3, March.

52.   Nirmala Lakshman, 'Employment Guarantee: Signs of Transformation', *The Hindu*, 11 May 2006.

53.   See, for example, Institute of Manpower Management (2009). *All India Report on Evaluation of NREGA: A Survey of Twenty Districts*, New Delhi, June. Available at www.indiaenvironmentportal.org.in/reports.../all-India-report-evaluation-nrega-survey-twenty-districts.

54.   See 'Performance Audit of Implementation of National Rural Employment Guarantee Act (NREGA)', in *Performance Audit Report No. XXXXII*, 2008. Available at http://www.icisa.cag.gov.in/performance%20audit/Performance%20

Audit%20Reports/Performance%20Audit%20%20Report%20on%20
National%20Rural%20Employment%20Guarantee%20Act/introduction.pdf
(accessed on 7 January 2012).

55. Ibid.

56. In 2010–11, of the Rs 79,387 crore allocation for rural development,
Rs 40,100 crores went to MGNREGA. Accountability Initiative, Budget
Briefs, Rural Development, Government of India, Centre for Policy Research,
New Delhi, 2011.

57. Drèze, 'The Task of Making the PDS Work', *The Hindu*, 8 July 2010.

58. Siddhartha Varadarajan, 'Political Logic of Budget is that Welfarism Pays',
The Hindu, 7 July 2009.

59. Interview with Drèze.

60. K. Venkateshwarlu, 'National Rural Employment Guarantee Act in Place',
The Hindu, 3 February 2006.

61. The NREGA did not have a provision to pay wages in accordance with
the provisions of the Minimum Wages Act. The central government did not
fix NREGA wages at the statutory minimum fixed in each state even though
the chairperson of the NAC wrote to the prime minister with this proposal,
which in effect means that the government decided to violate its own law in the
implementation of its own flagship programme. Instead, the central government
in January 2011 decided to index the wage rate to the Consumer Prices Index
for Agricultural Labourers (CPIA). This decision was announced within days of
Prime Minister Manmohan Singh making it clear that the government cannot
set the NREGA wages at a statutory minimum in each state. The daily wage
rate in various states would be revised over the base rate frozen at Rs 100 in
April 2009. Editorial, 'A Half Step', *Economic and Political Weekly*, vol. XLVI,
no. 3, 15–21 January 2011.

62. Ruchi Gupta (2011a), 'Democracy and the Politics around NREGA',
Kafila, 10 January, Available at kafila.org/2011/.../10/democracy-and-the-
politics-around-nrega-ruchi-gupta.

63. Sainath, 'Welfarist Policies Won the Elections for Parties in India', *One
World South Asia*, 16 June 2009. Available at http://southasia.oneworld.net/
opinioncomment/welfarist-policies-won-the-elections-for-parties-in-india
(accessed on 20 November 2010).

64. Drèze related this story in the interview on 16 February 2010. Palm of
the hand is the election symbol of the Congress party.

65. National Election Study, 'How India Voted', Report of the NES 2009,
The Hindu, 24 May 2009.

66. Ibid.

67. Interview with Sen, 23 July 2010.

68. Ibid.

7   Co-opting the Minorities

The UPA government, formed after one of the worst incidents of mass communal violence in Independent India, the 2002 Gujarat riots, promised an overall revival of secular and inclusive politics. More concretely, it promised an end to the kind of violence witnessed in Gujarat by tabling the Communal Violence (Prevention, Control and Rehabilitation of Victims) Bill in the Parliament. Second, more significantly, the Congress party's manifesto vowed to do something about the development of minorities by promising to establish a committee to examine the socio-economic conditions of Muslims. This was in response to a pervasive feeling that deprivation in India was widespread and was not confined to a single community or group, and yet official discourse had revolved essentially around caste-based discrimination, by implication leaving unaddressed many other critical areas of deprivation and discrimination.

MINORITY DISCOURSE

Nehru sought to create a secular state which would respect all religions equally and also prevent violence against minorities. Political secularism was one of the principal pillars of the liberal democratic state in India. Secularism was not an option but an absolute necessity in the context of India's extraordinary diversity and pluralism. This alone can provide a climate for equal rights for all citizens, regardless of religion, ethnicity, or culture. Nehruvian secularism, for all its flaws, was an integral part of an effort to build a plural conception of nationhood in extremely difficult political circumstances. Even in the face of pressures from the Hindu right, Nehru never countenanced a political role for religion because that would jeopardize national integrity. The great triumph of the Congress in this regard was that every political party now claims to be secular. The secular consensus held dominant sway over public life well beyond the Nehru era, facing a serious challenge only in the late 1980s. The breakdown of the Nehruvian consensus paved the way for the emergence of the BJP's brand of majoritarian politics. The original concept of India as a nation based on civic rather than ethnic identity was sharply undermined as increasing numbers of middle-class Hindus bought into the idea that the Hindu majority has been denied its due dominance of the public sphere.[1] As India's political landscape fractured with the rise of political parties based on religion, caste, and region, the Congress went into a long decline, and with that Muslims lost their cover because the Congress majority fell to an upsurge of Hindu nationalism. While the BJP and the Sangh Parivar appeared to be determined to mount a challenge to the secular and democratic orientation of the state, 'the failure of the Congress to grasp the true import of this contributed in large measure to the increasing alienation of the minority communities'.[2] The rise of majoritarianism represented a formidable challenge because the target of its ire was the secular national ethos. What gave Hindutva its cutting edge was the sustained campaign against secularism and its unrelenting attacks on minority rights, arguing that it amounted to an appeasement of the minorities, especially Muslims.[3]

However, the 2004 parliamentary elections, which saw the defeat of the NDA, were a pointer to the limits of the reach of the Hindutva campaign. What appeared to be tripping up the Congress in the recent past was its failure to sharply demarcate itself in opposition to the BJP's position. Following the violence against Muslims in Gujarat in 2002, the Congress response was surprisingly muted. After the defeat in the Gujarat and Madhya Pradesh state elections, the party recognized that there was a need to radically recast its political approach (see Chapter 3). The flirtation with majoritarianism had proved a debilitating experience for the nation as a whole, and in particular the Congress which paid high political and electoral costs for dabbling in it. Moreover, as we have noted earlier, the Gujarat factor was an important reason behind the NDA's dramatic defeat. The most striking aspect of this electoral turnaround 'and one with far-reaching implications was the shattering of the myth assiduously promoted by Hindu nationalists that their campaign for a Hindu India was conquering more and more political ground'.[4] By contrast, the Congress's renewed emphasis on secular governance and cultural pluralism helped the party to recover its reputation as the protector of minorities, which had suffered since the demolition of the

Babri Masjid when, feeling betrayed, Muslims began voting for regional parties rather than the Congress. This trend was reversed and they began returning to the Congress fold in 2004.

After coming to power in May 2004, the UPA launched a changed policy discourse on minorities with an emphasis on the idea of promoting diversity and pluralism in public institutions. This led to questioning the basic distinction between the cultural rights and social and economic rights of minorities. The experience of the past decades had exposed the fact that formal equality was not sufficient, and that it was important to go beyond it towards substantive equality.[5] Secularism, on which rested the notion of minority rights, though extremely important, did not confront material inequalities. Although the Constitution set out a conception of secular, universal citizenship, it had also sought to accommodate the claims of ascriptively disadvantaged groups. Rather than adopting an identical strategy towards various communities, the state had devised different institutional mechanisms and policies to recognize and address their interests.[6] One thing was clear from the outset: religious communities will not be the subject of state intervention, especially in regard to development, as these groups did not have shared material interests whereas Dalits, regardless of their economic standing, had suffered caste injustice. As far as issues of substantive development were concerned, only SCs and STs were considered relevant for this purpose as they were seen to have faced historical disadvantage and exclusion from the public domain because of the caste system. On the other hand, when it came to minorities, especially Muslims, the historical experience of Partition and the discourse of communalism versus secularism and nationalism versus separatism defined the official approach.[7] Indian Muslims were seen in the national political imagination primarily through the prism of identity politics, with rights articulated chiefly in terms of their right to freedom of religion and cultural and educational rights to establish and administer educational institutions of their choice, and to retain separate personal laws. No specific economic and social policies were designed to target minority communities, in contrast to disadvantaged caste groups who have been the beneficiaries of numerous social policies and measures that seek to promote their social development. The latter were viewed as development subjects with economic deprivation, social exclusion, and political under-representation as their defining characteristics, requiring the state to address these through various kinds of affirmative action.

However, the constitutional and political framework recognized the existence of religious communities, although only for the protection of religious and cultural diversity. There was therefore no serious engagement with the question of the social and material development of minorities until the submission of the *Sachar Committee Report*.[8] The terms of political engagement had been defined by the Congress in the decades immediately after Independence. It set itself up as the chief benefactor of Muslims and defined the parameters of public debate. It defined which interests were important and required protection, and determined the range of acceptable views on issues relevant to minorities.[9] Congress politics targeted minorities through their community membership whereas the government's development policies bypassed them in view of their membership of a religious community. Issues relating to education, health, housing, and employment were rarely ever raised by the Congress and its Muslim interlocutors who found it easier to mobilize the community through identity-related issues. Such a position suited entrenched interests within such Muslim politics as existed. For example, bodies like the All India Muslim Personal Law Board exercised unjustified authority in any discussion of these matters. Most Muslim politicians owed their authority to the Congress rather than to any genuinely substantive links to their communities.[10]

By the time the Congress returned to power in 2004, it was amply clear that the problems of minorities, and Muslims in particular, necessitated going beyond identity politics and the customary allegiance to secularism and pluralism. It demanded a willingness to face up to the implications of giving an excessive emphasis to identity and the concomitant disregard of equal rights and equal access of citizens to the government and the benefits of development. In the long term, the trade-off between two sets of rights had resulted in a weakening rather than an empowerment of the minorities through distributional policies. The minorities were placed at a disadvantage because the state earmarked them for special attention with regard to cultural rights but denied them crucial state support in other vital areas of well being, except the right to set up educational institutions.[11] This began to change in the first decade of the twenty-first century as they were for the first time seen as possible subjects of development in India.

A 'NEW DEAL' FOR MINORITIES

The Congress's altered position on the broader concerns of minorities emerged in the context of debates on widening the notion of discrimination and the exclusion of minorities from development, and also because of the strong support the party and its allies received from Muslims, who had been pressing the Congress to consider religion as a valid ground for beneficiary-oriented policies, in the 2004 parliamentary elections. Indeed, had Muslims not mobilized to an unprecedented degree, the Congress would never have won sufficient seats in those elections to cobble together a ruling coalition. In this regard, Muslims claim a kind of ownership of the UPA regime. The aggregate results from constituencies with differing Muslim vote percentages from the earlier elections indicated a definite decline of Muslim support for the Congress from the 1989 elections until 1998. This anti-Congress propensity had been largely reversed by 2004. The post-poll survey conducted by the CSDS showed that 53 per cent of Muslims voted for the Congress and only 11.2 per cent for the BJP-led alliance, and the bulk of the latter, voted not for the BJP but for its regional allies. According to this survey the party received the highest share of votes among Muslims. Some of this vote went to the regional parties and to the Left parties in Kerala, West Bengal, and Andhra Pradesh. This minority support was crucial for the UPA victory in several states. The Congress and its allies received 79 per cent of the vote in Bihar, 78 per cent in Tamil Nadu, 66 per cent in Assam, 60 per cent in Gujarat, 55 per cent in Karnataka, and 47 per cent in Maharashtra.[12] Therefore, electoral considerations, if not a commitment to secularism, was a powerful incentive to focus on minority concerns. This was an opportune moment for the ruling party to attend to their problems and have them participate more fully in India's progress.

In these circumstances, it was imperative for the Congress government not only to provide security but also to take concrete measures to advance the socio-economic empowerment of Muslims. Sonia Gandhi acknowledged that the 'under-representation in public life and public employment of considerable sections of the Muslim population ought to be a matter of concern in terms of equity and social justice. Differentiations of this kind are unacceptable in a modern society because they retard the overall progress of India itself.'[13] She called for the need 'to move the debate from the general to the specific and direct effort at producing results in a specified time frame' in an effort to make the minorities 'stake-holders in the new India that is emerging'.[14]

This reflected a significant departure, with the Congress beginning to focus on the economic and social development of minorities rather than only identity understood in terms of safeguarding Muslim personal law. The idea of a 'new deal' for minorities was strongly implicit in Manmohan Singh's observation at the chief ministers' conclave in Nainital in August 2006, where he urged the need to improve the understanding of minorities and pay special attention to their enrolment in schools and their participation in employment which is much lower than the state averages.[15]

Post 2004, the political discourse began to consider minorities as relevant for development, especially those sections among them who were socially and economically backward. The UPA government set in motion a large number of specific proposals and schemes for the welfare of minorities and some measures intended primarily for the Muslim minority. In the context of the NDA's shock defeat, the NCMP had acquired an overtly secular dimension. Driven by the socio-political configuration of the ruling coalition, the government promised inclusiveness in policy and development.[16] It was also obvious from the commitments in the NCMP, which included the formation of the Sachar Committee, the National Commission for Religious and Linguistic Minorities, the National Commission for Minority Education, the Prime Minister's 15-Point Programme for Minorities, and the creation of a Ministry of Minority Affairs (MMA). The Prime Minister's 15-Point Programme for Minorities was renamed as Prime Minister's New 15-Point Programme (15-PP) for the Welfare of Minorities to sharply focus action on issues linked to the social, educational, and economic uplift of minorities and provide for outlays in certain schemes to be so earmarked that progress could be monitored.[17]

The creation of the MMA in 2006 was a political step to demonstrate an acceptance of the category of minority for the purpose of policymaking for development. Five years after its formation, the MMA had done very little for minority development. Salman Khurshid, Minister of Minority Affairs under UPA-2, termed it 'powerless and redundant'.[18] He said: 'That unlike most demands-driven Ministries, the MMA lacked real power and could not effectively intervene on behalf of minorities. The Ministry acted mostly as a post-office, forwarding requests and recommendations to Ministries that actually took decisions.'[19] 'Ideally, there should be no MMA as it provides fodder for anti-minority rhetoric. Programmes and schemes for minorities can be handled by line ministries and the respective line departments and ought to be an integral part of various ministries.'[20] The decision to establish an MMA was intended to satisfy the Muslim clamour for a separate ministry devoted to their welfare as there was a widespread sense that line ministries ignore minority issues, or worse, discriminate against them in basic provisioning of public goods. Besides, the Congress could claim political credit for the creation of a separate ministry. But it was clearly a lightweight ministry, lacking institutional and political heft as well as sufficient influence with other ministries and governments to ensure compliance with minority-focused development objectives. Its own capacity weaknesses have meant that rather than devising schemes and guidelines for need-based interventions for minorities, it has taken the easy route of falling back on existing flagship schemes, tying in the success of its own programmes with those of the corresponding programmes. The MMA started in 2006 with five schemes and a budget allocation of Rs 130.89 crores. By 2009, it was running 12 schemes on a budget of Rs 2,600 crores. The MMA's overall allocation was Rs 7,000 crores, which is 0.32 per cent of the Eleventh Plan outlay.[21] Overall, it has made little headway in pushing the minority development agenda with the central and state governments and agencies through capacity building and sensitization, or within the minority communities themselves through outreach programmes.

More significant was the appointment of a Prime Minister's High Level Committee headed by Justice Rajinder Sachar to examine the socio-economic status of Muslims.[22] Belonging to a minority community himself, Manmohan Singh was sympathetic to the idea of setting up such a committee.[23] He recognized that government programmes have not had their desired effect in providing the basic needs of minorities. In effect, there was an implicit admission that Congress opposition to communal politics and violence notwithstanding, the state had over the past six decades or more failed to properly recognize the fact of deprivation and had done very little for the welfare and empowerment of minorities. The party had to recognize that the condition of Muslims was bad and Congress governments, despite all the rhetoric and promises, had failed to ameliorate it.

The *Sachar Committee Report* highlighted the deep deficiencies and deprivation of the Muslim community.[24] The cabinet approved its recommendations and the MMA was designated as the nodal ministry to monitor implementation. The BJP labelled it as another divisive ploy of the Congress in power. It dubbed the very appointment of the Sachar Committee as an act of Muslim appeasement whereas many in the Congress maintained that it had nailed the Hindu right wing propaganda that it pampered Muslims. Even when faced with the facts about Muslims being quite deprived despite the so-called 'appeasement' policies of the Congress, the BJP kept harping on it. Rejecting the *Sachar Committee Report*, its leaders said it would impair harmony and spread hatred in society. Sushma Swaraj said: 'The committee has done much hard work, but it is in a wrong direction. The Committee reflects a pseudo-vision; it is full of biases and prejudices; it would not improve the lot of Muslims.'[25] From the BJP's reaction it became clear that if there is one issue on which Congress could differentiate itself from its leading rival, it was the question of minority welfare. Even so, the Congress did not really push the government to seriously implement the Sachar Committee recommendations.

Muslims, like other deprived groups, faced multiple challenges relating to security, identity, and equity.[26] The Sachar Committee revealed that they lagged behind in every aspect of socio-economic development.[27] Their status in contemporary India was not very different from that of Dalits in the mid-twentieth century, which led to constitutionally mandated affirmative action in their favour. At Independence, Dalits were the most deprived and discriminated community but they have experienced a measure of upward mobility over the past 60 years, thanks to affirmative action. The noteworthy point was that deprivation and disadvantage of Muslims may have increased in contrast to the SCs. If we take 1947 as the baseline, Muslims have suffered downward mobility. They are, in consequence, under-represented in the political, administrative, and security structures of the state. Whichever way we look at it, the *Sachar Committee Report* provides extensive data to bolster the case for government intervention in favour of the development of minorities, though not for treating the Muslim community as an undifferentiated community.

The UPA government's response to the Sachar Committee recommendations has been at best half-hearted, lacking the political will to pioneer bold policies that can overcome structural disadvantages that derive from membership of a minority community. While the government embraced all the recommendations of the Sachar Committee, in implementing them it has placed greater stress on the community-specific programmes than on mainstreaming minority development to enable Muslims to get an equitable share in finance, education, and health services and to bring them within the ambit of income- and poverty-based programmes.[28] Many of the minority-specific initiatives are a rehash of the already existing Prime Minister's 15-PP for the Welfare of Minorities announced in 2005. In addition to minority scholarships, the UPA government rolled out a Multi-Sectoral Development Programme (MSDP) in 90 minority-concentration districts in 2008–9. It is important to note that these districts were not identified on the basis of one single minority, that is, the Muslim minority, but all minorities. This programme was a follow-up to the *Sachar Committee Report's* finding that Muslims are concentrated in locations with poor infrastructural facilities, and therefore the emphasis of government intervention should be infrastructure-related.[29]

The MSDP, based on the area development approach, was directed at improving the overall parameters of minority-concentration districts by topping up the funds of ongoing government schemes and public provisioning rather than those that would specifically target specific deprivations of Muslims. It was intended for the development of the area rather than minorities specifically, and certainly not Muslims alone. Under this approach, it was theoretically possible to raise the district's overall development indicators, while making little impact on that of Muslims.[30] Efforts were initially made by districts and states to propose projects aimed at Muslims under the MSDP but these were later reworked to fit the area-based projects whose benefits would also flow to Muslims and minorities living there.[31] By creating facilities such as a primary health centre in a village with a high concentration of Muslims, or an Industrial Training Institute (ITI) in the district, it was hoped that Muslims too would be able to make use of those facilities. A better way might have been to make blocks, even villages and hamlets, rather than districts, the unit for planning projects.[32] Low budgetary support and poor implementation of the flagship MSDP were further compromised by poor utilization: less than 20 per cent of the funds earmarked for the programme.[33] Importantly, the government did not put in place a proper assessment and monitoring system other than a Planning Commission Steering Committee for this purpose.

The real issue was the UPA government's reluctance to go beyond the area development approach for fear that any minority-specific scheme runs the risk of being challenged in courts whereas the area development programme has not attracted any legal challenge. The UPA time and again argued that minority-specific schemes contravene constitutional provisions which prohibit discrimination on grounds of religion, and therefore risk being struck down by the courts. But it did introduce minority scholarship schemes which have passed the constitutional test and the courts ruled that these do not violate the constitutional principles of equality or affect any of the Fundamental Rights guaranteed to the members of the other communities.[34] Only schemes directed at the entire community or only for a single minority community run the risk of falling foul of the Constitution. Nonetheless, because of these unwarranted fears, a Minority Sub-Plan (MSP) did not find favour with the MMA or the Planning Commission.[35] The proposal for an MSP mooted during the discussions on the Eleventh Plan provoked considerable opposition at various levels of the government, including the Planning Commission. The objection was driven by the argument that a minority sub-plan was unconstitutional because the constitutional status of minorities was different from that of SCs and STs.[36] The same kind of opposition to fiscal priority can be gauged from the controversy provoked by the prime minister's statement at the meeting of the NDC in December 2006. Calling for an India that is 'prosperous and equitable, caring and inclusive', the prime minister said:

I believe our collective priorities are clear: agriculture, irrigation and water resources, health, education, critical investment in rural infrastructure and the essential public investment needs of general infrastructure, along with programmes for the upliftment of SCs/STs, OBCs, minorities and women and children. The component plans for SCs and STs will need to be revitalized. We will have to devise innovative plans to ensure that minorities, particularly the Muslim minority, are empowered to share equitably in the fruits of development.[37]

The BJP and RSS immediately objected to the suggestion of fiscal priority. Condemning the prime minister's statement, L.K. Advani, the Leader of the Opposition, said: 'There are crores in the country below the poverty line, living in miserable conditions. When the prime minister talks about priority of claims I would expect him to say that the first claim on our resources should be of those below the poverty line, particularly the Dalits and tribals and backwards.'[38]

Defending the prime minister, the deputy chairman of the Planning Commission countered that 'the development deficit cannot be swept under the carpet. Inclusiveness, which is the theme of the Approach to the Eleventh Plan, does not mean anything if these issues are not taken care of.'[39]

The UPA government could have given a higher priority and greater financial allocations to programmes for disadvantaged sections of minorities but there were very few such schemes, and the few that there were did not receive substantial funds. Apart from under-funding of centrally sponsored programmes for minority development, most issues, such as education, security, and employment, fall under the purview of state governments and much programmes and hand out money depends upon the states and their political will to implement centrally sponsored schemes.[40] The UPA government's basic error lay in making the MMA the nodal agency for implementing the *Sachar Committee Report* recommendations, most of which required mainstreaming and greater inclusion of Muslims in existing government programmes. On the other hand, having made MMA the pivot for the implementation of the programme for minorities, this ministry did not introduce minority-specific initiatives beyond the MSDP and scholarships. What is more, these minority-specific programmes were generally uncoordinated and therefore unlikely to have a significant impact on minorities.

In short, the very government which appointed the Sachar Committee had not shown the political will to implement its recommendations. An Expert Group on Diversity Index had in 2008 recommended the setting up of Diversity Commission and Diversity Implementation Boards as institutional mechanisms for affirmative action and policy targeting.[41] Another Expert Group Report that year suggested the creation of an Equal Opportunity Commission to give shape to the equality jurisprudence of the Constitution and ensure inclusive growth.[42] Neither of these recommendations has been implemented. Even so, the Congress highlighted the minority-specific schemes in its election manifesto and campaigns to gain political mileage.

UNDER-REPRESENTATION AND QUOTAS

The development deficit has been compounded by the inadequate participation of minorities in the governance structures. But if there were a large number of Muslims in the government and legislatures they might be able to articulate and press for such policies. Muslim under-representation in these institutions is well known but it is yet to be squarely faced and consciously reversed. The absence of Muslims in the corridors of power and decision-making is just as stark today as when Nehru first drew attention to it over 55 years ago. As part of its 15-point programme, the UPA had announced that special consideration would be given to the recruitment of minorities in central and state services along with the PSUs. Following this, the Department of Personnel Training (DoPT) issued a circular in January 2007, asking all the ministries to consider minority candidates during recruitments and also asked the secretaries to ensure that the selection committees had at least one minority member. Nonetheless, a review carried out by the government found that the minority community members' figure was a mere 5 per cent of the total direct recruitments made by various ministries during 2007–8.[43]

Better representation of Muslims in government jobs would help in at least getting their voice heard in public institutions. Not much progress has been made in this context as there was a pervasive sense that Muslims, like other disadvantaged groups, were beneficiaries of the reservations regime and therefore their under-representation was either because they cannot qualify for the civil services due to lack of education or because they preferred self-employment. Muslim OBCs were entitled to reservations in the OBC quota in public employment but not many have actually got jobs under these.[44] The Sachar Committee made a strong case for boosting the community's share in jobs and education but it did not recommend separate reservations for Muslims; in fact, the committee was divided down the middle on the issue.[45] One reason for this was that the UPA government appointed the National Commission for Religious and Linguistic Minorities (NCRLM) in 2004 to specifically examine the extension of reservations to minorities and also to the SCs and STs. Reservations did not fall within the purview of the Sachar Committee, and therefore members opposed to reservations rightly argued that it would not be advisable to go beyond the committee's terms of reference.[46] In the end, the Sachar Committee favoured mainstreaming and in this context it recommended 'equitable' distribution of available jobs in the public sector amongst Muslims and 'incentives to the private sector to encourage diversity in the workforce'.[47]

Headed by Justice Ranganath Mishra, the NCRLM was a fulfilment of the Congress election manifesto promise to recommend solutions to resolve the economic and social backwardness of minorities and criteria for defining backwardness among the minorities.[48] The Commission recommended 10 per cent reservation for Muslims and 5 per cent for other minorities in government jobs[49] and favoured an amendment to the presidential order to give SC status to Dalits in all religions.[50] It recommended that there should be no discrimination in the provision of reservations to those who come from the same social background and performed the same occupations as SC Hindus.

The strong evidence of under-representation of Muslims in public institutions and the NCRLM's recommendations bolstered the long-standing demand for reservations.[51] The Congress responded by promising to implement the NCRLM recommendations. The Supreme Court's ruling in March 2010 which permitted the Andhra Pradesh government to provide 4 per cent reservation in jobs and education to 14 backward Muslim groups added to the pressure on the Congress to implement its promise. The interim ruling overturned the decision of a seven-judge Constitution bench of the Andhra Pradesh High Court which had quashed the state government's proposal on the grounds that it was unconstitutional to earmark reservations on a religious basis. This judgement was cited by the votaries of reservation to argue that there were no constitutional hurdles to its implementation. Arjun Singh wanted an early decision by party leadership on the recommendation of the NCRLM on reservation for Muslims and Dalit Christians saying 'we cannot just sleep over it (report)'.[52] To a question on whether the Congress agreed with this remark, party spokesperson Abhishek Singhvi said: 'It is this party and the government, which had initiated the process. So there is no question of disowning. There is no question of sleeping over it.'[53] 'There is a case for reservation for backwards and backwardness is spread across all religions,' he added.

This recharged the debate on reservations for Muslims and gave rise to media speculation that the Congress actually planned to give reservations to Muslims in jobs and education. Upbeat and optimistic statements by Congress leaders from time to time fuelled these hopes, leading many Muslims to believe that there is a clear intention to extend reservation in public employment to the community. It was difficult, if not impossible, to implement Muslim reservation because of opposition to religion-based reservations. Besides the Congress was apprehensive that a Muslim quota would give the BJP a handle to attack the party.

Two weeks before the submission of the *Sachar Committee Report*, Manmohan Singh, while addressing the Annual Conference of State Minorities Commissions on 2 November 2006, encouraged Muslim hopes of reservation when he underlined the need to provide a 'fair and legitimate share for minorities in central and state governments and in the private sector jobs'.[54] The BJP condemned this as nothing but vote-bank politics and minority appeasement. Describing 'fair share of minorities in government' as a 'dangerous doctrine', the BJP spokespersons said that any such move had the potential to divide the nation and that 'the party would fight it tooth and nail'.[55] It categorically rejected the idea of 'fair share' and accused the Congress of 'completely surrendering itself to the politics of minorityism' and lending support to this 'divisive demand either overtly or covertly'.[56] At the party plenary in Hyderabad from 21–3 January 2006, the Congress very firmly condemned 'the view espoused by some narrow minded political parties that policy interventions to address the concerns of minorities, as perceived by them, amounts to minority appeasement. Such a view is devoid of any understanding of the founding principles of our Constitution as, indeed, of the spirit in which the Freedom Movement brought together people of all faiths and communities.'[57]

Notwithstanding such rhetoric, affirmative action, even with a 'creamy layer' condition, would have faced serious hurdles. It was important to remember that despite schemes for disadvantaged minorities having passed the constitutional test, there was opposition to special treatment for them. What's more, there were practical constraints, most notably the Supreme-Court-approved ceiling that quotas cannot exceed 50 per cent, which makes it impossible to go beyond this limit without a constitutional amendment, although Tamil Nadu and Karnataka have reservations far in excess of that and the courts have been unable to curtail it.

One way of implementing NCRLM's recommendation would be to bring socially and educationally backward Muslims under the OBC category with a sub-quota to ensure they receive the benefits of reservation. But the Congress had to mull over the benefits of a sub-quota for Muslim OBCs against the prospect of annoying Hindu OBCs who would be directly affected by it as it would cut into the 27 per cent reserved for them. So, it could act as a double-edged sword in the northern states where it has to compete with caste-based parties for the votes of the deprived sections of society.[58]

The Congress was disinclined to implement the NCRLM's recommendations of extending SC quota facilities to Dalit Muslims and Christians who have been demanding it for decades for fear of a political backlash, claiming that a national consensus is needed on the issue. There was, in fact, an even stronger hostility to the very idea of including non-Hindus in the SC list which for all practical purposes is an extended Hindu category. Even if the Congress was inclined, it would be subject to huge pressure from Dalit MPs cutting across parties who opposed amendment to the presidential order.[59] Upper-caste MPs also opposed it for fear that it would encourage Hindu Dalits to convert to Islam and Christianity. Not surprisingly, the party backtracked on reservations. But on the campaign trail in 2004 and 2009 it was not reluctant, indeed, only too willing, to highlight reservations, notably those in Andhra Pradesh and Karnataka under Congress governments. The reason for this was obvious. Promises of community-specific programmes were an effective way of marshalling Muslim support and garnering political mileage for the party even when the government took refuge under legal constraints to rationalize that minority programmes were legally indefensible.

VIOLENCE AND DISCRIMINATION

The pogrom in Gujarat in early 2002 was a watershed in the history of Independent India. Details of the events which led to the riots in Gujarat at the end of February 2002 are well known. The scale and pattern of violence have been extensively reported in the press and examined by human rights organizations.[60] The National Human Rights Commission's (NHRC) investigation into the violence reported evidence of a complete breakdown of law and order in Gujarat and found irrefutable evidence of the government's unwillingness to control the violence.[61] Violence took the form of well-orchestrated attacks by Hindu militants aided and abetted both by the state security forces and local politicians who encouraged rioters by supplying them with information, weapons, and assurances of legal immunity.[62]

Most of the major cases of mass violence have entailed investigations by numerous commissions of inquiry and civil society groups. The failings of the state administration in dealing with the violence were clear from the reports of the commissions of inquiry. Each has, more or less, drawn the same conclusions: the police failed to act with impartiality;

the top brass rarely acted on its own and almost invariably looked to the political leadership for direction; the miscreants exploited every such delay in action by indulging in looting and arson. In the post-violence phase, from the registration of cases, to the gathering of evidence, to the prosecution of the accused, to the delivery of justice in courts, the judicial process has been allowed to become a casualty to political processes or executive fiat.[63] This was an all too familiar story of the state and its law enforcement agencies failing to deliver justice. Whether it was the industrial disaster in the Union Carbide plant in Bhopal, which killed 4,000 people immediately and several thousand over the years, the 1984 anti-Sikh riots, or the 1992 Ayodhya demolition, 'the state has been unable to punish the perpetrators or adequately compensate victims'.[64]

With the phenomenon of Hindutva receding from the centre of political discourse, it had become possible to rebuild the faith of minority communities in the capacity of the political and judicial system to deliver justice. The Prevention of Terrorism Act (POTA) was repealed.[65] The Congress promised to prevent a Gujarat-type massacre from taking place while it was in the central government, and no major Hindu–Muslim riots occurred during the five years of UPA. Most of this success must be attributed to the state governments which control law and order at the local level.[66] However, the central government too deserves credit for acting decisively on the one or two occasions when it appeared that the state governments were prepared to allow events to take place and there was a high risk that this would lead to large-scale communal violence. After the demolition of the 200-year-old tomb of Sufi saint Hazrat Rasheeduddin Chishti in Vadodara, in Gujarat in April 2006, violence broke out in which two people were murdered and dozens injured.[67] The riots ended quickly because the Congress government at the Centre warned the BJP government in Gujarat that it would impose central rule if the riots were not immediately quelled.[68] The one exception to this was the UPA's inability to prevent episodes of anti-Christian violence, principally in Orissa, but also in Karnataka and some other states. The prime minister described the attacks on Christians in Orissa as a 'shame on the nation' and spoke to the Orissa chief minister to urge him to 'restore normality' but evidently threatened no stronger central action.[69]

Early on in his administration, Manmohan Singh publicly voiced his concern about the Gujarat violence as well as the anti-Sikh riots in 1984 and expressed his determination that an atmosphere should be created wherein such incidents never occur again. The names of the politicians, officials, and policemen who colluded in the pogrom in Gujarat in 2002 are known, however no action has been taken against them. By contrast, within weeks of the Mumbai terrorist attacks in November 2008, the anti-terror law was passed. But seven years after Gujarat, the passage of the promised law to deal with communal violence faced considerable opposition.[70] This is because communal violence or mob violence is not treated as a crime as shocking as terrorism commited through bomb blasts.[71] Muslims convicted in terrorist cases have been punished, and in fact have frequently been given death sentences, while those responsible for violence against Muslims have been let off or not punished at all even though several hundred Muslims have been killed in such violence.[72] Suspects from the minority communities are routinely denied bail, unlike those from the majority community. As a consequence, Muslims have lost faith in the state and its instruments because of the institutional bias that pervades the functioning of public institutions.[73]

SUBSTANTIVE EQUALITY?

An important question was why a political system based on equal rights of citizenship and a political party which depended critically on the minority vote should have failed to deal with minority claims to equality and public goods. More importantly, why has this gap in inequalities persisted despite the dramatic growth and major changes in the economy and polity, especially the 'social revolution' that has brought power to the disadvantaged castes, apparent from the unmistakable change in the social composition of the political elite?[74] This was because certain classes, castes, and communities have a strong hold over the state and have been able to take advantage of opportunities, and given this proximity and participation in government, and blocked opportunities for certain others. The empowerment and advancement of minorities entails sharing the shrinking pool of government jobs and scarce resources among various disadvantaged groups, which can engender conflict and competition.

For a long time, minority development deficit was brushed under the carpet in the name of national unity as any reference to minority deprivation was seen to threaten the social fabric and strengthen communalism. This approach assumed that the best way of serving the interests of minority groups was to focus on the cultural rights of minorities, and their economic improvement would occur under the overall socio-economic development of the country. The Muslim community was preoccupied with identity issues that all too often trump distributive issues. However, the politics of Muslims has changed and is similar to the other disadvantaged groups who have struggled for a greater share in power and governance. The centre of gravity has moved away from traditional elites to more underprivileged sections of the people and their leaders who are comparatively more concerned with the welfare and well-being of their constituents. The demolition of the Babri Masjid brought about a radical change in the orientation and disposition of Muslims producing a shift in political discourse among minorities, which is increasingly in favour of empowerment and a greater willingness to demand their rights as citizens and a due share in governance. Despite an unmistakable sense of hurt and anguish, the tranquil and calm reaction of Muslims everywhere to the majority judgement of the Allahabad High Court in the Ayodhya case in October 2010, which justified the demolition, demonstrates the changed priorities of Muslims who are no longer obsessed by identity politics.[75] The judgement ignored the overtly political nature of the Ramajanmabhoomi movement and yet Muslims did not react to it.[76]

Manmohan Singh demonstrated boldness in setting up the Sachar Committee which was an important intervention in the policy discourse and the established paradigm. In the end, it benefited the Congress because Muslims felt the government was listening to them.[77] Under the UPA, the Congress has doubtless shown greater concern for minority development but it still lacked the political will to translate this recognition into substantive intervention. The big three leaders—Sonia Gandhi, Manmohan Singh, and Rahul Gandhi—have, since the submission of the *Sachar Committee Report*, hardly ever mentioned it or the development deficit it exposed presumably because these were 'contentious' issues.[78] All three have avoided engaging with these so-called controversial issues, as a result of which the party hasn't quite come to grips with what needs to be done on the Sachar Committee recommendations.[79] Not surprisingly, the discussion in the Congress does not go very far because of the reluctance of top leaders to take on board these issues. While Muslim leaders obviously hesitate to push the issue, most of the other leaders take recourse to the fear of backlash which puts a stop to any discussion.[80] As a consequence, the Congress can take the issue only up to a point, largely to win minority support, and then push the broader agenda of inclusive growth to tackle problems of under-representation.

This is because the Congress does not want to be seen to be adhering to a Muslim-centric approach, which is quite logical. Even secular leaders worry about the political costs of minority-specific, and even more about Muslim-specific, measures which, they fear, will provoke a political reaction, especially from the BJP. As a party, it is visibly wary of the BJP which is hostile to minority schemes and puts the Congress on the defensive by accusing it of vote bank politics. This defensiveness stems from the assumption that the BJP represents all Hindus and so if the BJP is critical, then it must signal 'Hindu unhappiness', which the Congress can ill-afford. The party therefore feels it has to tread carefully for fear that its actions can lend credibility to the BJP's allegations of minority appeasement.

As for voters, while they are not opposed to minority development, it ranks low in their order of priorities. Of all the groups, the middle classes are generally not in favour of minority-specific measures and would not be keen to support such initiatives. This has an impact on the Congress as it has to bear this in mind and not get overly focused on minority issues at the expense of overall development and majority community concerns. Moreover, it can take Muslims for granted as they can be expected to vote against the BJP, but it cannot do the same with regard to the majority community. This delicate balancing between the concerns of the majority and minority communities accounts for the equivocation during the Ayodhya movement and the inaction on the *Sachar Committee Report*. Ramachandra Guha aptly sums up the problem: 'The Congress seeks to exploit the Muslims politically. 'The BJP chooses to demonize them ideologically (but also with a political purpose). The Congress wishes to take care of the (sometimes spurious) religious and cultural needs of Muslims, rather than advance their real, tangible, economic and material interests. The BJP denies that they have any needs or interests at all.'[81]

Striking a balance between secularism and plurality in a way that gives Muslims what is due to them as equal citizens has proved to be an enormous challenge for the Congress and India's democracy as a whole. While considerable effort has been expended on redressing caste injustice, there is a persisting reluctance to compensate for the minority development deficit. Congress leadership can take up social justice for Dalits and OBCs as there is a national consensus on the subject. The Lok Sabha approved 27 per cent reservation for OBCs in central educational institutions by a voice vote, which means that there was such unanimity that there was no need for a formal vote. The UPA government did not need a special commission to recommend this; they just went ahead and did it. In the case of Muslims, for reasons explored earlier, the Congress seems to be unwilling to substantially mainstream minority development within existing development programmes. Also, again for political reasons, the party is not inclined to spend serious money on minority-specific measures and is even less inclined to devise special plans or take affirmative action in education and jobs.

Thanks to the focus on inclusive politics and growth, public debate has opened up to issues regarding the multiple axes of discrimination in contemporary India as well as the measures necessary to remedy this.[82] The big shift lies in broadening the concept of equality to take into account the multiple grounds of discrimination. The institutional response, though limited, has focused attention on the deprivation and development of Muslims with an acknowledgement that a minority development deficit exists. This recognition has set in motion the process of taking the minority question out of the nationalism–communalism problematic of the past.

NOTES

1. Malini Parthasarathy, 'Manufacturing Hatred: Bombay Attacks Show Up India's Growing Divide', *The New York Times*, 3 September 2003.

2. Parthasarathy, 'Reinvigorate Secular Nationalism', *The Hindu*, 25 September 2008.

3. This contravened the very idea of equality: of equal respect for religions and equality of citizenship in a democracy. For a discussion of this interconnection, see Sumit Sarkar (2001), 'Indian Democracy: The Historical Inheritance', in Atul Kohli (ed.), *The Success of India's Democracy*, Cambridge University Press, Cambridge, pp. 23–46.

4. Parthasarathy (2005), 'Constructing a False Reality', *Seminar*, no. 545, January.

186   CONGRESS AFTER INDIRA

5.   Neera Chandhoke (2010), 'Secularism', in Niraja Gopal Jayal and
Pratap Bhanu Mehta (eds), *The Oxford Companion to Politics in India*, Oxford
University Press, New Delhi, pp. 333–46, esp. p. 345.

6.   See Zoya Hasan (2009), *Politics of Inclusion: Castes, Minorities, and
Affirmative Action*, 2nd edition, Oxford University Press, New Delhi.

7.   Barbara Metcalf (1995), 'Presidential Address: Too Little and Too Much:
Reflections of the Muslims in the History of India', *Journal of Asian Studies*,
vol. 54, no. 4, November, pp. 951–67.

8.   Government of India (2006a), 'Social, Economic and Educational Status
of the Muslim Community in India: A Report', Prime Minister's High Level
Committee, Cabinet Secretariat, New Delhi. Available at http://minorityaffairs.
gov.in/sites/upload_files/MMA/files/pdfs/sachar_comm.pdf.

9.   See Zoya Hasan and Ritu Menon (2006), *In a Minority: Essays on Muslim
Women in India*, Oxford University Press, New Delhi.

10.   Mushirul Hasan (1998), *Legacy of a Divided Nation: India's Muslims since
Independence*, Oxford University Press, New Delhi.

11.   Rajeev Dhavan (1987), 'Religious Freedom in India', *American Journal of
Comparative Law*, vol. 35, no. 1, Winter, pp. 209–54.

12.   CSDS/Lokniti, 'How India Voted: Verdict 2004', post-poll survey, *The
Hindu*, 20 May 2004.

13.   Speech of Sonia Gandhi, chairperson of the UPA, at the inauguration of
the India Islamic Cultural Centre, New Delhi, published in *Congress Sandesh*,
July 2006.

14.   Ibid.

15.   PM's speech reported in *Asian Age*, 25 September 2006.

16.   Saba Naqvi, 'Ghost of an Office', *Outlook*, 17 April 2006.

17.   The Prime Minister's 15-Point Programme covers: (*a*) enhancing opportunities
for education; (*b*) equitable share in economic activities and employment;
(*c*) improving the conditions of living of minorities; and (*d*) prevention and
control of communal riots.

18.   Vidya Subrahmaniam, 'An Opportunity to Redeem Ministry of Minority
Affairs', *The Hindu*, 20 January 2011.

19.   In a 2009 interview to *The Hindu*, Salman Khurshid admitted that 'the
MMA had no major role in the lives of minorities except to award scholarships,
which could have been handled by any other Ministry'. Ibid.

20.   Interview with Abusaleh Shariff, Member-Secretary, Prime Minister's High
Level Committee, New Delhi, 28 October 2010.

21.   Centre for Budget and Governance Accountability (CBGA) (2009), 'How
Did the UPA Spend Our Money?' A report card on the track record of the UPA',
CBGA, New Delhi, 17 February. Available at http://www.cbgaindia.org/files/
budget_responses/Response%20to%20Union%20Budget%202011.pdf.

22.   In March 2005, UPA government appointed a High Level Committee
under the chairmanship of Justice Rajinder Sachar to study the social, educational

and economic status of the Muslim community. A notification issued on 9 March 2005 states that:

As it has been noted that there is lack of authentic information about the social, economic and educational status of the Muslim community of India which comes in the way of planning, formulating and implementing specific interventions, policies and programmes to address the issues relating to the socio-economic backwardness of this community, Government has constituted a High level Committee to prepare a comprehensive report covering these aspects.

Members of the Committee: Justice Rajinder Sachar was appointed Chairperson and Syed Hamid, T.K. Oommen, M.A. Basith, Rakesh Basant, and Akhtar Majeed were members while Abusaleh Shariff was Member Secretary. Notification No. 850/3/C/3/05-Pol. Prime Minister's Office, dated 9 March 2005, P.V., *Sachar Committee Report*.

23. Interview with T.K. Oommen, Member, Prime Minister's High Level Committee, 20 October 2010.

24. Government of India, 'Social, Economic and Educational Status of the Muslim Community in India'. Prime Minister's High Level Committee, also referred to as Sachar Committee, submitted its report to the Prime Minister on 17 November 2006. Henceforth referred to as *Sachar Committee Report*.

25. 'Panel Right on Empowerment, Wrong on Bengal, Says Left', *The Indian Express*, 1 December 2006.

26. Government of India, 'Social, Economic and Educational Status of the Muslim Community in India'.

27. The Sachar Committee used data from the Census of India, National Sample Surveys, and data from banking and financial institutions, government commissions, ministries, public sector undertakings, universities, and so on. For details on data used by the Sachar Committee, see Government of India, 'Social, Economic and Educational Status of the Muslim Community in India', pp. 5–6.

28. The UPA government focused on minority-specific programmes such as madarsa modernization even though the *Sachar Committee Report* figures show that only 4 per cent Muslims go to madarsas.

29. The MSDP is a centrally sponsored development programme for 90 minority-concentration districts, 338 Class 1 towns, and 1,228 blocks where minority population is 25 per cent or more of the population. For more details, see http://www.minorityaffairs.gov.in/msdp (accessed on 28 May 2011).

30. Centre of Equity Studies (CES) (2011), *Promises to Keep: Investigating Government's Response to the Sachar Committee Recommendations*, Study Report, New Delhi, August. Available at www.scribd.com/doc/52913174/sachar-final.

31. The total allocation for the MSDP was Rs 3,780 crores, but the reported expenditure undertaken by the states until mid-2011 was a mere Rs 940 crores. MMA, Government of India Empowered Committee meeting minutes, and extracts of select minutes of the empowered committee. Cited in CES, *Promises to Keep*.

32. Ibid.

33. Shariff, 'Muslims: The Lamb's Share', *Outlook*, 23 August 2010.

34. Four petitions in the Bombay, Gujarat, and Delhi high courts questioned the Merit-cum-Means Scholarship scheme for students of minority communities on the ground that it discriminates against students belonging to the majority community only on the ground of religion, and hence it was unconstitutional. The minority scholarship schemes passed the constitutional test. The Bombay High Court judgement (2010) affirmed that these schemes were not constitutionally invalid and had no adverse impact on students of majority community. It held that the funds used to minimize inequalities among minority communities by adopting various social and welfare activities would in no way violate the constitutional principles of equality or affect any of the Fundamental Rights guaranteed to the members of the other communities. WP (PIL) No. 84/2008 *Sanjiv Gajanan Punalekar vs Union of India* and WP (PIL) 254/2009 in the High Court of the Judicature at Bombay. This view was also supported by the decision of Gujarat High Court in *Vijay Harischandra Patel vs the Union of India* (2009).

35. Government of India (2006b), 'Report of the Working Group on Empowering the Minorities for the Eleventh Five Year Plan (2007–12)', Planning Commission, New Delhi. Available at http://planningcommission.nic.in/aboutus/committee/index.php?about=wrkg2_13.htm.

36. See Hasan, *Politics of Inclusion*, Chapter 6.

37. Prime Minister of India, Press Releases, 10 December 2006, New Delhi, Clarifications on PM's reference to 'First Claim on Resources'. Available at http://www.pmindia.nic.in (accessed on 22 December 2011).

38. 'Advani Demands Withdrawal of PM's Remarks', *Hindustan Times*, 11 December 2006.

39. Ibid.

40. After the creation of MMA, institutional arrangements for the implementation of minority schemes were made by the state governments but the institutional strength and absorptive capacities at the state and district levels are still very weak in many states even today, admitted the MMA. This response was submitted to the NAC on the Study Report of the CES, *Promises to Keep*.

41. Report of the Expert Group on Diversity Index, submitted to the Ministry of Minority Affairs, Government of India, 2008. Available at www.minorityaffairs.gov.in/sites/upload_files/moma/files/.../di_expgrp.pdf (accessed on 7 August 2011).

42. Madhava Menon (2008), *Equal Opportunity Commission: What, Why and How?* Report submitted to MMA, Government of India. Available at www.minorityaffairs.gov.in/sites/upload_files/moma/files/pdfs/eoc_wwh.pdf. The expert group constituted by the MMA recommended that the Equal Opportunity Commission (EOC) will cover all deprived and discriminated groups. In August 2010, the GoM decided that the mandate of the EOC when it is set up would

have to be confined to minorities. This recommendation was made after most ministries shot down the proposal for an EOC with a mandate to cover multiple groups across religious barriers.

43.   Cithara Paul, 'Minorities Got Only 5 Per Cent of the Jobs', *The Indian Express*, 25 June 2008.

44.   Hasan, *Politics of Inclusion*, p. 180.

45.   Interview with Oommen.

46.   Ibid.

47.   Government of India, 'Social, Economic and Educational Status of the Muslim Community in India', p. 252.

48.   Government of India (2007), 'Report of National Commission for Religious and Linguistic Minorities, Ministry of Minority Affairs', New Delhi. Available at http://minorityaffairs.gov.in/newsite/ncrlm/ncrlm.asp.

49.   As an alternative, the NCRLM recommended that out of the 27 per cent OBC quota, 8.4 percent sub quota be marked for minorities of which 6 per cent could be for Muslims. Available at http://minorityaffairs.gov.in/sites/upload_files/MMA/files/pdfs/volume-1.pdf (accessed on 24 August 2011) and favoured an amendment to the presidential order to give SC status to Dalits in all religions.

50.   In 1950, the president issued the Constitution (SC) order specifying who the SCs were. The order states: 'No person who professes a religion different from the Hindu or the Sikh religion shall be deemed to be a member of the SCs.' This order has been amended twice, once in 1956 to include Sikhs and again in 1990 to include the neo-Buddhists. The order of 1950 established state-specific lists which identified castes that fell into these categories. For details on the demand of Dalit Muslims and Christians for inclusion in the SC category and the UPA government's response, see Chapter 8 in Hasan, *Politics of Inclusion*.

51.   For a discussion of the Muslim demand for reservations, see Chapter 6 in ibid., pp. 159–95.

52.   'Don't Sleep over the Ranganath Commission Report: Arjun', *Outlook*, 24 March 2010.

53.   Ibid.

54.   'PM Inaugurates National Conference of State Minorities Commissions', 2 November 2006. Available at http://www.pmindia.nic.in (accessed on 6 February 2010).

55.   Ibid.

56.   Ibid.

57.   'Resolution on Political Affairs', introduction by Arjun Singh. Available at http://aicc.org.in/new/82ndplenary-cong-session-detail-php?id-3 (accessed on 13 August 2011).

58.   On 22 December 2011, the UPA government decided to provide a sub-quota of 4.5 per cent for minorities within the existing 27 per cent reservation for OBCs, a move which came ahead of the Uttar Pradesh Assembly elections in February 2012. The decision paved way for reservation in government jobs and

educational institutions for minorities as defined in section 2 (C) of the National Commission for Minorities Act, 1992 which include Muslims, Sikhs, Christians, Buddhists and Zoroastrians (Parsis). 'UP Polls Ahead, Govt Clears 4.5% Minority Quota within OBC 27%', *The Indian Express*, 23 December 2011.

59.   See Chapter 7 in Hasan, *Politics of Inclusion*, pp. 196–226.

60.   The Gujarat violence has been documented in many reports: *Crime against Humanity: An Inquiry into the Carnage in Gujarat*. Vols I, II, III. *Concerned Citizen's Tribunal: Gujarat 2002*. Available at http://www.sabrang.com/tribunal/tribunal2.pdf (accessed on 25 July 2010); *Genocide in Gujarat: The Sangh Parivar, Narendra Modi, and the Government of Gujarat*, Coalition against Genocide, 2 March 2005. Available at http://coalitionagainst genocide.org (accessed on 30 March 2012); *State-Sponsored Carnage in Gujarat*, March 2002, available at http://www.sacw.net/Gujarat2002/GujCarnage.html; For details of the Gujarat government's response to the riots, see '"We Have No Orders to Save You", State Participation and Complicity in Communal Violence in Gujarat', *Human Rights Watch*, vol. 14, no. 3C (2002). Available at http://coalitionagainst genocide.org/ reports/2002/hrw (accessed on 30 March 2012).

61.   Report on the visit of NHRC team headed by the chairperson, NHRC, to Ahmedabad, Vadodra, and Godhra from 19 to 22 March 2002. Available at http://nhrc.nic.in/whatsnew.htm#gr1 (accessed on 6 January 2012). An excerpt from the preliminary report of the NHRC is available at http://www.sabrang. com/cc/archive/2002/marapril/nhrc.htm (accessed on 6 January 2012).

62.   On this aspect, see cover story 'Communal Fascism in Gujarat: Appeasing the Hindu Right on Ayodhya', *Frontline*, vol. 19, no. 6, 29 March 2002.

63.   See V. Venkatesan, 'For a Fair Trial', *Frontline*, vol. 20, no. 17, 16–29 August 2003; and Sukumar Muralidharan, 'Gujarat: Quest for Justice', *Frontline*, vol. 20, no. 17, 16–29 August 2003.

64.   Editorial, *The Times of India*, 9 June 2010.

65.   The POTA, enacted in June 2002, which the NDA government insisted was the best remedy to deal with terrorist activities in India, was repealed by the UPA. The abolition of POTA was one of the first major policy decisions of UPA after taking office in May 2004. According to the Home Ministry, some 800 people have been arrested and jailed under POTA and 4,000 people were booked under the Act. Background information on repressive laws in India available at www.binayaksen.net/download/indian_repressive_laws.pdf (accessed on 6 January 2012).

66.   Steven Wilkinson (2004), *Votes and Violence: Electoral Competition and Ethnic Riots*, Cambridge University Press, New York.

67.   Dionne Bunsha, 'Killing Zeal', *Frontline*, vol. 23, no. 9, 19 May 2006.

68.   The dispute was over the local city council's decision to demolish a shrine of Sufi saint Hazrat Rasheed Uddin Chishti. The overwhelmingly BJP dominated council voted for its removal, claiming that it was an encroachment and obstructed traffic. See reports in Harsh Mander, 'Wages of Hate', *Hindustan*

Times, 8 May 2006 and Shabnam Hashmi, 'Emboldened in Baroda, Gujarat's Fascists Bask in the Sun', *The Times of India*, Hyderabad, 15 May 2006.

69. 'A Shame on Nation: Manmohan', *The Hindu*, 29 August 2008.

70. The Congress Party's 2004 election manifesto promised that it would enact a comprehensive law on communal violence in all its forms and manifestations, providing for investigations by a central agency, prosecution by special courts, and payment of uniform compensation for loss of life, honour, and property. The Communal Violence (Prevention, Control and Rehabilitation of Victims) Bill proposed by the government in 2005 has undergone changes over a period. The NAC formed a drafting committee headed by the Solicitor General of India, Gopal Subramaniam, to prepare the Communal and Sectarian Violence Bill in August 2010. The bill has been renamed as the Prevention of Communal and Targeted Violence (Access to Justice and Reparations) Bill, 2011. The passage of proposed law has faced considerable opposition both in the government and outside.

71. See Hasan (2006b), 'Mass Violence and the Wheels of Indian (In)Justice', in Amrita Basu and Srirupa Roy (eds), *Violence and Democracy in India*, Seagull Books, Calcutta.

72. Dileep Padgaonkar, 'Blood in Mumbai', *The Washington Post*, 28 November 2008.

73. This was one of the most significant findings of the National Community for Minorities (NCM) visits to violence-affected areas in Gujarat, Maharashtra, Andhra Pradesh, Orissa, and Karnataka in 2006. Report of the National Commission for Minorities' visit to Gujarat, 13–17 October 2006. Available at http://www.cjponline.org/gujaratTrials/statecomp/pdf%20files/pdfs/2006%20 october%20reprt%20of%20the%20NCM.pdf (accessed on 5 August 2009).

74. See Christophe Jaffrelot (2009b), 'Introduction', in Christophe Jaffrelot and Sanjay Kumar (eds), *Rise of the Plebians: The Changing Face of Indian Legislative Assemblies*, Routledge, New Delhi.

75. The use of faith as a legitimate argument for awarding the space under the central dome of the Babri Masjid (where the idols of Ram Lalla are placed) to the Hindu plaintiffs by the high court discomfited not just jurists and constitutional experts but also a broad swathe of citizenry who had reason to question the prioritization of faith over fact. There are three obvious problems with the Allahabad High Court judgement. The first was the obliteration of the distinction between fact and faith; the second was the distinction between negotiation and adjudication; and the third was the acceptance of the demolition of the Babri Masjid as a fait accompli. See Venkitesh Ramakrishnan (2010), 'In the Name of Faith', *Frontline*, vol. 27, no. 21, 9–22 October.

76. T.R. Andhyarujina, 'A Verdict that Legitimizes the Masjid Demolition', *The Hindu*, 5 October 2010.

77. Interview with Arjun Singh, 20 November 2009.

78.   Interview with Digvijay Singh, 19 December 2009.

79.   Digvijay Singh in an interview (19 December 2009) said that he had advised Rahul Gandhi to stay away from three contentious issues: minority character for Jamia Millia Islamia and Aligarh Muslim University; NCRLM recommendation of SC status for Dalit Christians and Muslims; and sub-quota for Muslim OBCs.

80.   Interview with Digvijay Singh, 19 December 2009.

81.   Ramachandra Guha, 'A Triple Tragedy', *The Telegraph*, 25 October 2008.

82.   Tarunabh Khaitan, 'Dealing with Discrimination', *Frontline*, vol. 25, no. 10, 10–23 May 2008.

8   Indo-US Nuclear Deal and Great Power Ambitions

Foreign policy is integral to domestic politics but it has not been a major issue in Indian politics (until the controversy over the Indo-US nuclear deal erupted) largely because voters have more pressing concerns such as livelihood, social security, and governance. The nuclear deal approved by the International Atomic Energy Agency (IAEA) in October 2008 symbolized a turning point in Indo-US relations, very significantly changing the contours of India's foreign policy. This chapter does not purport to discuss the shifts in foreign policy or the strategic partnership with the US. It is principally concerned with the domestic politics of the nuclear deal (rather than the nitty-gritty of the deal itself) in the context of the broader debate over the shifts in Congress politics. It tracks the choices, actions, and tensions within the leadership over prevailing ideologies and policies and belief systems, and the influence of powerful interests and the middle classes in pushing for new policies. In this case, the leitmotif was closer ties with the US, which eventually led to the break up with the Left parties. From this point of view, the parting of ways between the Congress and the Left parties reshaped Congress politics; that is to say, from this point on the party was freed from Left pressure to pursue its own agenda which diverged from that of the Left. The Congress–Left standoff occurred against the background of two distinct ruptures in the internal and external environments: the end of dirigisme (see Chapter 2)[1] and bipolarity after the end of the Cold War which effected a major shift in policy towards the US. In the post-Indira Gandhi, post-liberalization Congress, improvement of Indo-US relations mattered to the leadership but it had to expend considerable political capital to forge closer ties with the US and, above all, to break the deadlock over the nuclear issue.

MANMOHAN SINGH'S DOCTRINE OF ECONOMIC AND FOREIGN POLICY CONVERGENCE WITH THE US

The Indo-US nuclear deal put to test not only the UPA–Left relationship but also the Sonia Gandhi–Manmohan Singh partnership. The pro-US shift in foreign policy, a process accelerated under the UPA, became a key area of contention between the Congress and the Left parties as also, to start with, between the government and the party. The push for this acceleration originated from the US side.[1] The end of the Cold War changed American attitudes to India. Evidence of this was clear in the close attention paid to India by presidents as radically different as Bill Clinton and George W. Bush. Bush, soon after he was inaugurated as the president in January 2001, decided to speed up this process by signalling his willingness to enter into an Indo-US nuclear deal which would effectively rewrite both American domestic and international rules and norms in India's favour, in return for the latter's durable strategic repositioning in relation to the US.[2]

On the Indian side, Manmohan Singh was the greatest advocate of stronger engagement with the US. He gave the utmost priority to building strategic ties with the US, which he believed would advance India's economic, technological, and security interests. The 'Manmohan Singh doctrine',[3] as it has been termed by some commentators, is premised on linking the idea of India's economic resurgence, its 'emergence' as a 'major economic power', to India's place in the world. This idea had come to define foreign policy under the UPA.[4] Following the Manmohan Singh doctrine, the Congress government set about building strong ties with Washington based on close economic and diplomatic cooperation.[5] Singh played a decisive role when India opened up its economy to and he now wanted to promote a paradigm shift in foreign policy as a natural corollary to the economic shift. This was the handiwork of a small group of senior politicians, strategic advisors, and bureaucrats. This process was executive and technocrat-led, and very similar in its modus operandi to the 1991 economic liberalization (see Chapter 2). While some analysts complained that such a major shift in policy lacked a grand vision on the scale of Beijing's 'peaceful rise' doctrine, Sunil Khilnani points out that: 'Formulating a decisive strategy is much more difficult in an open democracy with many different definitions of the national interest. This lack of cohesion was not necessarily a disadvantage.'[6]

Indo-US relations began becoming especially warm from the early 1990s with the growing salience of the economic dimension of foreign policy.[7] The enlargement of Indo-US relations owed its genesis to economic liberalization coupled with the huge market potential it opened up. Middle class professionals, business groups, and the media favoured closer engagement with the US, especially large business enterprises and leading sections of the corporate sector also saw great opportunities coming their way from closer ties with the US. A survey in 2007 by the US-based Pew Research Centre confirms that India's middle classes were more pro-US than those in most other countries; in fact, they were quite strongly inclined towards the US.[8] As many as 71 per cent had a favourable opinion of the US, the highest proportion among the 16 countries surveyed, compared with 54 per cent three years ago.[9]

During this period, there has also been large-scale migration of Indians, especially professionals and the skilled, to the US, and they exert great influence over India's policy towards that country, as indeed US policy towards India.[10] Some of the fastest growing sectors of the economy, such as information technology, have benefited from forging back-office ties with American companies. These sectors were eager to forge a political alliance with the US, a logical step if India were to integrate in the world economy and become a major player on the world stage. Since 1991, Americans began viewing India as a vast emerging market and offering the prospect of providing an avenue for considerable business profits.

In the aftermath of the collapse of the Soviet Union and the US preponderance in a unipolar world, India's priorities changed rapidly. It wanted to be seen as a friend of the US and adjusted itself speedily to the end of the Cold War as well as the strategic consequences of growing integration with the global economy. Policy-makers and the elite were convinced that economic liberalization would work only if US companies invested in India. Sections of the Congress leadership sought to distance the party from traditional foreign policy planks as it began opening up the economy. By the end of the Narasimha Rao government's term, foreign policy had moved on. The prospect of a stronger relationship with the US suggested a radical change for a party that had since the time of Nehru and Indira Gandhi taken pride in the vision of India being a leader of the developing world and had consciously adopted a policy of non-alignment, which clearly indicated its reservations about superpower hegemony.

The India–US partnership had come a long way during the NDA government which had set in motion a process that laid the foundation for a dramatic upswing in the relationship. The decision to go nuclear in May 1998 was a turning point in this process.[11] The NDA's minister of external affairs, Jaswant Singh, and the US deputy secretary of state, Strobe Talbott, held talks that formed the basis of a determined effort to deal with Indo-US divergence over non-proliferation and technology transfers that had been blocked since the nuclear tests of 1974. The problem of fuel shortage for the nuclear plants was aggravated after the 1998 tests.

When the UPA came to power in 2004, it was not expected that the foreign policy trajectory charted out by the Vajpayee government would gather speed. After all, the UPA came to power with the support of the Left parties promising an independent foreign policy bearing in mind its past traditions. This policy would seek to promote multi-polarity in world relations and oppose all attempts at unipolarity. There was much speculation about a return to the doctrine of non-alignment or at least a stronger defence of multilateralism given that there were large numbers of Congress leaders who still believed in it. The Left parties expected the Congress to take corrective steps to reinstate an independent foreign policy that had been jolted by the manifest proximity to the US under the NDA.[12] Very soon they began to be disheartened and criticized Manmohan Singh for continuing the 'pro-US tilt' pursued by the NDA regime.[13] As the UPA government sought to break out of the non-alignment framework with its own discourse of 'national interest',[14] it was keen to take the Indo-US relationship to an unprecedented level, despite the Left's opposition and the unease of many Congress members.[15]

Important steps taken by the UPA government brought the ruling elites of Washington and New Delhi closer together. India voted with the US against Iran at the IAEA in September 2005 although it could have got away with an abstention. 'India's decision was an internal one,' but it was intended 'to placate the US'.[16] Again India voted for a Western-sponsored resolution in November 2005 for a referral of Iran's nuclear programme to the UN Security Council for minor breaches of IAEA rules, and once again the government showed a willingness to consider the American demand not to proceed with the Iran–Pakistan–India gas pipeline.[17] It was a significant move away from past traditions as the Congress and its nationalist leadership had virtually invented non-alignment and an independent foreign policy. It is apparent that repeated support for US actions on Iran was one of the conditions of India's nuclear deal with the US, which was given the final seal of approval by President Bush during the July 2005 visit of the Prime Minister Manmohan Singh to Washington. The strategic relationship was the rationale for the Indo-US nuclear deal and defence cooperation framework.[18]

INDO-US NUCLEAR DEAL AND THE STRATEGIC PARTNERSHIP

The Indo-US strategic partnership faced considerable opposition from the Left parties. The conflict began when the UPA government signed the New Framework for the US–India Defence Relationship with the US in July 2005, thus extending the 'Next Steps in Strategic Partnership' signed earlier in 2001 by the NDA government. The US-India Defence Relationship commits India to a wide range of military ties, and was surprisingly subjected to far less scrutiny and criticism than the Indo-US nuclear deal. This entails collaborative multinational operations, strengthening military capabilities to promote security, a defence strategy dialogue and intelligence exchanges, and encourages India to buy its military hardware from the US.[19]

The Left parties opposed the defence pact but did not as a consequence withdraw support to the UPA. If there was one issue of principle on which they could have withdrawn support, it was this agreement. Not having withdrawn support on the defence agreement which actually established a strategic partnership, the Left's position was considerably weaker when it eventually decided to cut ties with the UPA. Although it opposed the pact, it perhaps did not want to bring down the government after just a year and may have believed that that through pressure and smart manoeuvring in the Congress–Left coordination committee it might be able to block the continuation of this strategic partnership.

This was followed by the India–US nuclear deal, which would de facto admit India to the nuclear club and would lift restrictions that apply to all outside the club.[20] Manmohan Singh's visit to the US in 2005 laid the grounds for this 'coming out', coinciding with the completion of the Next Steps in Strategic Partnership (NSSP) initiative launched in January 2004. The joint statement on 13 January 2004 set out the broad contours of the

US–India nuclear energy cooperation in future.[21] From July 2005, both India and the US agreed to a number of initiatives required under the joint statement.[22] Five rounds of negotiations culminated in the India–US Civil Nuclear Cooperation Initiative: Bilateral Agreement on Peaceful Nuclear Cooperation, known as the '123 Agreement', in July 2007.[23] Under this ambitious plan, India agreed to effect a separation between its civil and military nuclear facilities and place all its civil nuclear facilities under IAEA safeguards and, in exchange, the US agreed to work towards full civil nuclear cooperation with India. It would make India a recognized member of the nuclear club, a closed circle of nations circumscribed by the Nuclear Non-Proliferation Treaty (NPT), which India has refused to sign. The agreement, as Foreign Secretary Shiv Shankar Menon put it, 'is the first step in dismantling the technology denial regime', and 'transform its [India's] relationship with the US from one of sanctions to a strategic partnership'.[24] It was regarded as a breakthrough because it would enable India to obtain equipment, technology, and fuel also from countries such as Russia, France, the United Kingdom, and Australia. Its proponents claimed that the end to discriminatory sanctions would open avenues to non-nuclear technologies denied since the 1974 Pokharan tests and also the import of nuclear materials for civilian programme regarded as indispensable for energy security. The technological upgradation entailed would have a multiplier effect. Siddharth Varadarajan described the negotiations which culminated in the nuclear deal as one of those decisive moments in international politics 'when two powers who have been courting each other for some time decide finally to cross the point of no return. The US and India have "come out", so to speak, and the world will never be the same again.'[25]

The nuclear deal was not, however, a stand-alone measure. It was the basis for forging a broader strategic alliance, among other things, to counter China. The US policy was driven by its overriding concern to maintain its global primacy in view of a rapidly rising China. India was viewed in a new light, with the US seeing it as playing a greater role in the coming decades. The US recognized that India's profile would only grow and that a certain amount of friction in the India–China bilateral relationship was inevitable. Both were major powers in Asia with a high likelihood of security competition and conflict between them. Former Foreign Secretary Shyam Saran observed: 'For the US, India can be relied upon to emerge as a counterweight to China. This was the bedrock of the India–US strategic partnership.'[26] Ashley J. Tellis, who was closely involved in the negotiation of the Indo-US civilian nuclear agreement, and whose report on India–US relations formed an important input for the Bush administration's thinking, stated explicitly that allowing India to access US nuclear material and equipment would make New Delhi more likely to help further US strategic goals in the region. '[It] would buttress [India's] potential utility as a hedge against a rising China, encourage it to pursue economic and strategic policies aligned with US interests, and shape its choices in regard to global energy stability.'[27]

The overweening reason for the Bush administration to show a willingness to get the Nuclear Suppliers Group (NSG) to lift restrictions on India was that the strategic and military payoffs were huge. Significantly, the UPA government too did not shy away from projecting the nuclear deal as the cornerstone of a strategic alliance with the US. Later it tried to de-Americanize the deal when it faced massive criticism by saying that it sought to facilitate nuclear cooperation with China, Russia, and France. Energy security was supposedly the prime driver of the nuclear deal, suggesting that nuclear power could be the answer to India's electricity needs in the short or even medium term.[28] It was presented as the panacea to the enormous energy needs of a rapidly growing economy and would reduce oil consumption and power shortages.[29] The prime minister observed that 'no government can afford to shirk the responsibility of ensuring energy security and hope to find favour with the people'.[30] Kapil Sibal, Minister of Science and Technology, claimed that the 'Indo-US nuclear deal is about bijlee [electricity], not about Bush'.[31] All along, the UPA government spokespersons emphasized the agreement's energy benefits, but there was no official document outlining the future energy scenario and making out the case for nuclear energy. Nuclear energy gets a passing mention in the Approach Paper of the Eleventh Plan. This is not surprising as nuclear energy contributed less than 3 per cent of the country's total electricity generation. A. Gopalakrishnan, former chairman of the Atomic Energy Regulatory Board, questioned the government's premise of promoting the deal primarily to enhance the country's energy security.[32]

India's foremost interest was to end its nuclear isolation in order to procure the uranium required by its nuclear reactors and nuclear-processing. Russia was constrained, given the NSG restrictions, from supplying uranium to non-NPT countries. For this, India needed a waiver which only the US could swing at the NSG. The next steps in cooperation between India and the US in the nuclear sphere therefore had to go beyond what had been put in place by the NDA. Indeed, the partnership and cooperation between India and the US were expanded and strengthened by the UPA.

As for the Congress, the nuclear deal was a window of opportunity to pursue the quest for global prestige and establish India as a great power.[33] It was keen to fund a place for India on the global high table. It was part of a larger game plan premised on Washington's offer to help India become a great power in the twenty-first century and by dangling the carrot of endorsing India's bid for a permanent seat in the United Nations Security Council (UNSC), albeit without veto power. Recognition of India as a great power has long been the dream of India's policymakers and elite; achieving it, they believed, would enhance, not limit strategic autonomy. Making a statement in Parliament on 13 August 2007, Manmohan Singh maintained that this agreement with the US will open doors in capitals across the world.[34] For him, ending nuclear isolation and addressing India's energy needs was paramount and could not be sacrificed, and on the way it would open the way for the country's recognition as a global power.

The Congress faced severe problems in selling the nuclear deal to the country, however. The scientific community's criticism proved the most difficult to handle. Influential sections of this community argued that the separation of civilian and military facilities would be difficult and would moreover jeopardize research and development in the nuclear weapons programme and the production facilities required for a nuclear deterrent.[35] They also cautioned the government against putting too much trust in the US in quest of the waiver. This expression of doubt by specialists who were at the cutting edge of nuclear development and who had been directly affected by US sanctions on technology transfer gave rise to a fair degree of scepticism regarding the deal.

The BJP, having been the driving force behind the Indo-US rapprochement, made its displeasure clear from the very outset. It described the nuclear deal as a great and terrible mistake, and one that the UPA government should back out of at the earliest. Taking the national security high ground, the party outlined three areas of concern: its impact on India's nuclear deterrence, the sovereignty of India's foreign policy, and the future independence of its nuclear policy. It reduced the question of independence and sovereignty to a single issue of the right to conduct nuclear tests. L.K. Advani argued that in the name of energy autonomy, the UPA government had surrendered its strategic autonomy and its right to determine the kind of nuclear deterrence India needed based on its own threat perception.[36] The BJP's critique lacked credibility because its own foreign policy was even more closely aligned with the US than the Congress Party's. For the BJP, it was not the nuclear deal or strategic partnership they were opposing but simply the UPA government. They were hostile to it because they wanted the government to fall and anything that could further that goal would have their full support. That is why the BJP's disagreement lacked conviction because, given an opportunity, it would have endorsed the same agreement or even a less favourable one. Pratap Bhanu Mehta appositely remarks that: 'The BJP could not shake off the suspicion that it will sell the store for even less.'[37] The regional parties did not have a strong position on the issue, although the BSP did withdraw support from the UPA in 2008 even before the Left had done so, apparently because of its opposition to the deal. The UPA allies—the NCP, RJD, LJP, and DMK—stood firmly behind the government. The Samajwadi Party made a lot of noise against the deal but in the end it was this party that saved the government by offering the support of its 34 MPs when the Left parties withdrew support. Thanks to some skilful planning, and months of behind-the-scene negotiations, the Samajwadi Party bailed out the Congress.

CONGRESS SUPPORT FOR THE NUCLEAR DEAL

Initially, the Congress was cold to the Indo-US nuclear deal. Most leaders were not alarmed by the defence deal because they felt Manmohan Singh was simply pursuing what Rao had begun. Soon, scepticism ran high with the use of such phrases as 'sell-out' and 'betrayal'. Several leaders railed against what they labelled 'anti–aam aadmi and pro-US policies'. Even before Manmohan Singh had returned after signing the joint statement, there were strong murmurs of dissent. When he addressed the CWC in July 2005, Manmohan Singh faced questions from senior members such as M.L. Fotedar and Ambika Soni.[38]

Former External Affairs Minister Natwar Singh highlights Sonia Gandhi's early misgivings on the issue: Initially, she was not in favour of the deal, he said: 'She reprimanded me for signing the Indo-US Joint Statement. No sooner had the Indian delegation returned after signing the Joint Statement she called me over and upbraided me by saying, "Natwar, what have you gone and done. This deal is not acceptable to most Indians".'[39]

Natwar Singh and Aiyar were two leaders critical of the strategic embrace with the US but the former had to resign from the government on 7 December 2005 because of allegations of kickbacks in the food-for-oil scandal[40] and Aiyar was shifted from the crucial Ministry of Gas and Petroleum to Panchayati Raj on 29 January 2006 because he pushed hard for the Iran–Pakistan–India gas pipeline which the Americans were none too happy about.[41] The point is that the Congress was not enthusiastic about the Indo-US strategic partnership but it did not temper the rush to embrace the US in various spheres, especially military and defence cooperation.

Apart from critics within her own party, Sonia Gandhi was under pressure from the Left parties to reject the deal. She seemed persuaded by their argument that it was not in India's national interest to sign the deal and, what is more, it was against the party's heritage of non-alignment. This impression gained ground because she maintained a studied silence on the matter for several months after the Indo-US Joint Statement (July 2005). At the *Hindustan Times* Summit in October 2007, she said the Left's opposition 'is not unreasonable'.[42] She did not throw her weight behind the deal until late 2007.

Both Sonia Gandhi and Manmohan Singh had appeared reconciled to the postponement of the deal. In October 2007, Manmohan Singh famously said that if the India–US nuclear deal did not go through, he would be disappointed, but that would not be 'the end of life'.[43] This was interpreted as his acceptance that it was not politically feasible to push the deal through in the teeth of the opposition led by the Left parties. It is obvious from subsequent events that he never gave up on the nuclear deal although other UPA leaders indicated that they would not pursue it at the risk of losing the Left's support, and hence the government.

There was no serious discussion on the nuclear deal in any forum of the Congress. The party had not prepared the ground for this radical reorientation in foreign policy to explain the reasons for its espousal of nuclear deal. It did not mount a nationwide public campaign to showcase the nuclear deal as part of a larger change in strategic policy that did not relate only to the US. This put the party on the defensive as it did not sufficiently highlight that similar deals were to be signed with France and Russia, a point that could have balanced out the perception that the Manmohan Singh administration was giving undue emphasis to the relationship with the US. Malini Parthasarathy notes that 'the failure to respond quickly and persuasively to the trenchant public criticism by the Left parties of the Prime Minister's stance on the deal testifies to a continuing structural weakness in the party organisation—the acute lack of communication skills, crucial to any political mobilisation effort'.[44]

The critical moment came when the Congress had to choose between completing the UPA's elected term of five years and ending it prematurely by pursuing the commitment it had made to the Bush administration to operationalize the deal. Most party leaders and other constituents of the UPA did not see much sense in fast tracking the nuclear deal which, they believed, would end up losing both the government and the deal, and hence were dismayed by the readiness to sacrifice the government in order to operationalize the deal with a 'discredited Bush'.

A few months earlier the prime minister had gone public on the nuclear issue in an unusually combative interview with *The Telegraph*.[45] In the interview, Manmohan Singh staunchly defended the deal, attacked its critics, and dared the Left to withdraw support to the UPA.[46] To *The Telegraph*, Singh said: 'I told them it is not possible to renegotiate the deal. It is an honourable deal, the cabinet has approved it, we cannot go back on it. I told them to do whatever they want to do; if they want to withdraw support, so be it.' He defended his efforts on the grounds that support for a strong Indo-US relationship cut across party lines and maintained that public opinion favoured closer engagement.[47]

Thereafter, the media was awash with editorials and commentary urging the UPA to call the Left's bluff even if it resulted in the fall of the government. Much of the commentary emphasized the fact that under India's Constitution the government need not submit treaties to Parliament for approval.[48] *The Economic Times* editorial, entitled 'Time to Call Left's Bluff', began by noting that: 'Both Prime Minister Singh and Congress president Sonia Gandhi have spoken strongly in favour of going ahead with the nuclear deal even at the cost of losing the Left's support. We welcome this attempt to call the Left's bluff on the nuclear deal, which is entirely in India's interest.'[49] The editorial concluded on the note that: 'The Congress has an opportunity to demonstrate its resolve to stand by what is in India's interest. The government must go ahead with the nuclear deal and send a signal that it will not compromise on core issues which further national interests. If the Left withdraws support, so be it. Even if general elections are held a few months ahead of schedule, it is a risk worth taking.[50] In a lead editorial, *The Times of India* on a similar vein strongly urged the UPA to press forward with implementation of the Indo-US nuclear accord: 'Now that the US administration has indicated that it will continue to push for the nuclear deal in the US Congress till January 19—its last day in power—the UPA government can't prevaricate in sync with the Left because timelines are short....'[51]

Not only did Manmohan Singh dare the Left parties to withdraw support, but also envisioned the nuclear deal with the US as the centrepiece of a larger world view and India's place in the world. For him, just as 1991 was a landmark in terms of economic policy, 2007 was another to facilitate India's integration with the rest of the world community and the concomitant gains in terms of access to markets, fuel, and technologies. In 1991, Singh had pursued a liberal–reformist approach which he described as 'enlightened national interest', even as his detractors denounced him for compromising national interest.[52] According to Aiyar, 'Manmohan Singh's exclusivist focus on accelerated growth cannot be sustained unless foreign policy is made the handmaiden of economic policy.'[53]

Despite the prime minister's high-risk manoeuvre, an influential section of the Congress remained apprehensive about the nuclear deal and more generally about the pro-US stance adversely affecting the party's Muslim support base.[54] Muslim participation in protest rallies and marches against George Bush was a matter of concern with party leaders claiming that the foreign policy debate was being 'communalized' because Muslim organizations had demonstrated against Bush when he visited India in 2006. Issuing a sharp rebuff to the protests against Bush's India visit, Sonia Gandhi said that it is indeed sad that some parties have tried to communalize our foreign policy for short-term electoral gains.[55]

Nonetheless, the Congress changed its stance only after the top leadership was convinced that the nuclear deal was unlikely to have much resonance with voters, Muslims included. This assessment proved to be correct as the deal was a non-issue in the 2009 elections. All political parties were guilty of playing the Muslim card, including the Left.[56] The

205 INDO-US NUCLEAR DEAL AND GREAT POWER AMBITIONS

CPI (M) was clearly worried about Muslim opposition to the deal. It cautioned the Samajwadi Party against its decision to bail out the UPA government because it claimed that the majority of Muslims opposed the deal.[57] A CSDS survey which asked a range of questions concerning this and related issues found that there was very little difference in the response of Muslims and non-Muslims to the issue.[58] This became clear from the rejection of the Left parties in the 2009 parliamentary elections in West Bengal and Kerala despite their stout opposition to the Indo-US nuclear deal.

Even though the Congress officially supported Manmohan Singh on the 123 Agreement,[59] only a handful of leaders, such as M. Veerappa Moily and Sibal, were strongly with Manmohan Singh.[60] Mukherjee, Antony, Arjun Singh, and Aiyar were sceptical. Many of them failed to understand the UPA government's hurry to push the deal through. However, the dissenting leaders did not openly question the official line of support on the issue, they opposed the timing, but not the deal as such.[61] Anyway in the end, those in favour of the deal prevailed upon the political leadership to support Manmohan Singh. Sonia Gandhi treaded cautiously as she was averse to any step that might precipitate a crisis in the UPA and result in snapping links with the Left parties on the issue. At the same time, she was 'mindful of the fact that he [Manmohan Singh] enjoys tremendous respect and admiration in Western capitals'.[62] The prime minister's foreign policy team helped in selling the deal, especially its development and energy benefits, to the top leadership.[63] They convinced the core group that the deal was in the national interest, given that it ended India's nuclear isolation and would help to tackle growing economy's energy needs and the severe shortage of fuel across the country's nuclear installations.[64] The top leadership was eventually persuaded by the benefits that would accrue to India in terms of not just technology, fuel supplies, energy, and so on, but, more importantly, also the prestige entry into the nuclear club would bring to India.[65] All in all, Sonia Gandhi appeared to have been convinced that the nuclear deal was beneficial for her party and was satisfied that: 'Our government has entered into this agreement, after tough negotiations. The agreement fulfills all the assurances that the Prime Minister has given repeatedly in Parliament. The objectives of technological self-reliance and national sovereignty have been and will continue to be fully protected. I congratulate our Prime Minister and his team for this accomplishment.'[66] Once she had taken a clear stand in support of the nuclear deal, the party rallied behind Manmohan Singh. It rejected the suggestion that the prime minister and the party president were not upholding an independent foreign policy.

In the final analysis, the support of the Congress was crucial in tilting the scale in favour of the nuclear deal. This can be attributed at least in part to its desire to court the influential middle class constituency and Indian capital which favours greater engagement with the US. More importantly, Manmohan Singh had the support of these sections and the media because he did for the economy what they thought needed to be done. Whilst the strategic relationship with the US may not have been a premeditated strategy to win the support of the elite and middle classes, the Congress's pro-US tilt had the potential to wean them away from the BJP. The Manmohan Singh doctrine of a convergence of the economic and foreign policies of the two countries appealed to the natural predisposition of these classes towards the US, magnified multifold in the post-liberalization period.

LEFT–CONGRESS FACE-OFF AND THE PARTING OF WAYS

The nuclear deal brought to the fore two diametrically opposite perspectives, especially in terms of policy towards the US, one represented by Manmohan Singh and the other by Prakash Karat. The CPI (M) had for long espoused the position that after the collapse of the Soviet Union and given the expansionism of the US under George Bush, the contradiction between the US and developing countries such as India is the primary contradiction of our times. The NCMP acknowledged that the UPA will pursue 'closer engagement and relations with the US' but this can only happen in the context of maintaining 'the independence of India's foreign policy position on all regional and global issues'. The CPI (M) took this to be the core of UPA's commitment to stand by multilateralism in foreign policy. It regarded the subsequent portrayal of the Indo-US strategic partnership as the mainspring of Congress's foreign policy as a complete betrayal of the NCMP. It opposed the one-sided nuclear agreement because it was the centrepiece of the plan to draw India into the US camp, and this will impinge on India's sovereignty and erode India's autonomy in running her nuclear programme, including the freedom to test nuclear weapons.[67] Fears of losing autonomy in foreign policy were countered by the UPA through its repeated assertion that it would maintain an independent foreign policy, but this lacked conviction after the vote against Iran in the IAEA during the run up to the deal. More specifically, the CPI (M) questioned the public justification given for the deal, that it would deal with India's energy needs, arguing that nuclear energy was not going to meet more than 5 per cent to 6 per cent of India's energy requirements. It was unrealistic of the Congress, in a coalition heavily dependent on the Left parties for survival, to have expected them to look the other way when its government waded into such contentious territory as strategic relations with the US.

Conveying his party's disagreement with the deal, Prakash Karat cited the 'widespread opposition' to the agreement and the fact that adequate discussion was not held on the issue before India entered into agreements with the US.[68] It reminded the Congress that the UPA had only come into existence because the Left parties had provided decisive support in view of their commitment to install a secular dispensation at the Centre and despite the fact that of the 61 Left MPs, 54 of them came to the Lok Sabha defeating Congress candidates. It asked the government not to proceed with the next steps towards the operationalization of the deal which has 'adverse consequences for an independent foreign policy, sovereignty, and the economic interests of the people'.[69] In August 2007, the Left had put the government on notice and warned: 'save the deal or the government'.[70] The Left made it clear that its differences with the government were sufficiently serious for it to withdraw support if the UPA went ahead with operationalizing the deal.

The Congress was presented with a difficult choice: risk losing the Left's support and face an early election, or give up on the deal and save the government. Making a tactical retreat, the UPA informed the Left parties in November 2007 that the government would not go ahead with the operationalization of the 123 Agreement before the joint UPA–Left committee arrived at an agreement based on its talks with the IAEA regarding the safeguards agreement.[71] At the same time, the government had clearly refused to put the deal in cold storage and claimed that 'informal negotiations' with the IAEA and the NSG, with whom agreements had to be initialled before the US Congress ratified the deal, would continue while the committee examined it.[72] Manmohan Singh gave an assurance that once the process was over, he would bring it before Parliament and abide by the verdict of the

House.[73] This assurance given at a meeting attended by Manmohan Singh, Sonia Gandhi, Mukherjee, Prakash Karat, and A.B. Bardhan in November 2007 was accepted by the Left leaders present in the meeting. The prime minister was extremely keen that the deal should go through and he was looking for an opportunity to press ahead with the negotiations with the IAEA. In view of these assurances, the Left leaders acceded to the government's request that they be allowed to go to the IAEA although it was obvious that the IAEA accord was a pact created to operationalize the India–US civil nuclear agreement. Against their better judgement 'that finalizing the agreement at the IAEA would put the nuclear deal on autopilot mode',[74] the Left leaders agreed to let the government start negotiations with the IAEA on condition that it would subsequently bring the same back to Parliament.[75] Mukherjee urged them to 'trust' the government because it had so far not taken any steps without their consent.[76] When these leaders gave an assurance Prakash Karat said, 'we thought yes, let them go, talk and come back. They are bringing this to the [UPA–Left nuclear] committee. When we object in the committee, they will not proceed. This is the assurance they gave us in November.'[77] This was, on the other hand, interpreted by the Congress as a green signal and the end of Left's resolute resistance to the deal. The Left parties had offered a window of opportunity which the government quickly grasped. This weakened its hand in the face off as it lost its trump card to delay the clearance of the India-specific safeguards agreement with the IAEA, which could have scuttled the deal.

Faced with the powerful US pressure to speed up the operationalization of the deal, the UPA government approached the IAEA in July 2008 for the India-Specific Safeguards Agreement.[78] The negotiation and the ratification process, its spokesman claimed, could not wait for the next meeting in September 2008 because a change in the composition of the board might imperil the draft agreement. By July 2008, the government was set on clinching the safeguards agreement which it refused to share with the Left leaders despite assurances that the outcome of the talks with the IAEA would be presented to the Congress–Left Coordination Committee before a final decision was taken.[79] In the event, the earlier decision endorsed by the Left parties to send the safeguards agreement to IAEA for its approval was a triumph for Manmohan Singh. The Congress achieved this by going back on its commitment that the outcome of the talks with the IAEA would be discussed in the Coordination Committee, which resulted in the severing of the UPA's link with the Left parties who had sustained it in power for over four years.

The Left parties underestimated Manmohan Singh's determination to push the nuclear deal through. In a high stakes game, the Congress outmanoeuvred the Left because the latter made the error of letting the government go to the IAEA to negotiate a safeguards agreement, confident that the UPA government would come back to them. They did not realize that there would be no way of stopping the government from ratifying the safeguards agreement once they had negotiated it. After the Congress took a strong stand, the Left's calculus crumbled; it found itself stranded between the government and the opposition.

The opponents of the nuclear deal were banking on the conflicting fears and ambitions within the Congress itself and the 'unequal' relationship between the prime minister and the Congress president to presuppose that Sonia Gandhi would exert her influence on Manmohan Singh because his lack of a personal political base reinforced his dependence on her for his political authority.[80] The division of labour between the two leaders led the media to project the impression that the executive was not in charge of the political agenda and the disingenuous perception that the prime minister lacked authority and would not be able to carry the deal through. The Left was banking on the left of centre group in the Congress to save the situation by advising Sonia Gandhi against the dangerous deal.[81] Above all, they misread Sonia Gandhi's position by misjudging her appreciation of the Left's arguments.[82] Her primary concern was not the Indo-US nuclear deal but the continuation of the UPA government under Singh.

Sonia Gandhi repeatedly stressed that there was no question of replacing Manmohan Singh with another leader. Replying to a question whether she had thought of any leader other than Manmohan Singh as prime minister, she emphatically said there had never been a doubt in her mind: 'No, never; absolutely not.'[83] She had made it clear to CPI (M) leaders that any moves to bind the government's negotiating powers on the deal were unacceptable because it would reflect an expression 'of no confidence' in the prime minister and the government's commitment to safeguarding India's national interests.[84] The Left parties, on the other hand, believed that her priority would be to save the alliance with the Left,[85] and she would be inclined to get rid of Singh.

Some Left leaders discerned a shift in her position from 2005 to 2008, pointing out that in the ultimate analysis, Sonia Gandhi supported the nuclear deal because of her intrinsic faith in Manmohan Singh. 'She was convinced that Doctor Saheb cannot sell the country's interest. Whatever decision he takes will be in the national interest. If Doctor Saheb is pushing the nuclear deal, then it must be in India's national interest.'[86] No matter what her stand on the intrinsic merits of the deal, it is clear that 'she had chosen to go along as she had nominated him to be the prime minister'.[87] Moreover, after November 2007, she felt the Left parties were not seriously opposed to the nuclear deal since they had allowed the government go to the IAEA.

The Left parties complained of being double-crossed by the Congress leadership. Asked if the CPI (M) had overestimated the trustworthiness of the Congress, Prakash Karat said: 'It seems like that,' adding, 'We should ask ourselves whether it was a mistake to believe in the word given by the Congress leadership which included the PM.'[88] This blunder was borne out of the miscalculation that the government would automatically fall when and if the Left parties withdrew support. It is also worth noting that the CPI(M) went along with the Congress in a moment of weakness when the Left Front in West Bengal was under attack for its ham-fisted response to the peasant protests in Nandigram.[89]

The Left parties withdrew support from the UPA government in the first week of July 2008, confident that both the deal and the government were 'doomed' without their support.[90] The government did not fall and the nuclear deal went through as the Congress had gone into overdrive trying to muster a majority. The Left parties had clearly not counted on the Samajwadi Party, which was opposed to the Congress and was a trusted ally of the CPI (M) for five years, to betray them and join forces with the Congress to save the Manmohan Singh government. Sonia Gandhi and Mukherjee were clear that on no account would the government be sacrificed. 'Deal is not more important than the government. That was the bottom line.'[91] Conscious of the possibility that the UPA government would be reduced to a minority in the countdown to the general elections of 2009, the party managers reckoned that the only way out of this predicament would be to seek support from another party and ensure the UPA's survival. Remarked Shyam Saran: 'The party went ahead with the deal once the Congress operators convinced the top leadership that the government would not fall. The deal wouldn't have gone through without the assurance that the departure of the Left would be more than made up by the support of the Samajwadi party.'[92]

The prime minister and his aides played a key role in bringing the Samajwadi Party on board, resulting in a political realignment to neutralize the loss of the support of the Left. In the trust vote on 22 July 2008, the UPA received 275 votes from the 541 members of the Lok Sabha. The victory was tainted by allegations of bribery and the manipulated absenteeism of MPs.[93] Three BJP MPs, in an unprecedented spectacle in parliamentary history, emptied two bagfuls of currency notes on the records table of the Lok Sabha, claiming it to be an advance from the Samajwadi Party to abstain from voting. Brushing aside these sleazy transactions, Mukherjee proclaimed that the trust vote was a 'legal, constitutional, and political victory'. US Embassy cables published by *The Hindu* exposed the murky aspect of the vote which was only suspected despite the dramatic display of bundles of currency notes in the Lok Sabha just before the crucial trust vote.[94]

The vote was the culmination of a major public debate and deal-making that divided all the leading institutions involved in the formulation of foreign and national security policy and parties which eventually had to take sides. The nuclear deal was debated in the Lok Sabha in July 2005 and February–March 2006, and then finally during the trust vote in August 2008. Both the Left and the BJP were not satisfied and protested that the UPA government had not made public the separation plan for India's civil and military nuclear facilities. The bruising battle kept the UPA government and its negotiators on their toes, working out the best terms and conditions on the nuclear deal, for instance, by keeping several plants off limits to inspectors.[95] In the end, the nuclear deal did address most of the major concerns the Department of Atomic Energy (DAE) and many critics had raised.[96]

NSG WAIVER AND THE DE FACTO RECOGNITION OF INDIA AS A NUCLEAR STATE

The political, bureaucratic, and security vanguard succeeded in bringing fundamental changes in India's nuclear policy in the face of considerable opposition and the 'biggest political crisis over a foreign policy issue in the nation's history'.[97] Only a technocratic leadership would have been sufficiently audacious to go ahead, without a national consensus and without the support of its critical allies, because it had the backing of the media, the middle classes, and, above all, the business groups, all sectors of society who matter in policymaking in the neo-liberal era.

The India-specific safeguards agreement was initialled by India and the IAEA immediately after the Left parties withdrew support to the government. On 6 September 2008, the NSG, after a 27 hour-long debate, overturned a 34-year-old ban against nuclear trade with India and approved the US–India nuclear trade agreement (the so-called 123 Agreement).[98] For the first time, the major powers agreed to resume nuclear trade with a country that possessed nuclear weapons but had neither signed the NPT nor acceded to any other nuclear restraint or disarmament agreement, including the Comprehensive Test Ban Treaty. The *Economic and Political Weekly* editorial noted that the waiver came about not for arms-control reasons, but because of strong-arm methods.[99] The CPI (M) described the NSG waiver 'a total surrender' and 'it is neither clean nor an unconditional waiver'.[100] On the other hand, Mukherjee declared in the Lok Sabha that the pact marked the end to 34 years of nuclear isolation and technology denial. 'To those who voice an ideological opposition to this pact, I would say once again that we have never compromised on our independent foreign policy. The deal does not in any way affect our strategic autonomy.'[101]

For the Congress, the nuclear deal redefined India's role in the world; it broke the regional chains and ushered its emergence as a major strategic force. [102] This extraordinary agreement was hailed as the arrival of India as a 'global power'.[103] The emergence of the global player was ministered by the US, and this brought India closer to Washington. In the words of Karl Inderfurth: 'After decades of being "estranged democracies", India and the United States entered a new era that can at best be described as "engaged democracies".'[104]

From the standpoint of the Congress, it was a good deal as it did not substantially cap India's nuclear capability. It believed that the NSG waiver and de facto recognition of India as a nuclear state appealed to the middle class, a constituency that was growing as the pace of economic liberalization gathered momentum. Bureaucrats, ex-bureaucrats, the corporate sector, national security elites, the media, and powerful American lobbies were all delighted that the nuclear deal had come through. These groups backed the deal for different reasons, though for domestic lobbies it was opening the way for recognition of India as a great power.[105] The corporate sector's support was the most explicit; it was keen to be allowed into nuclear power generation. The NSG waiver would open the doors for nuclear trade worth $40 billion.[106]

The NSG waiver was not quite as clean and unconditional as officially claimed. The statements of most countries interpreted the waiver as conditional upon India's commitment not to conduct nuclear tests and compliance with IAEA safeguards. Therefore, the significance of the nuclear deal must not be overstated. While it symbolized a recognition of India as a nuclear weapons power, access to advanced civilian nuclear technology remains uncertain and will in any case not seriously lessen its dependence on imported oil and natural gas. Most importantly, the NSG's plenary meeting in June 2011 adopted new guidelines on the transfer of sensitive nuclear technology, which will nullify the 'clean' waiver India received from the cartel in 2008 as far as the import of enrichment and reprocessing (ENR) equipment and technology is concerned.[107] The guidelines will exclude countries which are not signatories to the NPT and do not have a full-scope safeguards agreement allowing international inspections of all their nuclear facilities.[108] This decision targets India alone as it is the only country among the three non-NPT countries that was granted a waiver for nuclear commerce with NSC countries. The 123 Agreement had no reference to the US agreeing to transfer ENR technologies to non-NPT countries and was not part of the deal. This was contrary to Manmohan Singh's assurance to Parliament on 17 August 2006 that 'we will ensure that all restrictions on India have been lifted'.[109] This misconception persisted because this was the only way to sell the deal.

DE-LINKING FROM THE LEFT

The Left's clash with the Congress, most notably with Manmohan Singh, was driven by ideological differences. For the prime minister, the nuclear deal was a standout issue to define his legacy and contribution to the UPA. He believed it was vital to India's national interest and the best opportunity to push through an exceptional arrangement to normalize India's nuclear weapons and build a strategic alliance with the US before the completion of the term of the George Bush administration. For the Congress, a key issue was India's bid for global leadership achieved by his strong advocacy of a strategic alliance with the US. This is partly because the bond between 'nuclear capability and national prestige remains strong in the imagination of the Indian elite.'[110] India is an important global player on a whole range of international issues, which the elite and the middle classes believed would not have been possible without the nuclear deal and the de facto nuclear state status it had conferred.

Not surprisingly, Manmohan Singh considered the Indo-US deal the biggest foreign policy achievement of his government. He risked the survival of his government for a controversial deal which was important largely in symbolic terms as it provided a point of convergence for the strategic interests of the US and India.[111] Even so, India's most 'non-political' prime minister succeeded in the most politically daunting challenge of his career: he carried his party with him on the nuclear deal which redefined foreign and domestic policy. Unfazed by the political costs and domestic fallout of getting into the strategic clutches of the US, Singh decided to take the most consequential decision that any government had made in the realm of foreign policy. Apart from leaving behind an irreversible set of changes in foreign policy, just as he had done with regard to economic policy, he was eager 'to distance the Congress from the Left in a decisive, strategic manner'.[112] He was keen to unshackle the UPA from the constraints imposed by the Left through the NCMP and other means. In his speech to the trust vote (August 2008), Manmohan Singh spoke of two visions of India: UPA's secular vision and BJP's divisive one.[113] Although he never explicitly stated it, he may well have believed that there was a third position espoused by the Left which interfered with that of the Congress. By seeking to influence important sectors of policy-making, the Left parties were trying to create two polarities, Left-wing and Right-wing, that did not suit the politics of the Congress; in fact, in some instances, under Left pressure, it was compelled to take ideological positions it was otherwise loathe to adopt. In a direct attack on Prakash Karat, he said: 'Our friends in the Left should ponder over the company they are forced to keep because of miscalculations by their general secretary.'[114] This new-found confidence gave the Congress a fresh impetus to justify the nuclear deal even at the cost of jeopardizing a future entente with the Left. One Congress general secretary acknowledged this when he said freedom from Left parties was no mean achievement.[115] It was now free to follow its reform agenda and would be able to go all out to fight the Left parties in Kerala and West Bengal.[116] On the whole, the political pressures on the Congress were reduced and this opened up greater space to pursue its own political agenda. The showdown enabled the Congress in casting itself as the traditional custodian of national interest and advancing its version of nuclear nationalism. Furthermore, the Congress–Left alliance did not suit big business and corporate interests in India or the US because of the Left's capacity to influence economic policy and determine the degree of India's engagement with the US. In this context, it is important to remember that for the US,

the nuclear deal was of peripheral interest; what really mattered to Washington was its ability to shape India's strategic choices through military interoperability and acquisitions, and a range of other forms of engagement. The UPA–Left arrangement was the worst possible one from an American point of view because of the Left's ability to calibrate the degree of this engagement.[117]

The Left's disproportionate emphasis on the political dimensions of the nuclear deal and its climb down in the penultimate stages of negotiation quickened the parting of ways between the Congress and them. Undoubtedly, the Left's critique turned the Indo-US nuclear deal into an issue of major importance. The conflict revealed fundamental differences between the Congress and Left positions, which were clearly difficult to reconcile. The Left parties did not take these issues to the people in terms of mass campaigns; rather, it chose to pursue it in terms of opportunistic electoral alliances, such as the ill-advised move to stitch up a Third Front, losing as a result the main thrust of its opposition to the nuclear deal. In the final analysis, it failed to convince people that it was a bad deal.[118] This was in part because, like other political parties, the Left Front focused greater attention on the nuclear deal as the litmus test of national sovereignty than on the disarmament agenda and the government's overstated energy claims. The fallout was the Left's massive losses in the 2009 parliamentary elections and the 2011 assembly elections in West Bengal, which diminished its influence in national politics. As for the Congress, it won the battle against the Left, but lost the struggle to build a 'left-of-centre' UPA.

The passage of the nuclear deal indicated a change in the Congress position from coldness to clear support for the deal together with the strategic partnership with the US. The change in stance marked the emergence of an assertive Congress ready to take vital steps to press forward close ties with the US even though the balance of forces favoured an independent foreign policy. It is worth noting that the Left parties were able to gauge the import of the shift and the resultant standoff which involved a tussle between two world views: that of the 'new Congress', which had veered away from the Nehruvian path of non-alignment, and that represented by the Left parties which insisted on its greater relevance in the world order defined by US unilateralism. The Left's uneasiness with the Congress stand and the subsequent break-up of their alliance brought the Congress government closer to the US. It demonstrated the degree to which it was willing to go to adjust Indian policy to suit American interests and fast track US–India strategic relationship. The nuclear deal's significance, therefore, lies in what it reveals about Congress politics more than anything else— wrapping India more tightly in the embrace of American capital and its geopolitics. The subtext was the transformation of the state from a relatively autonomous Nehruvian state to one based on an integration of economic and foreign policy in keeping with the thrust of economic reforms.

NOTES

1.   See articles and reports by Ashley Tellis, 'The Transforming of U.S.–Indian Relationship and Its Significance for American Interests'. Available at http://npolicy.org/article_file/The_Transforming_US-Indian_Relationship_and_Its_Significance_for_American_Interests.pdf.

2.   Kanti Bajpai (2005), 'Where Are India and the US Heading', *Economic and Political Weekly*, vol. 40, no. 32, pp. 3577–81.

3.   Sanjaya Baru (2009b), 'India and the World: The Economics and Politics of the Manmohan Singh Doctrine in Foreign Policy', Institute of South Asian Studies, no. 53, 14 November, National University of Singapore, Institute of Singapore.

4.   N. Ravi, 'Missing the Wood for the Trees', *The Hindu*, 19 July 2008.

5.   Sunil Khilnani, 'New Delhi's Grand Strategy', *Newsweek*, 17 July 2009. Available at http://www.thedailybeast.com/newsweek/2009/07/17/delhi-s-grand-strategy.html (accessed on 28 December 2011).

6.   Ibid.

7.   C. Raja Mohan (2009), 'The Making of Indian Foreign Policy: The Role of Scholarship and Public Opinion', Institute of South Asian Studies, no. 73, 13 July, National University of Singapore, Institute of Singapore.

8.   Pew Research Center (2005), 'U.S. Image Up Slightly, But Still Negative', Pew Global Attitudes Project, 23 June. Available at http://www.pewglobal.org/2005/06/23/us-image-up-slightly-but-still-negative.

9.   Ibid.

10.   See Robert Hathaway, 'Unfinished Passage: India, Americans and the US Congress', *Washington Quarterly*, Spring 2001, pp. 21–34.

11.   Tellis, 'The Transforming of U.S.–Indian Relationship and Its Significance for American Interests'.

12.   Prakash Karat, interview on Rediff.com, 5 June 2008; Prakash Karat (2007), *Subordinate Ally: The Nuclear Deal and India–US Strategic Relations*, Leftword, New Delhi.

13.   Left statement on expectations of UPA pursuing an independent foreign policy quoted in 'Energy Security Not Assured: Left', *The Hindu*, 10 July 2008.

14.   Siddharth Varadarajan, 'Indian Capital, Foreign Policy', *The Hindu*, 15 August 2007.

15.   Christophe Jaffrelot (2009a), 'The Indo-US Rapprochment: State Driven or Middle Class Driven', *India Quarterly*, vol. 65, no. 1, pp. 1–14.

16.   Interview with Shyam Saran, former foreign secretary, New Delhi, 10 July 2010.

17.   The Left parties castigated the government for voting against Iran at the IAEA. The prime minister's remarks at a press conference in Washington after meeting George Bush in July 2005 that the pipeline project was fraught with risks, and that it will be difficult to find an international consortium to bankroll the costs, was seen by the Left as another example of his capitulation to the US.

18.   Praful Bidwai, 'Nuclear Deal at What Price?' *Frontline*, vol. 23, no. 5, 11–24 March 2006.

19.   Ibid.

20.   For a discussion of the dialogue between the US and India, see Harsh Pant (2011), *The US–India Nuclear Pact: Policy, Process and Great Power Politics*, Oxford University Press, New Delhi.

21.   'Joint Statement on Next Steps in Strategic Partnership'. Available at http://www.outlookindia.com/article.aspx?222620 (accessed on 24 December 2011).

22.   India, for instance, submitted a Nuclear Separation Plan 123 to the US in March 2006; the US Congress then passed the Henry J. Hyde United States–India Peaceful Atomic Energy Cooperation Act in December 2006; and both India and the US released the 123 Agreement on 15 August 2007 that seeks to translate the law into a mutually acceptable bilateral framework.

23.   '123' is named after Section 123 of the US Atomic Energy Act (AEA) which governs international nuclear cooperation by the US.

24.   Seema Sirohi, 'Raised to the Power of N...', *Outlook*, 22 September 2008.

25.   Varadarajan, 'The Truth Behind the Indo-U.S. Nuclear Deal', *The Hindu*, 28 July 2005.

26.   Interview with Saran.

27.   Tellis, 'The Transforming of U.S.– Indian Relationship and Its Significance for American Interests'.

28.   See Anil Kakodkar, 'The Fuel for a Billion Aspiring People and a Trillion Dollar Economy', *The Indian Express*, 21 September 2007. Kakodkar, Chairman of the Atomic Energy Commission, stated in this article that

India has been pursuing its robust three stage nuclear programme designed to maximize the energy potential from its domestic uranium and thorium resources and contribute around 25 per cent share of electricity generation in the country by the year 2050. The objective is to realize the huge energy potential that is realizable from these nuclear energy resources without having to add to the global carbon dioxide burden.

29.   See 'Energy Security Not Assured: Left', *The Hindu*, 10 July.

30.   Venkitesh Ramakrishnan, 'Nuclear Standoff', *Frontline*, vol. 24, no. 17, 25 August–5 September 2007.

31.   See 'Nuclear Deal Vital for Growth: Sibal', *The Hindu*, 30 September 2007.

32.   Quoted in 'Energy Security as a Scapegoat,' *Asian Age*, 13 August 2006.

33.   George Perkovich (2001), 'The Measure of India: What Makes Greatness', *Seminar*, no. 529, September; Stephen Cohen (2001), *Emerging Power: India*, Oxford University Press, New Delhi.

34.   Ramakrishnan, 'Nuclear Standoff'.

35.   Pant (2009), 'The US-India Nuclear Pact Policy: Process and Great Power Politics', *Asian Security*, vol. 5, no. 3, 2009, p. 278.

36.   L.K. Advani's interview published in *The Hindu*, 11 July 2008.

37.   Pratap Bhanu Mehta, 'House This for Clarity?' *The Indian Express*, 1 December 2007.

38.   Harish Khare, 'Team Manmohan at Work, At Last', *The Hindu*, 8 August 2005.

39.   Interview with Natwar Singh, MP Rajya Sabha, Minister for External Affairs, May 2004–December 2005, 20 December 2009.

40.   Natwar Singh, former external affairs minister, and the Congress party were listed in the Volcker Committee report released in October 2005 as non-contractual beneficiaries for procurement of contracts in the Oil-for-Food programme scam during the regime of Saddam Hussein. 'Volcker Report Names Natwar Singh and Congress Party as "beneficiaries"', *The Hindu*, 29 October 2005.

41.   The India cables sent on 30 January 2006 (51088: confidential) by Ambassador David C. Mulford to Washington stated that. 'The January 2006 Cabinet reshuffle, which saw the removal of "contentious and outspoken Iran pipeline advocate" Mani Shankar Aiyar and the appointment of "pro-US" Murli Deora as Petroleum Minister was described by the American Embassy as signifying a "determination to ensure that US/India relations continue to move ahead rapidly".' Suresh Nambath, "Pro-US Cabinet Reshuffle", *The Hindu*, 15 March 2011.

42.   'Dr Revises Diagnosis: If Deal Fails, Life Won't End', *The Indian Express*,

13 October 2007.

43.   'Left Welcomes Manmohan's Remarks', *The Hindu*, 12 October 2007.

44.   Malini Parthasarathy, 'The Congress Party's Last Chance', *The Hindu*, 8 July 2008.

45.   Manini Chatterji, 'Anguished PM to Left: If You Want to Withdraw, So Be It', *The Telegraph*, 11 August 2007.

46.   Ibid. Later in an interaction with women journalists, the prime minister publicly admitted that he would have resigned had the Indo-US nuclear deal not gone through. He said: 'I was quite clear [that] if the Indo-US nuclear deal had not gone through, I would have resigned.' Reported in *Hindustan Times*, 11 April 2010.

47.   Ibid.

48.   Somnath Chatterjee rejected the opposition's demand for a discussion on the Indo-US nuclear deal, saying that Parliament had no competence. Giving his ruling on the notices received under Rules 184 and 193 seeking a discussion on the prime minister's statement of 13 August 2007 regarding the Indo-US nuclear deal, Chatterjee observed that 'It is also well-established that there is no requirement to obtain ratification from Parliament of any treaty or agreement for its operation or enforcement. Thus, Parliament can only discuss any treaty or agreement entered into by the Government, without affecting its finality or enforceability'. 'Parliament Cannot Decide on Treaty or International Agreement: Somnath', *The Hindu*, 18 August 2008.

49.   See 'Time to Call the Left's Bluff', *The Economic Times*, 20 June 2008.

50.   The agreement allows 18 out of the 22 existing reactors and a fast breeder reactor under construction to remain outside the purview of IAEA inspection. The '123 agreement' provides that the US government can exercise its discretion to arrange for such supplies to continue from countries like France, Britain, land Russia. In any event, activation of the penalty will entail compensation. 'Make or Break', Editorial, *The Times of India*, 20 June 2008.

51.   *The Economic Times*, 'Time to Call the Left's Bluff'.

52.   Cited in Vidya Subrahmaniam, 'A Government and a Party in Combat Mode', *The Hindu*, 16 June 2006.

53.   Interview with Aiyar, 13 November 2009.

54.   Interview with Saran.

55.   Text of Sonia Gandhi's letter to party workers in the March issue of *Congress Sandesh*, reported in *The Indian Express*, 29 March 2006.

56.   Varadarajan (2008), 'Playing the Muslim Card on Nuclear Deal', *Economic and Political Weekly*, vol. XLIII, no. 28, 12 July.

57.   'To Warn SP, CPM Plays Religion Card: 'Muslim Majority Opposes Deal'', *The Indian Express*, 24 June 2008.

58.   Yogendra Yadav and Sanjay Kumar (2007), 'In a Mid-Term Poll, Nukes Won't Decide Votes', *The Indian Express*, 10 September.

59.   Purnima S. Tripathi (2008a), 'Restrained Dissent in the Congress',

Frontline, vol. 25, no. 14, 5–18 July.

60.   For a discussion of the advantages of the nuclear deal see Abhishek Singhvi, 'N-deal: Need for Less Fission and More Fusion', *The Times of India*, 11 September 2007.

61.   Ibid.

62.   Khare, 'The Making of a Prime Minister', *The Hindu*, 23 May 2004.

63.   This included India's Ambassador in Washington, Ronen Sen; National Security Adviser M.K. Narayanan; Foreign Secretary Shyam Saran; and Atomic Energy Commission Chairman Anil Kakodkar.

64.   Interview with Singhvi, 16 November 2010.

65.   Interview with Dixit, 8 January 2010.

66.   Sonia Gandhi's speech to the Congress Parliamentary Party Meeting, 14 August 2007. Available at aicc.org.in/new/president-speech-detail-3878.php. (accessed on 9 January 2012).

67.   Prakash Karat, 'Why the CPI(M) and the Left Oppose the Nuclear Deal', *The Hindu*, 20 August 2006.

68.   On this issue, see Ravi (2007), 'Will the Triumph Turn into Tragedy', *The Hindu*, 27 August.

69.   Prakash Karat, 'Why the CPI (M) and the Left Oppose the Nuclear Deal'.

70.   See *The Times of India*, 19 August 2007.

71.   After the standoff with the Left, the government agreed to set up the committee in September 2007 'to examine certain aspects of the bilateral agreement, implications of the Hyde Act on 123 agreement, and self-reliance in the nuclear sector, implications of the nuclear deal on foreign policy and security cooperation', thus covering all the areas of Left's concerns. Decision to set up a Committee reported in Smita Gupta, 'Blinkmanship', *Outlook*, 10 September 2007.

72.   Ramakrishnan, 'Tactical Moves', *Frontline*, vol. 24, no. 22, 3–16 November 2007.

73.   See 'Manmohan: Allow Us to Go to IAEA, NSG', *The Hindu*, 1 July 2008.

74.   'Ahead of Meet on N-deal, Left Offers Little Hope', *The Indian Express*, 17 June 2008.

75.   In his autobiography, Somnath Chatterjee, Speaker of the Lok Sabha who was expelled by the CPI (M) for refusing to resign as Speaker after the CPI (M) had withdrawn support, says, 'Prakash Karat met me at my residence a few days after the party had decided to withdraw support.... He said he felt insulted and betrayed... on the Indo-US nuclear deal. Because of what he called breach of promise, the party, according to him, had no option but to break with the UPA.' Somnath Chatterjee's comment quoted in *The Times of India*, 25 July 2010 and also see 'It Will Be More Difficult to Stop the Deal when the PM Comes Back to Parliament: Yechury', *The Hindu*, 1 July 2008.

76.   Mukherjee quoted in 'Pranab Meets Karat to Push N-deal', *India Today*, 17 June 2008.

77.   Prakash Karat's statement on the nuclear deal quoted in 'Mayawati for

PM, Karat Won't Tell Now', *The Telegraph*, 1 August 2008.

78.   The government also underlined that the safeguards agreement is unique because it recognizes India's strategic programme and clearly restricts all application of safeguards to the civilian side, and that IAEA's approval is a precondition for nuclear commerce with any country. Reported in *The Indian Express*, 7 June 2008.

79.   The CPI (M) said the government held back from the Left parties the fact that it was mandatory for it to go to the IAEA for an India-specific safeguards agreement. See 'Left Not Informed of Need to Go to IAEA', *The Hindu*, 1 July 2008. Also see report in 'CPM Charges Government with Betrayal, Disinformation', *The Economic Times*, 22 July 2008.

80.   Shankarshan Thakur, 'Nominee and Nominator', *The Telegraph*, 30 June 2008.

81.   Jayanth Jacob, 'Left Banks on Comrade Sonia', *The Telegraph*, 20 June 2007.

82.   Manini Chatterjee, 'Left Hears Break-Up Bell', *The Telegraph*, 25 June 2008.

83.   Excerpts from Sonia Gandhi's interaction. Available at www.infocera.com/Excerpts_from_Sonia_Gandhi_interaction_1821.htm (accessed on 10 January 2012).

84.   Vir Sanghvi, 'Deal or No Deal', *Hindustan Times*, 22 June 2008.

85.   Jacob, 'Left Banks on Comrade Sonia'.

86.   Interview with Sitaram Yechury.

87.   Interview with Aiyar, 13 November 2009.

88.   Interview of Prakash Karat published in *The Times of India*, 18 July 2008.

89.   On the orders of the Left Front government that was in power in West Bengal, over 4,000 heavily armed policemen entered the Nandigram area in January 2007 with the aim of quelling protests against the state government's plans to take over 10,000 acres of land for a Special Economic Zone (SEZ) to be developed by the Indonesia-based Salim Group. According to a report in *The Economic Times*, 11 people were killed in the resultant police firing. 'Nandigram Turns Blood Red', *The Economic Times*, 15 March 2007.

90.   'Prakash Karat Says Government and the Nuclear Deal Will Be Doomed' *The Hindu*, 21 July 2008.

91.   Interview with Saran.

92.   Ibid.

93.   For details on these allegations, see V. Venkatesan, 'Bartered Trust', *Frontline*, vol. 25, no. 16, 2–15 August 2008.

94.   Ibid.

95.   Khilnani, 'New Delhi's Grand Strategy'.

96.   Varadarajan, 'An Endgame with No Clear Winners', *The Hindu*, 23 July 2008.

97.   Raja Mohan, 'The Making of Indian Foreign Policy'.

98.   The bilateral agreement grants India access to US civil nuclear technology

and opens the door to trade with other countries in the future. In October 2009, India announced a plan to put 14 out of its 22 nuclear reactors under IAEA safeguards by 2014. As part of the deal, India agreed to divide its 22 nuclear facilities into two categories, civil and military, and submit 14 of its civilian facilities to IAEA inspection under a negotiated safeguards agreement to ensure non-diversion of imported material to military purposes. India can use the remaining eight reactors, and other facilities, to expand its nuclear arsenal and thus turn its back on nuclear disarmament, to which it promised to return four years ago.

99.   Editorial, *Economic and Political Weekly*, vol. 43, no. 37, 2008.

100.   Ibid.

101.   'Pranab: No Compromise on Independent Foreign Policy', *The Hindu*, 22 July 2008.

102.   Pant, 'Power Game in Asia Trips Nuclear Non-Proliferation', *YaleGlobal*, 12 August 2010. Available at http://yaleglobal.yale.edu/content/asia-trips-nuclear-non-proliferation?page=1 (accessed on 3 January 2012).

103.   For a contrary view that argues that India has quite a long way to go before it could become a world power, its growing economic and demographic assets notwithstanding, see David Malone (2011), *Does the Elephant Dance? Contemporary Indian Foreign Policy*. Oxford University Press, New Delhi.

104.   Karl. F. Inderfurth, 'The US and India Expanding Engagement Agenda', *The Hindu*, 10 September 2008.

105.   Baru (2009), 'The Growing Influence of Business and Media on Indian Foreign Policy', *India Review*, vol. 8, no. 3, July–September, pp. 266–85.

106.   Investment Commission headed by Ratan Tata extended strong support to the nuclear deal and made a strong pitch for allowing private sector's investment in nuclear power generation. See report 'Investment Panel Backs Nuclear Deal', *The Indian Express*, 5 July 2008.

107.   R. Ramachandran, 'On Slippery Ground', *Frontline*, vol. 28, no. 16, 30 July–12 August 2011.

108.   The new rules require the recipient state to sign the additional protocol. India has signed an Additional Protocol but that is India-specific. Indrani Bagchi, 'New NSG Rules Restrain N-Transfer to India', *The Times of India*, 30 July 2011.

109.   'Statement of the PM in the Rajya Sabha on the India-US Nuclear Agreement,' 17 August 2006. Available at pmindia.nic.in/parliament-all.php?pageid=3 (accessed on 16 January 2011).

110.   Sukumar Muralidharan describes the bond between 'nuclear capability and national prestige' as 'nationalist vanity', in his review article 'Explaining the Mundane, Excluding the Voices of Dissent', *Economic and Political Weekly*, vol XLVII, 14 January 2012, p. 37.

111.   Manmohan Singh's 'achievement' was hailed by the electronic media through a headline borrowed from the title of the popular Hindu film 'Singh is Kinng' released in 2008 just before the trust vote in the Lok Sabha on the nuclear deal on 22 July 2008. Television channels, for example, CNN-IBN,

used the title of the film as the headline and gave it top billing on the day of the confidence vote. Both *India Today* and *Outlook* ran this line on the cover story of their editions in the week of the trust vote.

112.   Bidwai, 'Completing the 1991 Agenda', *Frontline*, vol. 25, no. 16, 2–15 August 2008.

113.   Prime Minister's speech to the trust vote on 22 July 2008. Available at http://www.pmindia.nic.in/lspeech.asp?id=695 (accessed on 7 July 2011).

114.   'PM's Reply to the Debate on the Motion of No-confidence in the Lok Sabha', 22 July 2008. Available at pmindia.nic.in/pmsinparliament.php?nodeid=32 (accessed on 6 July 2010).

115.   Quoted in Tripathi, 'After the Hurrahs', *Frontline*, vol. 25, no. 16, 2–15 August 2008.

116.   Ibid.

117.   Varadarajan, 'An Endgame with No Clear Winners'.

118.   Prakash Karat admitted after the Left's stunning defeat in the West Bengal Assembly election in May 2011 that the Congress outmanoeuvred the Left. He remarked: 'We underestimated the Congress's experience in power-play and skills in political manoeuvring, more so when the USA was standing behind it.' Prakash Karat quoted in 'The Bengal Loss Is a Big Loss and Throws Up Many Challenges: Prakash Karat', *The Economic Times*, 14 May 2011.

Conclusion

Over the decades, Indian politics has become increasingly competitive and contentious. The momentum generated by the Congress's role in the freedom struggle helped the party to rule India almost continually for four decades and weather the damage inflicted by organizational erosion. Such an advantage could not continue forever. The organizational weakening was principally due to the centralization of the party and the concentration of power in the hands of Indira Gandhi and the political miscalculations of her successors. By the end of the 1980s, key groups in its social coalition had lost faith in the Congress's ability to represent their interests and advance their aspirations. The party's base withered away in the keystone states of Uttar Pradesh, Bihar, West Bengal, Andhra Pradesh, and Tamil Nadu and was much weaker in many others. All that remained of the Congress Party of old was its ties to the Nehru–Gandhi family. This excessive reliance on the charismatic appeal of the family was inadequate after the dramatic transformation of India's democracy in the 1990s which saw the rise of regional and lower caste-based parties and the diffusion of political power from New Delhi to the states.

From 1984 onwards, ruling parties, including the Congress and/or alliances at the national level, were voted out by the electorate in five of the six parliamentary elections. At the state level, ruling parties and alliances were defeated in over 70 per cent of assembly elections between 1989 and 2004. The Congress was acutely aware that its customary strategies of distribution of patronage to cultivate support to win elections were not yielding the same results. Post-liberalization, this was not working because political parties could no longer rely on incorporating voters, particularly poor voters, through patronage networks. At the state level, non-Congress parties stressed identity politics in efforts to polarize society, but these campaigns varied greatly, from Gujarat to Uttar Pradesh and Tamil Nadu. Many other parties have pursued development-oriented policies, albeit employing very different methods, to build social coalitions. The Congress too was in search of new political strategies and pursued a range of post-clientilistic methods. It began giving preference to issue-based politics as opposed to identity politics to counter its principal rivals: the BJP and regional parties which had traditionally espoused identity politics as the basis for securing support.

Against the background of significant reconfigurations of state–society relations and changes in the distribution of political authority from the 1980s, the high politics of this period showed major changes in Congress politics but these were neither singular nor cohesive. Three major changes brought about by Sonia Gandhi's leadership—the reassertion of secularism, an alliance with regional parties, and rapprochement with the Left parties—paved the way for a return of the Congress to power. In just under a decade under her leadership, the party's fortunes were reversed and it regained pre-eminence, a phenomenon that many had thought exceedingly improbable in the 1990s.

One remarkable feature of the Congress since the early 1990s was the tendency to move away from ideological frameworks. If asked what the Congress stood for, few leaders could give a coherent answer beyond expressing commitment to pluralism and social justice. One thing is clear: Congress has no ideology, only strategy. If there is one ideology that the party continues to represent, it is the ideology of power. Economic liberalization has accentuated this trend and brought individual and special interests into the open. Some of these shifts have occurred owing to the emergence of a worldwide economic order, typified by globalized financial markets, production, and marketing, and novel transnational regulatory structures which have shifted power more firmly from voters to capital. As a consequence, politics is everywhere market-driven. This shift is a strong tendency in the development of political parties globally. Both the Democratic Party in the US and the Labour Party in the UK, as well as many other parties of the Left have embraced free market policies first made acceptable by President Bill Clinton, and subsequently by Prime Minister Tony Blair. The Congress Party was certainly not immune to this trend. However, seen in a comparative perspective, the distinctiveness of the Congress lies in the fact that even though its policies were conditioned by global economic forces, at the same time, to dominate national politics, it went against the Washington consensus and introduced, for example, a mandatory right to employment and education to benefit the vulnerable and deprived sections of society. Policymaking under the Congress-led UPA (2004–9) was as sensitive to market sentiment as it was to the compulsions of democracy and the challenges of development in a largely poor country.

Out of power for eight years, Congress leaders began to recognize that the party needed to define what it stood for. This was a difficult question for a party that has thrived on an ambiguity which facilitated its claim to represent everyone and every interest. Balance, or the 'middle-path', as the plenary in 2010 to mark 125 years of the party's journey characterized it, has always been a strong feature of the Congress. Political resolutions from 1998 onwards reflect greater emphasis on pluralism and secularism, and the explicit understanding that the two are inseparable. The Gujarat violence of 2002 was a turning point in compelling the Congress to confront the BJP's divisive politics. Although the idea of soft Hindutva was coined by some senior leaders who tried to push the party to adopt this line, the majority in the party, and the top leadership in particular, was not swayed by it.

In 2004, the Congress was able to wrest power on the basis of its emphatic rejection of the BJP's divisive policies and its own insistence that India must remain a pluralistic nation in which all citizens are equal before the law. This election had once again shown that it is the pluralist character of the Congress that remains its unique selling point. With all its faults, it represents a non-parochial idea of India. This inclusivity helped it to reclaim the role of the dominant party in the coalition era. The symbolism of Sonia Gandhi and Manmohan Singh belonging to minority communities and occupying the top positions in the Congress and the UPA was a powerful refutation of the BJP's exclusivist idea of India. The combined leadership of Sonia Gandhi, representing the party's traditional commitment to the poor and the deprived, and Manmohan Singh, the reformer, taking India on a trajectory of economic growth, appealing to the middle classes, helped the Congress return to the centre of the political arena.

The UPA's political agenda focused on the principles of inclusive growth, an idea that the Congress promoted as the means to its reinvention. There are, however, two aspects to inclusive growth: the sustainability of the growth process and the strengthening of plural and secular politics. As the leading party of the UPA, the Congress had a particular responsibility to recognize that the vote for secular politics could not be separated from the demands of marginalized groups for fair treatment. Shedding much of its earlier ideological ambivalence, it was able to convince the voter that it could sustain the high growth trajectory without compromising on the imperative of pluralism and on ensuring equal access to the public domain and prosperity to all citizens.

Paralleling the return of the Congress to power, there was a sharp decline in the overall levels of ethnic and communal violence. Periodically, a few provocative events did occur, such as attacks on Christians in some states, but overall the balance-sheet was positive as the Congress promoted a plural ethos and, by and large, communal peace. Most importantly, it did not allow the BJP to resurrect the Hindutva campaigns and exert pressure on the cultural rights of the minorities, especially Muslims. In a related move, it initiated a fresh policy discourse on minorities. One initiative was commissioning the *Sachar Committee Report*, which highlighted the development deficit and deprivation of the Muslim community, thus exposing the hollowness of the propaganda of minority appeasement. The new deal for minorities has, however, got off to a weak start because the scale of government response was spectacularly parsimonious in relation to the funds necessary to deal with the huge development deficit. Eight years later, the government was still battling systemic resistance as well as opposition within its own ranks to special attention being accorded to minorities, and to Muslims in particular, and their welfare and mainstreaming their interests by confronting discrimination against them.

Major shifts in the economy and public policy have taken place under the Congress governments between 1984 and 2009. The party's economic resolutions over the years reflect the swing to a market-driven ideology and increased economic growth. Policies of liberalization undoubtedly stimulated a much higher level of economic activity in the private sector which powered high growth rates. The embrace of capitalism and the growing centrality of business groups to the process of economic growth, whether through the active promotion of the corporate sector or through the very framework of economic policies, was a reflection of a major structural transformation that has taken place thanks to Congress policies under Manmohan Singh. By 2009, the Congress had consolidated its claim to economic credibility through sustained high growth under its government even after the slowdown during the global recession, but, in the process, the locus of power had moved decisively to the corporate sector, as the events of last few years have shown.

Post-2004 has seen a profound change in India's relationship with the US, crafted by Manmohan Singh. The shift occurred in the context of a distinct rupture in the internal and external environments: the end of dirigisme and bipolarity in foreign policy which affected a major shift in policy towards the US. The nuclear deal signed in October 2008 symbolized a turning point in Indo-US relations, very significantly changing the trajectory of India's foreign policy from independence to a strategic partnership with the US. The passage of the nuclear deal indicated a transformation not just in India–US relations, but also in the Congress's position which went on to support a close relationship with the US at the expense of multilateralism. This was applauded by the AICC plenary in December 2010, especially the US endorsement of India's claim for a permanent seat in the UNSC. Such a possibility still remains some distance away, but President Barack Obama's endorsement of it during his India visit in November 2010 was seen as confirmation of the emergence of India as a 'global power'.

However, it is obvious that being a global power may mean nothing when millions of Indians lack food security, assured access to drinking water, health care, and education, as well as equality of opportunity. The rapidity of growth has only marginally touched the poor and the overall decline in poverty has not kept pace with the high growth of the economy. Congress politics has been captured by the rich but is sustained by the poor in the age of globalization. Even as disparities and inequalities have been an intrinsic part of India's high-growth economy, the state has thrown its weight behind the rich and powerful. The staggering fortunes of millionaires and billionaires, frequently accumulated through illegitimate means and a politics–business–bureaucracy alliance, indicate that this group has been the greatest beneficiary of globalization. But the need to promote the well-being of the people at large was also vitally important. The party could not have regained power in 2004 without the support of the poor even though in the past Congress governments had failed to deliver on the commitments to improve their conditions. Mindful of the incompleteness of the promise to build an egalitarian order, the Congress ambitiously set out to ensure that this changed. A significant feature, therefore, was its decision to position itself strategically as a party that placed great emphasis on the poor. The UPA government under its dispensation went on to commit massive resources to the social sector and an array of centrally sponsored schemes for poverty alleviation.

After 2004, Congress strategy was more development-centric and governance-focused than ideologically welfarist or distributive in a defined sense. For such an approach to succeed, the UPA had to deliver on tangible social policies like the NREGA. The real difference was that in the past the Congress had signalled intention but not implementation of welfare schemes. This time it was under pressure to go beyond intention and implement its promises. It had to adjust itself to a 'post-rhetorical' India where tall claims were insufficient. It is, however, difficult to discern in all this a well-thought-out and cohesive ideological shift even though after 2004 it had moved a little to the left of centre in comparison to its position in the 1990s.

The interesting point is that the Congress-led UPA made a strong political impact through the introduction of a rather large number of good social policies. The more perceptive leaders and strategists of the Congress were fully aware that the party organization was in shambles, and that for the party to sustain its revival, it had to rely on government intervention. The Congress has failed to undertake the party reforms necessary to strengthen its social base which can enable it to achieve the policy goals advanced by the leadership, and therefore it tends to rely on bold policy initiatives and on the formal administrative structures of the government to implement these initiatives. The proliferation of numerous centrally sponsored schemes and programmes was part of this 'scheme-oriented' advance underscoring the policy-driven thrust of Congress revival.

Nonetheless, for the Congress, the 'scheme-oriented' approach had served the deeper strategic purpose of neutralizing identity politics, and this has had a positive impact on its fortunes. It helped the Congress direct attention to distributive policies implemented from 2004 to 2009, which paid electoral dividends to the party. As the party took advantage of opportunities provided by these centrally sponsored schemes, it could challenge identity politics by bringing back into sharper focus policies that are likely to produce more equitable outcomes. This has created an environment in which policies and programmes are debated and discussed, and given final form. It constituted an important shift in public discourse even though it is too early to say that it will usher in a transition to post-identity politics. The three major policy issues taken up by the Congress engaged multiple social constituencies: NREGA with the poor; Sachar Committee aimed to win over Muslims with the promise to rectify the development deficit; and the nuclear deal had an appeal for the middle classes. This suggests that it was attempting to construct a social coalition of the middle classes, the poor, and the minorities.

By contrast, identity-based parties failed to win as many seats as they had hoped in the 2009 parliamentary elections. The Lok Sabha elections returned the UPA with a larger plurality than had been anticipated. The Congress on its own gained 61 seats more than its tally in 2004. The Third Front, which won only 79 seats, was devastated. The BJP won 112 seats, 25 less than its tally in 2004. This election was the third consecutive one in which the BJP dropped a significant share of its vote, which fell below its tally in 1991 when it had reached the point of take-off.

India has not returned to the Congress era, but the Congress could aspire to power because of its ideological and political flexibility and a political/institutional arrangement that enable it to incorporate and accommodate many social, economic, and political contradictions and interests in the emergent processes of India's economy and society. It possessed considerable elasticity which allows it to speak in multiple voices and work with multiple agendas, which significantly included the poor. It can accommodate conflicting interests, and therefore does not exclusively represent any single interest. Congress power derived from its ability to continue holding on to both ends of the contradiction—growth/distribution; rich/poor; majority/minority—within itself. It harks back to the older ideological and political flexibility for which the Congress was known and which gave voice to divergent interests.

This flexibility in the contemporary period was founded on two new processes. The first was the availability of increased government revenue which the ruling party can invest in addressing some of the pressing basic needs of the people without having to compromise on the profits of the corporate sector. Enhanced revenues have enabled the Congress to reach out to multiple constituencies. In all this, the larger aim was to refocus the debate on economic issues, on growth, but more crucially on the social agenda of development as its own distinct agenda. This blend of social welfare and the lure of the new economy saw the poor and middle classes gravitate towards the Congress.

The second were a set of contingent reasons, most notably the Congress–Left alliance, the foundation-stone of the UPA experiment, and the internal leverage it gave Sonia Gandhi in relation to the conservative lobbies in the UPA government. Acting as the UPA's conscience, it influenced its policies in a progressive direction. The political strategy was in this sense contingent on the specific circumstances that brought the Congress and the UPA to power. The UPA government could not have been formed without support from the Left, and the latter's insistence on a NCMP lent a progressive power and thrust to the coalition. In implementing the social and legislative agenda, the UPA faced serious resistance from within the ruling establishment and from outside the government. It is here that Left and its insistence on adhering to the NCMP played an important role in pushing the Congress to make its implementation a priority, and in the end deriving huge political benefits from it. At the same time, their opposition to economic reforms and the nuclear deal created sympathy for Manmohan Singh which helped the Congress to gain support among the middle classes. In hindsight, the importance of the Left support to the Congress and UPA cannot be overstated. It provided the Congress with the credibility to project itself as pro-people and, above all, neutralized the right-wing elements within the UPA government and the bureaucracy. However, if the Left's role was enabling, it was the Congress leadership which obviously played a decisive role in the political advance of the party through an inclusive platform. Sonia Gandhi's clout in the UPA, which enabled her to push the social agenda, derived in part from the Left Front's support, but also from the dramatic rise in her political stock following her refusal to yield to entreaties from her colleagues that she assume the post of prime minister in 2004.

The political upturn has, however, taken place without organizational reform, which raises serious doubts about its sustainability. As a mass party centred on political leadership, it has not paid much attention to its troubled organization, which has remained weak and ineffective and plagued by factional conflicts at all levels. The shift in the locus of power towards the party as a key element in the UPA's governing process did not encourage party rebuilding. Promises to reorganize and streamline the party have proved to be unsuccessful. Rhetoric about inner party democracy and election to party posts are confined to plenary sessions and forgotten thereafter. In theory, Congress holds elections to all party posts, but in fact, all important offices and positions continue to go to nominees in a party dominated by the culture of nomination. The consequence is that the 'world's largest democracy' is managed by an internally undemocratic party.

The Congress remains Delhi-centred and this has further eroded its organizational strength. Above all, its dependence on a single family at the top and smaller family fiefdoms in the states is unhealthy. It seeks to ride out crises by expecting the 'magic' of the Nehru–Gandhi family to bail it out every time. Most leaders are not engaged in political mobilization, movements, agitations, or concentrated constituency development because most of them have not emerged from grassroots politics or movements. The contrast between the party organization and leadership during the first three decades after Independence, when most Congress stalwarts were associated with political movements, and the first decade of this century is striking. The real change will come when it gets the right kind of state-level and local leadership: a modern, forward-looking, and compassionate leadership that strengthens the local foundations of party and democracy. The focus of the debate on leadership for building a 'new Congress' should, therefore, shift to the states.

The Congress was much stronger after it had won two consecutive elections, even if in coalition, in 2004 and 2009, something it had not done since 1984. But under UPA-2, it failed to capitalize on the momentum of change achieved under UPA-1. During UPA-1, the Left parties had put pressure on the government to fulfil its own manifesto which benefited the Congress electorally. But under UPA-2, there is no Left inside or outside pushing it towards policies and politics that are socially relevant and electorally viable. Moreover, pursuing a social agenda appears more difficult also because of a combination of crony capitalism and big money being able to make greater and greater inroads into the corridors of power. The increasing monetization of the political process, evident from the very large number of wealthy MPs and cabinet ministers backed by a state–business alliance at the apex, which has strengthened the neo-liberal regime, could produce conditions to unravel the social agenda which brought the Congress back to power.

While it is tempting to think that the Congress with 200 plus seats and the UPA-2 with 270 plus seats is likely to re-establish its dominance, the future of the Congress will depend upon its handling of the two critical issues which it must face in the months and years ahead—succession of the top leadership in government and party, and the need to regain key states permanently annexed by non-Congress parties. To what extent the pivot of the 'new Congress'—its inventive social coalition of the middle classes, the poor, and the minorities—would endure and help the party in meeting these challenges depends on the capacity to rebuild the party organization, assuring representation to the marginalized groups, and defining an overarching vision for a country that, on the one hand, is galloping ahead on a high growth path and, on the other, is divided by structural inequalities in the state and society. What is needed is a revitalized vision with much greater perspective and resoluteness to address issues of inequity and injustice. Only a coalition anchored to social democratic foundations can do so by trying to reconcile the modern goals of economic development with equity.

Bibliography

Ahluwalia, Isher Judge and I.M.D. Little (eds) (1998), 'Introduction', in *India's Economic Reforms and Development: Essays for Manmohan Singh*, Oxford University Press, New Delhi, pp. 1–20.

Aiyar, Mani Shankar (ed.) (1997), *Rajiv Gandhi's India*, 4 vols, UBSPD, New Delhi.

———— (2003), 'Can the Congress Find a Future', *Seminar*, no. 526, June, pp. 14–22.

———— (2010), 'Dilemma of Development and Democracy', 24 November. Available at www.cmsindia.org/ManiShankarAiyar24Nov2010.pdf (accessed on 29 December 2010).

Ananth, Krishna (2010), *India since Independence*, Pearson, New Delhi.

Bajpai, Kanti (2005), 'Where Are India and the US Heading', *Economic and Political Weekly*, vol. 40, no. 32, pp. 3577–81.

Bardhan, Pranab (2000), 'Political Economy of Reform in India', in Zoya Hasan (ed.), *Politics and the State in India*, Sage Publications, New Delhi, pp. 158–74.

———— (2009), 'Notes on the Political Economy of India's Tortuous Transition', *Economic and Political Weekly*, vol. XLIV, no. 49, pp. 31–6.

———— (2010), *Awakening Giants, Feet of Clay: Assessing the Economic Rise of China and India*, Oxford University Press, New Delhi.

Baru, Sanjaya (2009), 'The Growing Influence of Business and Media on Indian Foreign Policy', *India Review*, vol. 8, no. 3, July–September, pp. 266–85.

———— (2009b), 'India and the World: The Economics and Politics of the Manmohan Singh Doctrine in Foreign Policy', Institute of South Asian Studies, no. 53, 14 November, National University of Singapore, Institute of Singapore.

Bhalla, Sheila (2010), 'Inclusive Growth? Focus on Employment', Paper presented at The Institute for Human Development, 'The Challenge of Employment in India: Lessons from the Work of the NCEUS', The Institute for Human Development, 7–8 May 2010, New Delhi, mimeo.

Bhargava, Rajeev (2002), 'Liberal, Secular Democracy and Explanations of Hindu Nationalism', *Journal of Commonwealth and Comparative Politics*, vol. 40, no. 3, pp. 72–96.

Bijukumar, V. (2006), *Reinventing the Congress: Economic Policies and Strategies since 1991*, Rawat Publications, New Delhi.

Breman, Jan (2010), 'India's Social Question in a State of Denial', *Economic and Political Weekly*, vol. XLV, no. 23, 5 June, pp. 42–6.

Butler, David, Ashok Lahiri, and Prannoy Roy (1991), *India Decides: Elections 1953–1991*, Living Media India, New Delhi.

Byres, T.J. (ed.) (1997), 'Introduction: Development Planning and the Interventionist State versus Liberalization and the Neo-liberal State: India, 1989–1996', in *The State, Development Planning and Liberalization in India*, Oxford University Press, New Delhi.

——— (ed.) (1998), *The State, Development Planning and Liberalization in India*, Oxford University Press, New Delhi.

Centre for Budget and Governance Accountability (CBGA) (2009), 'How Did the UPA Spend Our Money: An Assessment of Expenditure Priorities and Resource Mobilisation Efforts by the UPA Government', CBGA, New Delhi. Available at http://www.cbgaindia.org/whats_new /How%20did%20the%20 UPA%20spend%20our%20money.pdf (accessed on 20 March 2011).

Centre of Equity Studies (CES) (2011), *Promises to Keep: Investigating Government's Response to the Sachar Committee Recommendations*, Study Report, New Delhi, August. Available at www.scribd.com/doc/52913174/ sachar-final (accessed on 13 August 2011).

Chakravarthy, Uma and Nandita Haksar (1987), *The Delhi Riots: Three Days in the Life of a Nation*, Lancer International, New Delhi.

Chandhoke, Neera (2010), 'Secularism', in Niraja Gopal Jayal and Pratap Bhanu Mehta (eds), *The Oxford Companion to Politics in India*, Oxford University Press, New Delhi, pp. 333–46.

Chandrasekhar, C.P. and Jayati Ghosh (2002), *The Market that Failed: A Decade of Neoliberal Economic Reforms in India*, Leftword Books, New Delhi.

——— (2007), 'Recent Trends in Employment in India and China: An Unfortunate Convergence?' *MacroScan*, 5 April. Available at www.macroscan. org/anl/apr07/pdf/india_china.pdf (accessed on 11 November 2010).

Chatterjee, Partha (2008), 'Democracy and Economic Transformation in India', *Economic and Political Weekly*, vol. 43, no. 16, 19–25 April, pp. 53–62.

Chatterjee, Somnath (2010), *Keeping the Faith: Memoirs of a Parliamentarian*, HarperCollins, New Delhi.

Chaudhuri, Jay (2010), 'Going to the Operating Room without a Diagnostic: Reforming Centrally Sponsored Schemes', *India Review*, vol. 9, no. 2, April–June, pp. 169–203.

Chelliah, Raja (1996), *Towards Sustainable Growth: Essays in Fiscal and Financial Sector Reforms in India*, Oxford University Press, New Delhi.

Chenoy, Kamal Mitra, S.P. Shukla, K.S. Subramanian, and Achin Vanaik (2000), *Gujarat Carnage 2002: A Report to the Nation*, April.

Cohen, Stephen (2001), *Emerging Power: India*, Oxford University Press, New Delhi.

Congress Sandesh (2000), 'Antony Committee Report', January. Available at www.congresssandesh.com/dec_jan_issue/cwc.html (accessed on 7 June 2009).

——— (2003), 'Nation Suffered Enough under the BJP: Sonia Gandhi', April. Available at www.congresssandesh.com/april-2003/report/2.html (accessed on 28 January 2012).

Corbridge, Stuart and John Harriss (2000), *Reinventing India: Liberalization, Hindu Nationalism, and Popular Democracy*, Oxford University Press, New Delhi.

CPI (M) (2006), *Policy Issues: Left Alternatives. Notes Submitted by the Left to the UPA Government on Some Important Policy Issues*, October, CPI(M) Publication, New Delhi.

Damodran, Harish (2008), *India's New Capitalists: Caste, Business and Industry in a Modern Nation*, Permanent Black, Delhi.

Das, Subrat and Yamini Mishra (2010), 'What Does Budget 2010 Imply for the Social Sector', *Economic and Political Weekly*, vol. XLV, no. 13, 27 March, pp. 64–8.

Deaton, Angus and Jean Drèze (2002), 'Poverty and Inequality in India: A Reexamination', *Economic and Political Weekly*, vol. 37, no. 36, 7–13 September, pp. 3729–48.

Dhavan, Rajeev (1987), 'Religious Freedom in India', *American Journal of Comparative Law*, vol. 35, no. 1, Winter, pp. 209–54.

——— (1994), 'The Ayodhya Judgment: Encoding Secularism in the Law', *Economic and Political Weekly*, vol. 29, no. 48, 26 November.

Drèze, Jean and Amartya Sen (2000), *Economic Development and Social Opportunity*, Oxford University Press, New Delhi.

Dubey, Muchkund and S.N. Jha (2002), *Social Development in India: The Policy Canvas: An Overview of the Last Fifty Years and Emerging Issues for the Twenty-First Century*, Council of Social Development, New Delhi.

Frankel, Francine (1990), 'India's Democracy in Transition', *World Policy Journal*, vol. 7, no. 3, Summer, pp. 521–55.

——— (2005), *India's Political Economy: 1947–2004, The Gradual Revolution*, 2nd edition, Oxford University Press, New Delhi.

Gandhi, Rajiv (1989), *Selected Speeches and Writings—1986*, Publications Division of the Ministry of Information and Broadcasting, New Delhi.

Gandhi, Sonia (2004a), *India Today* Conclave, 13 March. Available at www.congresssandesh.com/april-2004/speech1.html (accessed on 15 August 2010).

Gandhi, Sonia (2004b), Congress Parliamentary Party, *The Times of India*, 18 May.
——— (2006), Speech at AICC Plenary, Hyderabad, 21–3 January.
——— (2008), Speech at the *Hindustan Times* Leadership Summit, 21 November.
Ganguly, Sumit (2003), 'The Crisis of Indian Secularism', *Journal of Democracy*, vol. 14, no. 4, October, pp. 11–25.
Ghimre, Yubraj (1997), 'Search for New Power Centres', *Outlook*, 1 January.
Ghosh, Jayati (2006), 'The Right to Work and Recent Legislation in India', *Social Scientist*, vol. 34, nos 1 and 2, January–February, pp. 88–102. Available at indiabudget.nic.in/es2003-04/chapt2004/chap104.pdf (accessed on 14 January 2012).
Ghosh, Partha (2010), 'Foreign Policy and Indian Politics: Issues before the Fifteenth General Election', in A.K. Mehra (ed.), *Emerging Trends in Indian Politics: The Fifteenth General Election*, Routledge, New Delhi.
Godbole, Madhav (1996), *Unfinished Innings: Recollections and Reflections of a Civil Servant*, Orient Longman, New Delhi.
Goldman Sachs (2007), *BRICs and Beyond*. Chapter 1, 'India's Rising Growth Potential', Goldman Sachs Global Economics Department, New York. Available at http://www2.goldmansachs.com/ideas/brics/BRICS-and-Beyond.html (accessed on 24 December 2011).
Government of India (1987), *Economic Survey, 1986–7*, Ministry of Finance, New Delhi.
——— (1996), *Economic Survey of India, 1995–96*, Ministry of Finance, Economic Division. Available at ieo.org/surv001.html (accessed on 12 January 2012).
——— (2006a), 'Social, Economic and Educational Status of the Muslim Community in India: A Report', Prime Minister's High Level Committee, Cabinet Secretariat, New Delhi. Available at http://minorityaffairs.gov.in/sites/upload_files/MMA/files/pdfs/sachar_comm.pdf (accessed on 8 November 2011).
——— (2006b), 'Report of the Working Group on Empowering the Minorities for the Eleventh Five Year Plan (2007–12)', Planning Commission, New Delhi. Available at http://planningcommission.nic.in/aboutus/committee/index.php?about=wrkg2_13.htm (accessed on 17 November 2011).
——— (2006c), '*Towards Faster and More Inclusive Growth. An Approach to the 11th Five Year Plan*', Planning Commission, New Delhi, June. Available at planningcommission.nic.in/plans/planrel/apppap_11.pdf (accessed on 7 August 2010).
——— (2007), 'Report of National Commission for Religious and Linguistic Minorities', Ministry of Minority Affairs, New Delhi. Available at

http://minorityaffairs.gov.in/newsite/ncrlm/ ncrlm.asp (accessed on 8 January 2010).

Government of India (2008), Report of the National Commission for Enterprises in the Unorganized Sector (NCEUS) on *Conditions of Work and Promotion of Work and Livelihoods in the Unorganized Sector*, Ministry of Small Scale Industries, New Delhi.

———— (2009a), 'Report of the Expert Group to Review the Methodology for Estimation of Poverty', Planning Commission, New Delhi, November. Available at www.planningcommission.nic.in/reports/genrep/rep_pov.pdf (accessed on 14 February 2011).

———— (2009b), 'Report of the National Commission for Enterprises in the Unorganized Sector (NCEUS), vol. 1 Main Report and vol. II Annexures'. Available at www.cdhr.org.in/.../The_Challenge_of_Employment_in_India_(Vol.%20II)[1].pdf (accessed on 8 August 2011).

———— (2010), *Economic Survey, 2009–10*, Ministry of Finance, New Delhi.

Gowda, M.V.R. and E. Sridharan (2009), 'Parties and the Party System, 1947–2006', in Sumit Ganguly, Larry Diamond, and Marc Plattner (eds), *The State of India's Democracy*, Oxford University Press, New Delhi, pp. 3–25.

Guha, Ramachandra (2007), *India after Gandhi: The History of the World's Largest Democracy*, Picador, London.

Guha-Thakurta, Paranjoy (2009), 'NREGA', *Caravan*, vol. 2, no. 3, March.

Gupta, Ruchi (2011a). 'Democracy and the Politics around NREGA', Kafila, 10 January. Available at kafila.org/2011/.../10/democracy-and-the-politics-around-nrega-ruchi-gupta (accessed on 20 may 2011).

———— (2011b). 'Deconstructing the NAC', *Seminar*, no. 624, August, pp. 82–5.

Gupta, Shekhar (1990), 'The Gathering Storm', in Marshall Bouton and Philip Oldenberg (eds), *India Briefing*, Oxford University Press, New Delhi, pp. 25–49.

Hardgrave, Robert and Stanley Kochanek (1993), *Government and Politics in a Developing Nation*, Harcourt Brace Jovanovich, New York.

Harriss, John (2011), 'How Far Have India's Economic Reforms Been Guided by Compassion and Justice: Social Policy in the Neoliberal Era', in Sanjay Ruparelia, Sanjay Reddy, John Harriss, and Stuart Corbridge (eds), *Understanding India's New Political Economy: A Great Transformation?* Routledge, London, pp. 66–80.

Harvey, David (2005), *A Brief History of Neoliberalism*, The Clarendon Press, Oxford.

Hasan, Mushirul (1998), *Legacy of a Divided Nation: India's Muslims since Independence*, Oxford University Press, New Delhi.

Hasan, Zoya (1998a), *Quest for Power: Oppositional Movements and Post-Congress Politics in Uttar Pradesh*, Oxford University Press, New Delhi.

Hasan, Zoya (ed.) (1998b), 'Minority Identity, State Policy and the Political Process', in *Forging Identities: Gender, Communities and the State in India*, Kali for Women, Delhi, pp. 59–73.

——— (2006a), 'Bridging the Divide: Indian National Congress and Indian Democracy', *Contemporary South Asia*, vol. 1, no. 15, December, pp. 473–88.

——— (2006b), 'Mass Violence and the Wheels of Indian (In)Justice', in Amrita Basu and Srirupa Roy (eds), *Violence and Democracy in India*, Seagull Books, Kolkata, pp. 198–222.

——— (ed.) (2008), *Parties and Party Politics in India*, 5th impression, Oxford University Press, New Delhi.

——— (2009), *Politics of Inclusion: Castes, Minorities, and Affirmative Action*, 2nd edition, Oxford University Press, New Delhi.

Hasan, Zoya and Ritu Menon (eds) (2006), *In a Minority: Essays on Muslim Women in India*, Oxford University Press, New Delhi.

Human Rights Watch (2002), '"We Have No Orders to Save You", State Participation and Complicity in Communal Violence in Gujarat', vol 14, no. 3.

Institute of Manpower Management (2009), *All India Report on Evaluation of NREGA: A Survey of Twenty Districts*, New Delhi, June. Available at www.indiaenvironmentportal.org.in/reports.../all-india-report-evaluation-nrega-survey-twenty-districts (accessed on 24 May 2011).

Jaffrelot, Christophe (2009a), 'The Indo-US Rapprochment: State Driven or Middle Class Driven', *India Quarterly*, vol. 65, no. 1, pp. 1–14.

——— (2009b), 'Introduction', in Christophe Jaffrelot and Sanjay Kumar (eds), *Rise of the Plebians: The Changing Face of Indian Legislative Assemblies*, Routledge, New Delhi, pp. 1–26.

Jalan, Bimal (ed.) (1992), *The Indian Economy*, Oxford University Press, New Delhi.

Jeffrey, Robin (1994), 'Prime Minister and the Ruling Party', in James Manor (ed.), *Nehru to the Nineties: The Changing Office of the Prime Minister in India*, Hurst & Co., London, pp. 161–84.

Jenkins, Rob (1999), *Democratic Politics and Economic Reform in India*, Cambridge University Press, Cambridge.

Kale, Sunita (2009), 'Inside Out: India's Global Reorientation', *India Review*, vol. 8, no. 1, January–March, pp. 43–64.

Karat, Prakash (2007) *Subordinate Ally: The Nuclear Deal and India–US Strategic Relations*, Leftword, New Delhi.

Khare, Harish (2004), 'The Indian National Congress: Problems of Survival and Re-Invention', in Subrata Mitra, Mike Enskat, and Clemens Spieb (eds), *Political Parties in South Asia*, Praeger, London, pp. 31–54.

Kochanek, Stanley (1976), 'Mrs. Gandhi's Pyramid: The New Congress', in Henry Hart (ed.), *Indira Gandhi's India: A Political System Reappraised*, Westview Press, Boulder, Colorado, pp. 93–124.

———— (1987), 'Brief Case Politics in India: The Congress Party and the Business Elite', *Asian Survey*, vol. 27, no. 12, December, pp. 1278–301.

Kochanek, Stanley (1996), 'Liberalization and Business Lobbying in India', *Journal of Commonwealth and Comparative Politics*, vol. 34, no. 3, pp. 155–173.

Kohli, Atul (ed.) (1988), *India's Democracy: An Analysis of Changing State–Society Relations*, Princeton University Press, Princeton.

———— (1994), *Democracy and Discontent: India's Growing Crisis of Governability*, Cambridge University Press, Cambridge.

———— (ed.) (2001), *The Success of India's Democracy*, Cambridge University Press, Cambridge.

———— (2006), 'Politics and Redistribution in India'. Available at http://www.princeton.edu/~kohli/Politics%20and%20Redistribution%20in%20India.pdf (accessed on 27 March 2012).

———— (ed.) (2009a), 'Politics of Economic Growth in India, 1980–2005, Part I: The 1980s', in *Democracy and Development: From Socialism to Pro-Business*, Oxford University Press, New Delhi, pp. 140–64.

———— (2009b), 'Politics of Economic Liberalization in India', in *Democracy and Development in India: From Socialism to Pro-Business*, Oxford University Press, New Delhi, pp. 186–226.

Kurien, C.T. (1994), *Global Capitalism and the Indian Economy*, vol. 6, *Tracts for the Times*, Orient Longman, New Delhi.

———— (1996), *Economic Reforms and the People*, Madhyam Books, New Delhi.

Kreisberg, Paul (1987), 'Gandhi at Mid-Term', *Foreign Affairs*, Summer, pp. 1055–1076.

Lakin, Jason and N. Ravishankar (2006), 'Working for Votes: The Politics of Employment Guarantee in India', Paper presented to the American Political Science Association Meeting, Philadelphia, 31 August–31 September. Available at www.allacademic.com/meta/p151215_index.html (accessed on 24 August 2010)

Luce, Edward (2007) *In Spite of the Gods: The Strange Rise of Modern India*, Little Brown, paperback edition, Abacus, London.

MacAuslan, Ian (2008), 'India's National Rural Employment Guarantee Act: A Case Study of How Change Happens', Oxfam. Case study written as a contribution to *From Poverty to Power: How Active Citizens and Effective States Can Change the World*, Oxfam International. Available at http://www.oxfam.org.uk//resources/downloads/FP2P/FP2P_India_Nat520Rural_employ_gt. (accessed on 7 January 2012).

Malone, David (2011), *Does the Elephant Dance? Contemporary Indian Foreign Policy*, Oxford University Press, New Delhi.

Manor, James (1983), 'Anomie in Indian Politics: Origins and Potential Wider Impact', *Economic and Political Weekly*, vol. 18, no. 19/21, Annual Number, May, pp. 725–734.

Manor, James (1988), 'Parties and Party System', in Atul Kohli (ed.), *India's Democracy: An Analysis of Changing State–Society Relations*, Princeton University Press, Princeton, pp. 62–98.

——— (1990), 'India after the Dynasty', *Journal of Democracy*, vol. 1, no. 3, Summer.

——— (2003), 'Organizational Renewal', *Seminar*, no. 526, June, pp. 23–26.

——— (2011a), 'The Congress Party and the "Great Transformation"', in Sanjay Ruparelia, Sanjay Reddy, John Harriss, and Stuart Corbridge (eds), *Understanding India's New Political Economy: A Great Transformation?* Routledge, London.

——— (2011b), 'Did the Central Government's Poverty Initiatives Help to Re-elect It', in Lawrence Saez and Gurharpal Singh (eds), *New Dimensions of Politics in India: The United Progressive Alliance in Power*, Routledge, London, pp. 13–25.

Mehta, Pratap Bhanu (2001), 'Reform Political Parties First', *Seminar*, no. 497, January, pp. 16–19.

——— (2004), 'The End of Charisma', *Seminar*, no. 539, July.

Menon, Madhava (2008), *Equal Opportunity Commission: What, Why and How?* Report submitted to the Ministry of Minority Affairs, Government of India. Available at http://www.minorityaffairs.gov.in/sites/upload_files/moma/files/pdfs/eoc_wwh.pdf (accessed on 7 August 2011).

Metcalf, Barbara (1995), 'Presidential Address: Too Little and Too Much: Reflections on the Muslims in the History of India', *Journal of Asian Studies*, vol. 54, no. 4, November, pp. 951–67.

MGNREGA (2011), *Accountability Initiative, Budget Briefs, Rural Development*, Government of India (GoI), Centre for Policy Research, New Delhi.

Mitta, Manoj and H.S. Phoolka (2007), *When a Tree Shook Delhi: The 1984 Carnage and Its Aftermath*, Roli Books, New Delhi.

Mohanty, Mritiunjoy (2009), 'Lok Sabha Election: A Storm in the Teacup?' *Macroscan*, 18 May. Available at www.macroscan.org/cur/may09/cur180509Lok_Sabha_Election.htm (accessed on 14 January 2012).

Mooij, Jos (ed.) (2005), *The Politics of the Economic Reforms in India*, Sage Publications, New Delhi.

Morris-Jones, W.H. (1967), 'The Dilemma of Dominance', *Modern Asian Studies*, no. 1, pp. 102–132.

Mukherjee, Pranab (2009), *Congress and the Making of the Indian Nation*, vols 1 and 2, Academic Foundation Books, New Delhi.

Mukherji, Rahul (2009a), *India's Economic Transition: The Politics of Reforms*, Oxford University Press, New Delhi.

———— (2009b), 'State, Economic Growth and Development in India', *India Review*, vol. 8, no. 1, pp. 88–106.

Mukhopadhyay, Nilanjan (1994), *The Demolition: India at the Crossroads*, HarperCollins, New Delhi.

Muralidharan, Sukumar (2012), 'Explaining the Mundane, Excluding the Voices of Dissent', *Economic and Political Weekly*, vol. XLVII, 14 January, p. 37.

Nandy, Ashis, Shikha Trivedi, Shail Mayaram, and Achut Yagnik (1995), *Creating a Nationality: Ramjanmabhoomi Movement and the Fear of the Self*, Oxford University Press, New Delhi.

National Election Study (NES) (2009), 'How India Voted', Report of the NES 2009, *The Hindu*, 24 May.

National Human Rights Commission (NHRC) (2002), 'Report on the Visit of the NHRC Team headed by Chairperson, NHRC, to Ahmedabad, Vadodra and Godhra from 19 to 22 March'. Available at www.nhrc.nic.in/guj_finalorder.htm (accessed on 18 January 2011).

Nayar, Baldev Raj (1998), 'Political Structure and India's Economic Reforms of the 1990s', *Pacific Affairs*, vol. 71, no. 3, Autumn, pp. 335–58.

———— (2001a), *Globalization and Nationalism: The Changing Balance in India's Economic Policy 1950–2000*, Sage Publications, New Delhi.

———— (2001b), 'Opening Up and Openness of Indian Economy', *Economic and Political Weekly*, vol. 36, no. 37, 15–21 September, pp. 792–815.

———— (2005), 'India in 2004: Regime Change in a Divided Democracy', *Asian Survey*, vol. 45, no. 1, pp. 71–82.

Nayar, Baldev Raj and Samuel Paul (2003), *India in the World Order*, Cambridge University Press, Cambridge.

Ninan, T.N. (2008), 'Boom and Gloom', *Seminar*, no. 581, January, pp. 1–7.

Nussbaum, Martha (2007), *The Clash within: Democracy, Religious Violence and India's Future*, Harvard University Press, Cambridge, MA.

Palshikar, Suhas and Yogendra Yadav (1999), 'Electoral Politics in India, 1989–99', *Economic and Political Weekly*, vol. 34, nos 34 and 35, 21–28 August.

Panagariya, Arvind (2002), 'India in the 1980s and 1990s: A Triumph of Reform', 6 November. Available at http.www.imf.org (accessed on 27 December 2011).

Pant, Harsh (2009), 'The US-India Nuclear Pact Policy: Process and Great Power Politics', *Asian Security*, vol. 5, no. 3, pp. 273–95.

Pant, Harsh (2011), *The US-India Nuclear Pact: Policy, Process, and Great Power Politics*, Oxford University Press, New Delhi.

Parthasarathy, Malini (2005), 'Constructing a False Reality', *Seminar*, no. 545, January.

Parikh, Manju (1993), 'The Debacle at Ayodhya: Why Militant Hinduism Met with a Weak Response', *Asian Survey*, vol. 33, no. 19, July, pp. 173–84.

Patnaik, Prabhat and C.P. Chandrasekhar (1995), 'Indian Economy under "Structural Adjustment"', *Economic and Political Weekly*, vol. 30, no. 47, 25 November, pp. 3001–13.

Pedersen, Jorgen (2000), 'Explaining Economic Liberalization in India: State and Society Perspectives', *World Development*, vol. 28, no. 2, February, pp. 265–82.

People's Union for Democratic Rights and People's Union for Civil Liberties (1984), *Who Are the Guilty? Report of a Joint Inquiry into the Causes and Impact of the Riots in Delhi from 31 October to 10 November, 1984*, PUDR and PUCL, New Delhi.

Perkovich, George (2001), 'The Measure of India: What Makes Greatness', *Seminar*, no. 529, September.

Pew Research Center (2005), 'U.S. Image Up Slightly, but Still Negative', Pew Global Attitudes Project, 23 June. Available at http://www.pewglobal.org/2005/06/23/us-image-up-slightly-but-still-negative (accessed on 8 January 2012).

Pye, Lucian (2004), 'Why One-Party Systems Decline', in Ashutosh Varshney (ed.), *India and the Politics of Developing Countries: Essays in Memory of Myron Weiner*, Sage Publications, New Delhi.

Raja Mohan, C. (2009), 'The Making of Indian Foreign Policy: The Role of Scholarship and Public Opinion', Institute of South Asian Studies, no. 73, 13 July, National University of Singapore, Institute of Singapore.

Rangarajan, Mahesh (2005a), 'Congress in Coalition', *Seminar*, no. 545, January, pp. 30–4.

——— (2005b), 'Polity in Transition: India after the 2004 General Election', *Economic and Political Weekly*, vol. 40, no. 32, 6 August, pp. 3598–606.

——— (2007), 'Reviving the Congress', *Seminar*, no. 569, January, pp. 34–7.

Rao, Narasimha (2000), 'Essence of Liberalization: Means to Transform Society, Not a Business Ploy', The Second J.R.D. Tata Memorial Lecture delivered in New Delhi on 1 November 1999, *Mainstream*, 10 June 2010.

——— (2006), *Ayodhya: 6 December 1992*, Penguin Viking, Delhi.

Ruparelia, Sanjay (2005), 'Managing the United Progressive Alliance: The Challenges Ahead', *Economic and Political Weekly*, vol. 40, no. 24, 11 June, pp. 2407–12.

Ruparelia, Sanjay, Sanjay Reddy, John Harriss, and Stuart Corbridge (eds) (2011), *Understanding India's New Political Economy: A Great Transformation?* Routledge, London.

Sarkar, Sumit (2001), 'Indian Democracy: The Historical Inheritance', in Atul Kohli (ed.), *The Success of India's Democracy*, Cambridge University Press, Cambridge, pp. 23–46.

Saxena, Naresh C. (2007), 'Outlays and Outcomes', *Seminar*, no. 574, June.

Sen, Abhijit and Himanshu (2004), 'Poverty and Inequality in India', *Economic and Political Weekly*, vol. 39, 18 and 25 September, p. 4247 and pp. 4361–4375.

Sengupta, Arjun (1995), 'Financial Sector and Economic Reforms in India', *Economic and Political Weekly*, vol. 30, no. 1, 7 January, pp. 39–44.

Sengupta, Mitu (2008), 'How the State Changed Its Mind: Power, Politics and the Origins of India's Market Reforms', *Economic and Political Weekly*, vol. 43, no. 21, 24–30 May, pp. 35–42.

Singh, Manmohan (1993), 'India's Economic Policies: The Past Experiences and the New Initiatives', in Debandra K. Das (ed.), *Structural Adjustment in the Indian Economy*, Deep & Deep, New Delhi.

Sinha, Aseema (2007), 'Economic Growth and Political Accommodation', *Journal of Democracy*, vol. 18, no. 2, April, pp. 41–54.

Sisson, Richard and Ramashray Roy (eds) (1990), *Diversity and Dominance in Indian Politics: Changing Bases of Congress Support*, Sage Publications, New Delhi.

Sridharan, E. (2004a), 'The Growth and Sectoral Composition of India's Middle Class: Its Impact on the Politics of Economic Liberalization', *India Review*, vol. 3, no. 4, October, pp. 405–28.

——— (2004b), 'Electoral Coalitions in 2004 General Elections: Theory and Evidence', *Economic and Political Weekly*, vol. XXXIX, no. 51, 18–24 December, pp. 5418–25.

Srivastava, Sushil (1994), 'The Abuse of History: A Study of the White Papers on Ayodha', *Social Scientist*, vol. 22, nos 5/6, May–June.

Swaminathan, Madhura (2005), *The Public Distribution of Food in India*, Leftword Books, New Delhi.

Swamy, Arun (2004), 'Back to the Future: The Congress Party's Upset Victory in India's 14th General Elections', Occasional Paper Series, June, Asia Pacific Center for Security Studies, Honolulu. Available at http//www.dtic/mil.tr/ fulltext/u2/a446094.pdf (accessed on 26 July 2011).

Tambiah, Stanley (1997), *Levelling Crowds: Ethnonationalist Conflicts and Collective Violence in South Asia*, Vistaar Publications, New Delhi.

——— (1999), 'The Crisis of Secularism in India', in Rajeev Bhargava (ed.), *Secularism and Its Critics*, Oxford University Press, New Delhi, pp. 438–53.

Tata Institute of Social Sciences (TISS) (2005), 'Causes of Farmer Suicides: An Enquiry', 5 March, p. 11. Available at www.vnss-mission.gov.in/htmldocs/ Farmers_suicide_TISS_report.pdf (accessed on 1 January 2011).

Tellis, Ashley. Available at http://npolicy.org/article_file/The_Transforming_US- Indian_Relationship_and_Its_Significance_for_American_Interests.pdf last (accessed on 3 January 2012).

Tully, Mark and Satish Jacob (1985), *Amritsar: Mrs. Gandhi's Last Battle*, Rupa & Co., Delhi.

United Nations Development Programme (UNDP) (2003), *UN Human Development Report*, United Nations, Geneva.

van der Veer, Peter (1996), 'The Ruined Centre: Religion and Mass Politics in India', *Journal of International Affairs*, vol. 50, no. 1, Summer, pp. 255–77.

Varadarajan, Siddharth (2008), 'Playing the Muslim Card on Nuclear Deal', *Economic and Political Weekly*, vol. XLIII, no. 28, 12 July.

Varshney, Ashutosh (2007a), 'Mass Politics or Elite Politics? India's Economic Reforms in Comparative Perspective', in Rahul Mukherji (ed.), *India's Economic Transition: The Politics of Reforms*, Oxford University Press, New Delhi.

———— (2007b), 'India's Democratic Challenge', *Foreign Affairs*, vol. 86, no. 2, March–April, pp. 93–106.

Wallace, Paul and Ramashroy Roy (eds) (2000), *India's 1999 Elections and 20th Century Politics*, Sage Publications, New Delhi.

Weiner, Myron (1987), 'Rajiv Gandhi: A Mid-Term Assessment', in Marshall Bouton (ed.), *India Briefing*, Westview Press, Boulder, CA.

Wilkinson, Steven (2004), *Votes and Violence: Electoral Competition and Ethnic Riots*, Cambridge University Press, New York.

Yadav, Yogendra (1996), 'Reconfiguration of Indian Politics: State Assembly Elections, 1993–95', *Economic and Political Weekly*, vol. 31, nos 2/3, 13–20 January, pp. 94–105.

———— (1999a), 'Electoral Politics in the Time of Change: India's Third Electoral System, 1989–99', *Economic and Political Weekly*, vol. 34, nos 34 and 35, 21–8 August, pp. 2393–9.

———— (1999b), 'The United Colours of the Congress: Social Profile of Congress Voters, 1996 and 1998', *Economic and Political Weekly*, nos 34 and 35, 21–8 August, pp. 2518–28.

———— (2000). 'The Second Democratic Upsurge', in Francine Frankel, Zoya Hasan, Rajeev Bhargava, and Balveer Arora (eds), *Transforming India: Social Dynamics of Democracy*, Oxford University Press, New Delhi, pp. 120–45.

———— (2004), 'The Elusive Mandate of 2004', *Economic and Political Weekly*, vol. 39, no. 51, 18 December, pp. 5383–98.

Index